Amélie Nothomb

Belgian Francophone Library

Donald Flanell Friedman
General Editor

Vol. 16

PETER LANG
New York • Washington, D.C./Baltimore • Bern
Frankfurt am Main • Berlin • Brussels • Vienna • Oxford

Amélie Nothomb

Authorship, Identity and Narrative Practice

EDITED BY
Susan Bainbrigge and
Jeanette den Toonder

PETER LANG
New York • Washington, D.C./Baltimore • Bern
Frankfurt am Main • Berlin • Brussels • Vienna • Oxford

Library of Congress Cataloging-in-Publication Data

Amélie Nothomb: authorship, identity and narrative practice /
[edited by] Susan Bainbrigge and Jeanette den Toonder.
p. cm. — (Belgian francophone library; v. 16)
Includes bibliographical references.
1. Nothomb, Amélie—Criticism and interpretation. 2. Authorship in literature.
3. Identity (Psychology) in literature. 4. Narration (Rhetoric). I. Bainbrigge,
Susan. II. Toonder, Jeanette M. L. den. III. Series.
PQ2674.O778 Z54   843'.914—dc21   2002070491
ISBN 0-8204-6182-2
ISSN 1074-6757

Bibliographic information published by **Die Deutsche Bibliothek**.
Die Deutsche Bibliothek lists this publication in the 'Deutsche
Nationalbibliografie'; detailed bibliographic data is available
on the Internet at http://dnb.ddb.de

Cover photo: Amélie Nothomb by Renaud Montfourny,
courtesy of the author and Editions Albin Michel

The paper in this book meets the guidelines for permanence and durability
of the Committee on Production Guidelines for Book Longevity
of the Council of Library Resources.

© 2003 Peter Lang Publishing, Inc., New York
275 Seventh Avenue, 28th Floor, New York, NY 10001
www.peterlangusa.com

Printed in Germany

CONTENTS

NARRATIVE PRACTICE

TRANSLATING AMÉLIE NOTHOMB

ACKNOWLEDGEMENTS

We would like to thank all those involved in the Amélie Nothomb project, from its beginnings as an informal reading group to the conference held at the University of Edinburgh in November 2001. The conference would not have been possible without the secretarial support of Joanne Naysmith and the financial support of the *Centre d'études francophones belges* and the Faculty of Arts, University of Edinburgh as well as the British Academy. We are also grateful for the funds from the Faculty Research Group which made the publication possible.

We gratefully acknowledge the expert help provided by the team at Peter Lang. Our series editor Donald Flanell Friedman was instrumental in getting the project off the ground and we thank him for his unfailing enthusiasm and for his assistance in gleaning financial support from the Belgian Ministry of Culture to assist with production costs. Thanks also to David Gascoigne for his thoughtful comments and advice on the manuscript.

Special thanks go to Professor John Renwick for getting the ball rolling; the reading group for so many lively discussions about Amélie Nothomb's books; France Sharratt for transcribing the interview and Katherine Ashley for the translation. Amélie Nothomb has been very generous with her time and we extend our heartfelt thanks to her for her interest and encouragement. Finally, a big thanks to our colleagues at Edinburgh for their good humour and moral support.

We are grateful to the editors of the journal *Religiologiques* for permission to print Laureline Amanieux's article, an amended version of which appeared in French in the Spring 2002 issue.

Magritte's *Le Miroir magique,* is reproduced here with permission from the Artists Rights Society, New York, and ADAGP, Paris.

The photograph of Amélie Nothomb is reproduced on the front cover with the permission of the photographer, Renaud Montfourny, and the Éditions Albin Michel.

Jacques de Decker

PREFACE: NOTHOMB AVEC UN B COMME BELGIQUE

Dans la ville écossaise d'Édimbourg, au mois de novembre 2001, le colloque 'Autour d'Amélie Nothomb' fut une merveilleuse occasion de deviser de la pensée et de l'œuvre de la plus jeune et la plus célèbre des femmes de lettres belges. Ces journées qui constituent la première vaste contribution scientifique à la connaissance de la diva de la littérature belge d'aujourd'hui, ont donné lieu à la publication du présent volume.

J'aimerais renvoyer d'abord au livre le plus récent d'Amélie Nothomb, *Cosmétique de l'ennemi*. Avec ce titre, elle annonce la couleur de son dixième livre: cet intitulé est un écho évident à son initial *Hygiène de l'assassin*. Au point que l'on est en droit de parler de syntagme figé: arrivée à son dixième livre publié (j'y insiste), elle marque le pas, et revient sur les lieux de son premier crime. Elle aurait pu aussi bien appeler son ouvrage *Hygiène de l'assassin Deux* ou *Hygiène de l'assassin: Le retour*. Pourquoi lui en faire grief? Reproche-t-on à un musicien ou à un peintre de revenir au même motif?

Notre auteur, on s'en est déjà bien aperçu, dans *Mercure* notamment, aime le roman gothique et le fantastique. Mais la parution de *Cosmétique de l'ennemi* a rendu d'autant plus opportune l'organisation de ces journées d'études à Édimbourg. Ce livre garantit l'actualité du colloque, parce qu'Amélie Nothomb y rend un hommage appuyé au Stevenson de *Docteur Jekyll et Mister Hyde*. Que notre forcenée des meilleures ventes ait trouvé une part de son inspiration chez le plus illustre écrivain né à Édimbourg a donc trouvé un parfait écho académique...

Élargissons le propos à ce que l'on pourrait appeler le phénomène Nothomb. Car écrire un best-seller à 24 ans, publier, avec une régularité horlogère, un livre à chaque rentrée depuis lors, faire grimper impavidement les tirages de ses titres jusqu'à se retrouver dans les listes des meilleures ventes avec deux, voire trois ouvrages parus chaque fois à un an de distance, faire s'entredéchirer les éditeurs étrangers à la

Jacques de Decker

PREFACE: NOTHOMB WITH A
B AS IN BELGIUM

In November 2001, in the Scottish city of Edinburgh, the conference 'Autour d'Amélie Nothomb' was a wonderful opportunity to discuss the philosophy and the works of Belgium's youngest and most famous woman of letters. This was the first occasion to bring together wide-ranging academic studies focusing on the young star of Belgian literature, and it has given rise to the publication of the current volume.

May I begin by referring to Amélie Nothomb's most recent work, *Cosmétique de l'ennemi.* The title itself sets the tone for her tenth book and clearly echoes her first work, *Hygiène de l'assassin,* to the point that we could allow ourselves to talk of her use of the set phrase. With this her *tenth* published book, she has marked time and gone back to the scene of her first crime. She could have called her work *Hygiène de l'assassin Deux* or *Hygiène de l'assassin: Le retour.* And why should we take her to task for that? Does one reproach a musician or a painter for returning to the same motif?

We have already noticed, for example in *Mercure,* that our author likes the gothic novel and the fantastic. However, the publication of *Cosmétique de l'ennemi* has made this conference in Edinburgh even more appropriate as that book itself guarantees the topicality of the colloquium: in *Cosmétique de l'ennemi,* Amélie Nothomb pays a glowing tribute to Stevenson's *Doctor Jekyll and Mister Hyde.* How appropriate that our zealously prolific best-selling author has found some inspiration in Edinburgh's most famous writer.

Let us broaden the context to consider what might be called the Nothomb phenomenon. Writing a best seller at the age of twenty-four, publishing a book every year since then with clockwork-like regularity, pushing up print runs of her books quite fearlessly to the point of finding herself on the bestseller list with two, sometimes even three works appearing every year at the same time, causing foreign editors

Foire de Francfort pour les droits d'un roman écrit en langue française, emporter l'adhésion des académiciens français (après avoir eu droit, insistons-y, aux lauriers de leurs confrères belges), tout cela est, reconnaissons-le, de l'ordre du phénomène. Nothomb a fait de l'exceptionnel son ordinaire.

La question est: que trouve à Nothomb sa foule de lecteurs à travers le monde? Le corpus se compose de dix livres, dont neuf romans et une pièce de théâtre, *Les Combustibles*. Les neuf romans se partagent en diverses catégories. Ceux qui font une place royale au dialogue, si grande que, la confusion aidant, la pièce fut présentée, sans vergogne, comme un roman elle aussi: il s'agit de *Hygiène de l'assassin*, des *Catilinaires*, et maintenant de *Cosmétique de l'ennemi*. Ceux qui sont écrits à la troisième personne (la trilogie *Péplum, Attentat, Mercure*), et ceux où l'auteur se raconte en disant 'je'. Cette dernière manière lui a inspiré ses meilleurs livres, et, ce qui ne gâche rien, valu ses plus grands succès: *Le Sabotage amoureux, Stupeur et tremblements* et *Métaphysique des tubes*.

À trois reprises, elle y explore les souvenirs hors du commun que lui ont procurés son enfance de fille de diplomate belge en Orient. *Le Sabotage amoureux* racontait ses jeux d'enfants dans le quartier des ambassades de Pékin: une sorte de *Guerre des boutons* cosmopolite et asiatique. *Stupeur et tremblements* relatait ses débuts dans la vie professionnelle au Japon, qui entraîna sa rupture définitive avec le principe de réalité. Et *Métaphysique des tubes* explique qu'il n'y a pas d'âge pour se poser les questions des fins dernières: elle s'y souvient d'un mal-être éprouvé lorsqu'elle n'avait pas trois ans, et qui la mena jusqu'à une tentative de suicide dans un étang à carpes, drame ontologique que les grandes personnes se hâtèrent bien sûr de considérer comme un accident.

Si l'on s'interroge sur le phénoménal succès de l'auteur, il est bon de s'attarder à ces trois récits (les livres d'Amélie Nothomb dépassent rarement les 150.000 signes, un lecteur entraîné les lit sur le temps d'un trajet Paris-Bruxelles en Thalys), parce qu'ils sont tous construits sur un conflit avec le monde. Dans *Le Sabotage amoureux,* l'enfant invente le réel, le construit à sa guise, y puise de profondes détresses quelquefois (l'amour sans retour, thème récurrent, est déjà présent dans ce livre), mais dans *Stupeur et tremblements* les contraintes du système social et professionnel sont telles qu'elles provoquent une révolte sans appel, et dans *Métaphysique des tubes,* il s'agit tout simplement du refus d'exister, de se mêler à la vie, d'avoir partie liée avec elle.

Les angoisses que Nothomb fait émerger au jour sont primitives, viscérales, et chacun peut s'y retrouver, ou y retrouver les premiers échos d'une sorte de tragédie originelle. Dans cette expression du mal-être foncier, de la déréliction de se trouver *jeté-là* dans le marasme du réel, Nothomb puise des fables qui parlent à chacun de nous, pour peu que l'on se souvienne de ses premiers vertiges et de ses premiers rejets.

Amélie a trouvé son issue à elle: elle passe par l'écriture, qui lui procure un évident soulagement, et une jouissance qui peut être contagieuse. La certitude intime que ses malaises sont sans remède lui insuffle, depuis le début, un humour désespéré qui jaillit de sa phrase subtilement piégée, de son vocabulaire habilement

at the Frankfurt Book fair to fight over the rights to a novel written in French, winning the members of the *Académie française* to her cause (not forgetting, of course, the awards already made to her by their Belgian counterparts). All this is clearly in the realms of the phenomenal. What for others would be extraordinary achievements are, with Nothomb, her own usual performance.

The question is, what brings crowds of readers all over the world especially to Nothomb? The corpus consists of ten book: nine novels and a play, *Les Combustibles*. The nine novels can be divided into different categories. There are those in which the dialogue has pride of place (such as *Hygiène de l'assassin, Les Catilinaires,* and now, *Cosmétique de l'ennemi*) and this to such an extent that, heightening the uncertainty as to the generic nature of the text, when she did write a play, it too was unapologetically presented as a novel. There are those written in the third person (the trilogy *Péplum, Attentat, Mercure*), and others in which the author speaks about herself in the first person. The latter method has inspired *Le Sabotage amoureux, Stupeur et tremblements* and *Métaphysique des tubes*, her best works, and, without in any way detracting from them, this method has also brought her her greatest success.

On three occasions in these books she explores the exceptional memories that her childhood as a Belgian diplomat's daughter in the Far East have given her. *Le Sabotage amoureux* recounted the childhood games in and around the area in Peking where the Embassies were situated, like a kind of cosmopolitan, Asian *Guerre des boutons. Stupeur et tremblements* told the story of her first experience of Japanese professional life, and brought about her definitive break with realism. *Métaphysique des tubes* explains that there is no 'right' age at which to wonder about mortality. She remembers a feeling of malaise when she wasn't even three years old, which led to a suicide attempt in a pond full of carp, an ontological drama that the grown-ups of course were quick to call an accident.

If we think about the phenomenal success of the author, it's worth lingering over these three stories (Amélie Nothomb's books are rarely more than 150 pages long, short enough for an experienced reader caught up in the momentum to read them in the time it takes for the Thalys to go from Paris to Brussels), because they are all based on a conflict with the world. In *Le Sabotage amoureux,* the child invents reality, fashions it as she wishes, and sometimes gets from it profound distress (unrequited love, a recurring theme, is already present in this work) but in *Stupeur et tremblements* the constraints of the social and professional structures are such that they provoke a revolt that permits no going back, and in *Métaphysique des tubes* it is a question quite simply of refusing to exist, to be involved in life, to play any part in it.

The anxieties that Nothomb brings to light are primitive, visceral, and anyone can identify with them, or recognize in them the first echoes of a kind of primal tragedy. By voicing that fundamental uneasiness with self, by depicting what it feels like to find oneself abandoned in the midst of life's dreariness, Nothomb creates fables that have meaning for every one of us, if only we can remember our first moments of disorientation and the first time we felt rejection.

Amélie has found her own solution: through the act of writing, which brings her

sélectionné. Son hygiène mentale passe par le style, qui est souvent brillant, parce qu'un cynisme de bon ton y va de pair avec une drôlerie d'excellente compagnie. Amélie Nothomb a été bien élevée, et elle ne le renie pas, elle sait comment décocher des flèches assassines sans se départir d'un sourire d'hôtesse exemplaire. Elle est, en ce sens, la digne héritière de ces grandes bourgeoises et aristocrates qui ont su déboulonner avec toute l'élégance voulue les univers où elles se débattaient: elle est, tout compte fait, proche de Jane Austen, de Louise de Vilmorin, mais qui seraient devenues belges.

Car Amélie Nothomb, avec un b comme Belgique, est belge, comme son illustre nom l'indique, et elle ne se soigne pas pour autant, trop certaine, comme elle le dit dans son avant-dernier livre, que Dieu l'est certainement aussi, puisqu'elle eut la certitude, autour de trente-six mois, d'être son incarnation.

obvious relief and an enjoyment which can be contagious. Being absolutely convinced that her suffering is incurable instils from the beginning a desperate humour which wells up from her carefully double-edged phrase, and from her cleverly selected vocabulary. Her often brilliant style plays a crucial part in ensuring her mental well-being because a tasteful cynicism goes hand in hand with a perfectly matched comedy. Amélie Nothomb has been well brought up, she does not deny this and she knows how to shoot deadly arrows without losing the perfect smile of the society hostess. In that sense, she is the worthy heiress to those great middle-class and aristocratic women who knew how to dismantle with such elegance the worlds in which they struggled. She is, all said and done, close to what Jane Austen or Louise de Vilmorin would have been, had they been Belgian.

For Amélie Nothomb, with a b as in Belgium, is Belgian, as her illustrious name indicates. She does not make a big issue of the fact, since, as she says in her penultimate book, God is too, because she was convinced at the age of thirty-six months of being his incarnation.

Translated by Susan Bainbrigge and Jeanette den Toonder

Susan Bainbrigge and Jeanette den Toonder

INTRODUCTION

Biographical Information

Amélie Nothomb, of Belgian origin, was born in Kobe, Japan, in 1967. A diplomat's daughter, she grew up in the Far East, and was seventeen before she visited Europe. So totally different was it from what she had imagined through her extensive reading of European literature that the experience was to inform her development as a writer. She studied Romance Philology at the *Université Libre de Bruxelles,* but more importantly, she also started writing during this period, a time in which she felt alienated and misunderstood. Struck by what she terms a chronic writing disease ('la maladie de l'écriture'), Amélie Nothomb has become a famously prolific writer who published her first novel at the age of twenty-five. In particular, winning the *Grand Prix du roman de l'Académie française* in 1999 for *Stupeur et tremblements* has really put her name on the literary map.[1]

Now based in Brussels and Paris, she attracts a variety of readers, from teenagers to performers and theatre directors keen to dramatize her work, to the literary establishment (initially causing a flurry of interest when *Hygiène de l'assassin* was suspected by one well-known editor of being a hoax from an established author and definitely not the work of a novice).[2] She is said to please her audiences because her novels are short reads as well as being highly imaginative, a blend of dark humour and comical reflections, intellectual tour de force and comedy. In each work, she combines the acutely personal with grand philosophical questions about the nature of existence. This ability to combine the public and private, the microcosm and the macrocosm so deftly is perhaps in part due to her particularly cosmopolitan upbringing, Nothomb even referring to herself as 'une apatride belge', the seemingly contradictory terms somehow encapsulating her peculiar position in which Belgian identity is both affirmed and renounced.[3] She has been known to refer to herself, albeit slightly tongue-in-cheek, as 'une héritière du surréalisme belge'.[4] And yet this association is not that far-fetched, given the ways in which she juxtaposes fact and fantasy, overturns conventions, mocks and parodies institutions of all kinds, and uses intertextuality to surprise and provoke the reader.

Nothomb's phenomenal success goes far beyond Belgian and French borders, as her work has been translated into thirty languages (German, Catalan, Danish, Dutch, Greek, Japanese, Polish, Russian to name but a few). Despite this world-wide interest, to date only four titles have been translated into English, and no full-length study of the author exists in English.[5] Thus it is hoped that this volume will bring the writing of this prize-winning author to a wider audience.

It will become evident that Nothomb's œuvre flouts genre conventions and defies facile literary classification. Many genres are represented within the body of her work: autobiographical and semi-autobiographical texts, science fiction, fantasy, rewritings of fairy tales, epics and myths. Margaret-Anne Hutton has observed that despite the variety in Nothomb's wide-ranging œuvre, one recurring factor common to all her works can be traced: conflict of all kinds.[6] If sparks fly in all directions in the author's dialogues, meeting with her could not be more different, and we are grateful to Amélie Nothomb for granting us permission to print the interview in this volume.

A Brief Synopsis of Amélie Nothomb's Works

Prétextat Tach, protagonist of Nothomb's first novel, *Hygiène de l'assassin* (1992), is an arrogant, vulgar and misogynistic hulk who has just won the Nobel prize for his literary œuvre of twenty-two novels. He treats his opponents, five journalists who have come from all over the world to interview him, with the greatest contempt. The novelist's cruel cynicism and coarseness—journalists are, in his opinion, mere parasites living off creators whose work they haven't even read—quickly scare away the first four. But the last one, Nina, who knows his books in great detail, discovers the horrible secret that lies hidden in his literary works: as an adolescent, he strangled his cousin Léopoldine to prevent her from becoming a woman. In his own view, he saved her by giving her eternal youth. At the end of a biting and dazzling dialogue, the female journalist puts the monstrous Tach quite literally to silence. For this debut Nothomb received two prizes: the *Prix René-Fallet* and the *Prix Alain-Fournier*.

The second novel, *Le Sabotage amoureux* (1993), was also awarded the *Prix Alain-Fournier,* as well as the *Prix de la Vocation* and the *Prix Chardonne*. In this autobiographical text, Nothomb describes the closed world of a compound of foreign diplomats and their children in communist Beijing between 1972 and 1975. The narrative perspective is that of a seven-year-old girl. This young first-person narrator considers her bike to be a horse, quotes Wittgenstein and Baudelaire, reflects on beauty and war, ridicules adults and falls in love with the ravishing Elena. This authentic, absolute love is both fantastic and tragic, because unrequited. The story of 'loving sabotage' takes place in a setting of violence and ugliness, as the children, encompassing a variety of nationalities, are absorbed in one particular game: that of reliving their own Second World War.

A state of war also constitutes the background of *Les Combustibles* (1994), to date Nothomb's only play. In a besieged city, three characters — a Professor, his assistant Daniel and the student Marina — have taken refuge in the Professor's apartment. Outside, the bombing and shelling continue, whilst inside the pressing question of survival centres around one particular issue: how to fight against the cold? The only combustible item left in the house is in the Professor's library: his books. Soon the protagonists not only ask each other which book should be saved for last, but, more perversely, which book is worth giving up one single moment of physical warmth.

In *Les Catilinaires* (1995), yet another confined space constitutes the setting of the devastating events that ruin the lives of the protagonists. A retired couple, Émile and Juliette, have just moved to a house in the woods where they hope to quietly spend the last years of their life together. Their calm solitude is however cruelly disturbed by their obese neighbour, Palamède Bernardin, who, every day between four and six o'clock, invites himself into their house, gets himself settled down, hardly saying a word. His presence and silence drive the couple to distraction and the absurdity of the situation is enhanced when they discover the existence of Mme Bernardin who is so corpulent that she can hardly move. However, when Émile decides to act against the rude neighbour's undesired infiltration into their space, the roles of perpetrator and victim slowly become blurred . . . For this black comedy the author received the *Prix Paris Première* and the *Prix du jury Jean-Giono*.

The title of the fourth novel refers to a woman's garment that was worn in ancient times: *Péplum* (1996). In a book that combines science fiction, satire and historical events, ancient past and future times are linked together through the burying of Pompeii under the ashes of Vesuvius, in 79 A.D. During a short stay at the hospital, the writer A.N. wakes up in the 26th century and discovers that this volcanic eruption was provoked by future scientists in order to preserve the most beautiful example of a classical city. Her encounter with one of the major instigators, the scientist Celsius, results in a heated conversation in which a great number of topics are discussed. These include the great war that took place in the 22nd century; abstract issues such as the virtual and the real; travelling in time, but also timeless issues such as art, philosophy and morality.

In *Attentat* (1997) we are presented with the very unappealing Epiphane Otos, who, despite being aesthetically challenged with few redeeming features in the personality stakes, manages to become the darling of the modelling world, 'ambassadeur de la monstruosité internationale', and who falls in love with the young and beautiful Ethel. Like many of Nothomb's works, the theme of beauty is paramount, yet as the reference to Baudelaire confirms, 'Le beau est toujours bizarre' (*A* 39). This introduces us to the pathological extremes to which the protagonist will be driven in pursuit of the woman he desires. In an overturning of platitudes about beauty, Epiphane takes the reader on a fantastical journey, via his erotic and violent adolescent dreams, to his quest for Ethel which will take him to Japan, and to her violent death at his hands, ultimately leaving him with only his solitude and memories of her. *Attentat* concludes with Epiphane's contemplation of his murder of Ethel while he is imprisoned. Musing on his current situation, he notes that now he will have plenty of time at his disposal to write. Imprisonment is not as bad as all that, he ponders.

In *Mercure* (1998), the theme of freedom and imprisonment is pursued, in a mock Gothic tale. *Mercure* tells the story of the young Hazel Englert, who, since she was orphaned (in 1918), leads a secluded life on an island off the coast of Cherbourg with an old man, Omer Loncours. Led to believe that she has been badly disfigured by the bombardment which killed her parents, she is kept from seeing her reflection: there are no mirrors in the house, nor is there anything that would offer a reflection. Omer employs a nurse to look after Hazel. Françoise Chavaigne arrives and is dumbfounded by the ways in which her employer and her charge lead their lives. She makes it her mission to enlighten Hazel about her situation (the fact that she is not hideously disfigured but of breathtaking beauty), but will find to her horror that when she finally gets the chance to expose the old man's deception, Hazel's response is perhaps not what she had bargained for.

Stupeur et tremblements (1999) is written under the auspices of autobiography. Claimed to represent a year spent as a *stagiaire* in 1990 for a Japanese import-export company, the narrator takes us through the ritual humiliations at the hand of her superiors that become a fact of life, as she descends ever lower in the corporate ladder, finally ending up as a 'Dame Pipi'. A text that provoked outrage as well as acclaim, Nothomb sets up and dismantles stereotypes, in a genre which blends the real and the surreal. Amélie-san can one minute be describing her struggles with her boss's expense accounts, the next minute be cavorting naked out of hours in the office, or contemplating the vertiginous drop from the window . . . Funny, eloquent and imaginative, office politics and the abuse of hierarchies are all too recognizable in this compelling tale.

In *Métaphysique des tubes* (2000) the author takes us further back in time, to the portrayal of the narrator as an infant. What is more, an infant who thinks she is God. The first three years of the child's life in Japan are depicted from the perspective of an interior monologue in which the child's power to name even takes on biblical proportions. Family anecdotes become existential dramas in which the narrator has to overcome obstacle after obstacle to survive, questioning the ways of the world in the process.

Finally, the intimate dialogues of the earlier works bring the narrative in Nothomb's most recent publication, *Cosmétique de l'ennemi* (2001) back to the *huis clos*. Set in an airport lounge, two voices are heard in dialogue. One of them belongs to Jérôme Angust, the other to Textor Texel, an enigmatic other whose true identity is revealed at the end to be none other than Angust's alter ego. He remorselessly pursues Angust, so desperate is he for an ear to listen to his 'confessional', despite Angust's protestations; he is racked with guilt about a murder he believes he may have committed as a child, haunted by an 'ennemi intérieur', yet insistent at the same time in bringing his interlocutor's actions into perspective: the fact that it is Angust who is suspected of killing his wife and who effectively tortures himself via the words of Texel to the point of his own self-destruction.

Introduction to the Essays in this Volume

In the first section, 'Autobiography and Gender', questions concerning the juxtaposition of true and verifiable biographemes with situations and characters exaggerated to the point of the absurd will be discussed in relation to theories of reading and gender identity. Despite the fantastical and the absurd, the reader's disbelief is suspended all along as childhood becomes the nostalgic centre which offers the possibility of freedom to choose one's own gender. A sense of injustice concerning gender and the discovery of individual identity seem to coincide in the fragments of the author's childhood described in the autobiography.

In her article, Hélène Jaccomard examines the consequences that Nothomb's three autobiographical works, *Le Sabotage amoureux, Stupeur et tremblements* and *Métaphysique des tubes* have on the autobiographical pact. Jaccomard argues that memories in Nothomb's tales of childhood insist on the search for identity through language. Language expression is at the heart of the formation of the protagonist's metaphysical, national and gender identities, to the extent that storytelling is an inherent part of Nothomb's autobiographical style. Nothomb's personality remains a *self in fabula*, and is thus uncommitted to truthtelling.

The issue of gender inequality is discussed by Désirée Pries, who focuses on the image of the carp in *Métaphysique des tubes*. Through the dual image of the carp in this work — carps are a symbol for the masculine, but they are also evoked in feminine terms — the autobiographical account of Nothomb's earliest childhood memories is studied as a metaphor for the traumatic transformation of a young girl's body, which indicates the passage of childhood to adulthood. Pries demonstrates that the girl's attempt to remain pre-adolescent — by becoming anorexic or attempting suicide — results in a redefinition of the female body and in the conception of an alternative feminine identity.

Female and male bodies are the objects of study in the second section of this volume, 'Representations of the body'. In the first article of this section, Victoria Korzeniowska examines formal aspects of the presentation of the body in Nothomb's writing through elements of the fantastical and by focusing on the power of imagination. In *Stupeur et tremblements,* the patterns of the heroine's bodily movements play an important role in the construction of her reality and are counteracted by the use of imagination. Korzeniowska illustrates that corporeal interaction with space and the creative potential of imagination allow for resistance, subversion, transgression and free-thinking.

The idealization of female bodies, on the contrary, seems to reduce the freedom of stunningly beautiful female characters such as the young Hazel in *Mercure,* who lives in sequestration because her seventy-seven year old 'protector' yearns to possess her beauty. In a number of Nothomb's novels (for example *Hygiène de l'assassin, Attentat* and *Les Catilinaires*), the sublime beauty of a female protagonist contrasts sharply with a hideous male 'monster'. This image of an incompatible couple blurs commonplace conceptions that associate thinness with virtue and fatness with evil. Catherine Rodgers argues that the real nature of Nothombian beauty resides in its thinness, its virginity and its asexuality, which leaves no room for a female, adult, sexual body. Hence the promotion of an anorexic alternative that enables the female characters to maintain their childlike angelic appearance. They are flanked by hideous individuals: these are repulsive males whose objective is to control the Other.

Lénaïk Le Garrec explores this contrast between beauty and ugliness through the representations of male and female characters. In her study, the mirror plays an essential role, as this magical element not only reveals the protagonists' physical appearance, but also Nothomb's different conceptions of self. If the mirror confirms beauty, as in fairytales, and confronts—mostly male—characters with their unattractive features, it is also stressed that its nature can be deceptive. By focusing on the deceitful characteristics of angels and monsters, Le Garrec shows that Nothomb's works disrupt the established order by rejecting the norms of beauty, thus putting our superficial society on trial. Philippa Caine further explores the rupture of common dualisms by considering the deconstructive inscriptions of female corporeality in Nothomb's narratives. Caine uses the notion of 'entre-deux' writing to examine the associations of women's bodies with slenderness and beauty as well as with corpulence and abjection. These elements are related to certain dogmas of (Western) discourse—such as phallocentric fears of the 'fleshy' female body—that are effectively exploited in Nothomb's œuvre.

In the final contribution of this section, Jean-Marc Terrasse proposes to tackle the representation of monstrosity by using the Derridean notion of the 'monstre événementiel'. Terrasse's poetic exploration and deconstruction of male and female demons and angels focuses on their voices and silence, and on the ways in which they seek to enslave or love each other.

In the section devoted to Narrative Practice, the essays engage, to greater and lesser degrees, with the entirety of Nothomb's œuvre. They focus on stylistic aspects of her work and authorial preoccupations, in particular the use of dialogue; the role of humour; intertextuality and the relationship between author and reader; questions of authorship, status and canons of literature; linguistic virtuosity and figures of language; beginnings and endings.

Amélie Nothomb's ear for dialogue brings her (often monstrous) characters to life, whether it's the domineering writer Prétextat Tach of *Hygiène de l'assassin* who reduces all journalists to quivering wrecks, or the hideously ugly Epiphane Otos, the domineering protagonist of *Attentat*. Shirley Jordan explores this important feature of Nothomb's narrative practice in terms of the author's meditation on the interpersonal dynamics of power, analysing the presentation of combative relationships and paying attention to two particular arms in the author's weaponry: erudition and wit. She explores the function of the author's dialogic games in a broader context in order to assess their pertinence as vehicles for philosophical enquiry.

Claire Gorrara then examines the status of the author and authorship in the debate on literature's value to the individual and the collective which is presented in *Les Combustibles*. In this play, the values espoused by a trio in an unknown city under siege are put under the spotlight. Pursuing the intertextual vein here, parodic reworkings of genres such as *littérature engagée* raise important questions about the status of authors and critics, highlighting the demands upon the reader to be attentive and erudite too. The relationship between the erudite author and the literary world, and what Jordan calls her 'poetics of virtuosity', is then explored in terms of intertextuality by Susan Bainbrigge, who questions the nature of the relationship between author, intertext and reader in *Mercure,* paying particular attention to Nothomb's fascination for 19th century Romantic and Gothic literature. In this hybrid text the reader can only wonder at the image of the vertiginous 'escalier anachronique', an unstable escape route which enables the heroine of the story to flee her captor, and perhaps also a metaphor for the author's own writing practice.

In David Gascoigne's essay, parody and irony emerge in his study of the wide-ranging and highly coloured figures of language in Nothomb's textual landscapes. Within Nothomb's 'poetics of excess', he examines the origins of the voice, whether at its source an irritant, an intruder, or an unwelcome arrival in an ordered world provoking the primal scream. He charts in various texts the overwhelming feeling of power that is garnered by the act of naming, not forgetting the author's ritual or incantatory use of language as another means of reaching more searching and visceral levels of expression and provocation.

Laureline Amanieux identifies one particular influence on Nothomb: the image of Dionysus, and the pervasiveness of images of doubles and duality in her texts. She presents and compares several examples of Dionysian characters in order to demonstrate the ambivalence and necessity of their 'sublime' feelings and their monstrosity, and then goes on to argue that the author combines these dual feelings in the creative momentum of writing itself.

Linguistic skill is matched by complex narrative strategies; in particular, endings are the focus of articles by Mark Lee and Marinella Termite. Lee explores the writing of childhood's end in Nothomb's works, by drawing up an inventory of threshold scenes in different texts, and assessing the varied representations of them and their importance in the creation of the author's literary voice. Termite looks more generally at the ways in which the author concludes, especially her use of role reversal and alternative endings in texts which mirror the destructive titles assigned to them. Termite argues that Nothomb disrupts and subverts her narratives, defying in the process generic codes and conventions.

Andrew Wilson and Adriana Hunter's translations mark an important turning point in making Nothomb's works available to an English-speaking audience. They recount here the trials and tribulations of translation, offering insights into the process itself, and revealing personal affinities with the author which emerged as they grappled with the linguistic virtuosities of her prose. To close the volume we are delighted to present the transcription of an interview conducted with the author in January 2002 in which we discuss with her a number of the questions raised at the conference in the presentations and discussions.

Notes

1. Full references for Nothomb's works are listed in the bibliography.
2. See Yolande Helm, 'Amélie Nothomb: "l'enfant terrible" des lettres belges de langue française', *Études Francophones*, 11 (1996), 113–120 (p. 113).
3. 'De toute façon, je ne me sens bien nulle part. Cela s'appelle être apatride, j'imagine. Et cependant, si je ne suis chez moi nulle part, je n'en suis pas moins une apatride belge', in 'Une Apatride belge', *Belgique toujours grande et belle,* Revue de l'Université de Bruxelles (1998), ed. by Antoine Pickels and Jacques Sojcher (Bruxelles: Éditions Complexe, 1998), p. 409.
4. See interview in this volume, and Yolande Helm, op. cit., p. 115.
5. Scholarly articles on Nothomb's writing are listed in the bibliography.
6. '[. . .] si l'œuvre d'Amélie Nothomb échappe à la classification, on y retrouve pourtant un facteur commun sous la forme de trois niveaux de conflit: individuel (les personnages s'affrontent); collectif (mention de guerres dans tous les textes); lutte entre l'auteur et le lecteur', in '"Personne n'est indispensable, sauf l'ennemi": l'œuvre conflictuelle d'Amélie Nothomb', in *Nouvelles Écrivaines: nouvelles voix?,* ed. by Nathalie Morello and Catherine Rodgers (Amsterdam: Rodopi, 2002), pp. 111–27 (pp. 111–12). See also Évelyne Wilwerth, 'Amélie Nothomb: Sous le signe du cinglant', *Revue Générale,* 132, 6–7 (June–July 1997), 45–51.

AUTOBIOGRAPHY AND GENDER

Hélène Jaccomard

SELF IN FABULA: AMÉLIE NOTHOMB'S THREE AUTOBIOGRAPHICAL WORKS

*Le royaume du conte n'est autre chose que l'univers familial bien clos
et bien délimité où se joue le drame premier de l'homme.*[1]

Only a very young woman can honestly declare: 'Je me souviens très bien de mon enfance et de ma petite enfance'.[2] The conviction itself that our childhood memories are authentic, is hardly proof that they are. Sigmund Freud proposed fairly convincingly that memories are formed and constructed at the time of remembrance, to the extent that 'our memory is without memories'.[3] All the same, in a very rare self-reflexive comment in *Métaphysique des tubes* Nothomb reiterates her belief: 'Une affirmation aussi énorme—"je me souviens de tout"—n'a aucune chance d'être crue par quiconque. Cela n'a pas d'importance. S'agissant d'un énoncé aussi invérifiable, je vois moins que jamais l'intérêt d'être crédible'.[4] What happens then to the autobiographical project when the autobiographer is so naïve—or feigns naïvity—and discards cardinal autobiographical rules of truthtelling and verifiability at the stroke of a pen? Can the reader find her autobiographical texts satisfactory?

The autobiographical vein is not the main thrust of Amélie Nothomb's works to date, and judging from her latest novel, *Cosmétique de l'ennemi*,[5] she has, momentarily at least, stemmed the flow. Possibly because of her youth, the autobiographical impulse is also fairly sporadic, and does not appear to be a sustained, concerted attempt at writing an autobiography. Dates of publication, which are not necessarily proof of time of writing with Amélie Nothomb, do not correspond to the chronology of life events. *Métaphysique des tubes,* which came last, actually goes back further in time than the first, and the middle text (*Stupeur et tremblements*)[6] deals with a more recent event than the other two (see Appendix). Yet the autobiographical project is an ancient one, encapsulated in her vow to herself

as a three-year-old, conflating reminiscing with writing: 'Tu dois te souvenir! Tu dois te souvenir! Puisque tu ne vivras pas toujours au Japon, puisque tu seras chassée du jardin [. . .], tu as pour devoir de te rappeler ces trésors. Le souvenir a le même pouvoir que l'écriture [. . .]' (*MT* 139).

In this postmodern age, 'memories' and 'writing' are strangely uncomplicated words under Nothomb's pen, to the point that it begs the question: what do these fragments contribute to her early promise and, perhaps more importantly for the reader, to the ever problematic genre of autobiography? I'll take Nothomb's latest autobiographical publication, *Métaphysique des tubes*, the 'book of (her) genesis', as a canvas into which, when pertinent, threads from *Le Sabotage amoureux* and, to a lesser extent, *Stupeur et tremblements* can be woven. On this tapestry, three overlapping pictures of the protagonist emerge—as a metaphysical being, a gendered being, and a national being.

The striking beginning of *Métaphysique des tubes*—'Au commencement il n'y avait rien'—blends hyperbole and philosophy, the hallmark of all three works, and the ending: 'Ensuite il ne s'est plus rien passé'. The metaphysical terminology has overtones of Nietzschean and Sartrian philosophizing, and the irony of a 170-page text starting with the word nothing and finishing with 'rien' will strike more than one reader, in addition to the fact that on a factual level, it is clearly not true. The character continues to live; she even becomes a writer and a narrator who writes about other sequences of her ensuing life. The assertion ['Ensuite il ne s'est plus rien passé'] is true if we accord a philosophical meaning to the word nothing: nothing of value, nothing of note. Such an airy nihilism is not new, and can be associated with the cliché that infancy is a lost paradise as in a fable. Marguerite Yourcenar for instance, in her memoirs—where she studiously avoids talking about herself—cites a letter written as a child to her aunt following the death of her dog: 'C'est en somme ma première composition littéraire; j'aurais pu aussi bien m'en tenir là'.[7] Childhood is so significant that it can only be followed by a vacuous life where death or at least decline are the only likely prospects, or a literary career trying to recapture a lost innocence.

Richard N. Coe's seminal work, *When the Grass was Taller*, detects a decidedly mystical tendency in many of the six hundred of what he terms 'Childhoods' with a capital 'C', all texts dealing with the early years of life.[8] In particular 'l'enfant métaphysicien' is a recurrent topos of many autobiographies and is reminiscent of Jungian psychoanalytical models rather than Freudian ones. For instance, in the first volume of his autobiography, Michel Leiris sets about narrating 'la métaphysique de l'enfance'[9] (which, incidentally, might have provided Nothomb with her title). Many writers in Coe's corpus—to which we can now add Nothomb—believe in a communal subconscious, listing numerous cases of early irrational intuitions such as intimations of immortality. Nothomb's views of childhood and identity are then relatively commonplace in tales of childhood, yet they have rarely been pushed to their logical conclusions as in *Métaphysique des tubes* and *Le Sabotage amoureux*.

As an example among many, Nothomb claims the word 'death' was the sixth she

uttered. She 'discovered' death before discovering life: 'Mort! Qui mieux que moi savait? Le sens de ce mot, je venais à peine de le quitter [. . .] Qu'avaient-ils [ses parents] pensé que je faisais, dans mon berceau, pendant [deux ans et demi], sinon mourir ma vie, mourir le temps, mourir la peur, mourir le néant, mourir la torpeur?' (*MT* 54). The theme of 'death within life' pervades literature in general, and Nothomb's texts in particular, with an unusual degree of elaboration and transmutation: death is, at the very least, not the scarecrow adults assume it to be. In fact the four-year old Amélie courts death a few times, and if she doesn't tell her mother that she tried to commit suicide in the fish pond (*MT* 168) it's only to protect her from the truth. But if we are to believe Michel Picard, 'quand on parle de la mort, on parle toujours d'autre chose',[10] if we accept therefore that Death stands here as a mere decoy, Nothomb is speaking not of the death of her body, but that of a delusion. She loses her self-image as an ego endowed with willpower, supreme confidence, and acute consciousness. 'L'autre chose' Nothomb deals with, is the loss of the child's natural sense of the divine.

The author represents her former self as closer to unmediated truths via her natural mysticism, than any other person, any other adult. As Coe writes, 'the child, through its inspired fantasies is still able to participate more immediately than the average adult in the common, total past of the human race'.[11] However Nothomb goes much further than any of her predecessors in her insistence on the metaphysical nature of infancy. In fact, baby Amélie is beyond any adult-made philosophy, in a 'nothingness' outside any category imagined by man, be it time, movement, evolution, existence: 'être ou ne pas être, telle n'était pas sa question' (*MT* 13). The baby, 'God or the Plant', is the essence of a cosmic nothing, 'le rien' with only one force, its 'force d'inertie' (*MT* 15). The implication is that this baby in its claim to nihilism represents the purest condition imaginable, maybe a state all babies go through, if only for shorter periods of time than Amélie Nothomb, but which they forget about. She is unique in the sense that not only did she not forget that stage, but she can put into language what is in essence a non-language stage. 'Si jeune et déjà surdouée',[12] a critic comments ironically. Her remarkable feat is to make us forget that she is not writing her memories, be they early ones, but reconstructing pre-verbal sensations. In fact, this and the idea that a baby might feel like a God, or a cosmic entity, is carried out in the most serious tone by a narrator who is a typically Nothombian, argumentative, seemingly logical thinker au fait with Cartesian reasoning. An amusing metatextual comment can apply to this very text: the narrator mentions Slawomir Mrozek who is supposed to have written remarks on tubes that are either 'confondants de profondeur ou superbement désopilants' (*MT* 9). Both qualifications apply simultaneously to these texts whose serious tone is constantly undercut by irony.

In her 'book of genesis', *Métaphysique des tubes,* mock-serious flourish tinges the telling of each new phase of baby Amélie's life. Past her second birthday she grows out of the pure 'principle of Nirvana'[13] she embodied so far and for the next six months, she is mad with rage, a kind of wrath of God, which stems from her realization that she is not all-powerful, she is not in control of the world (*MT* 29). She will find peace a few months later. As with the sudden eruption of her divine anger, the causation of events is illogical. In a pastiche of a sacred text, the two-and-a half year old discovers a unique sense of identity. As in a fairy-tale she is bestowed a faith—the primacy of her Self—when eating a piece of chocolate (entering the 'oral stage' or experiencing the holy communion?) proffered by a good fairy (or rather, 'l'ange Gabriel' in keeping with the biblical overtones of the passage). This 'éveil au plaisir' via the marvellously symbolic Belgian chocolate, this moment of adumbration, is followed by the narrator's musing on the 'logical' links between self, voluptuousness, and memory, as if her design was to rewrite infant psychology and western philosophy and religion in one fell swoop. Facetious as it is, this sophistry nonetheless holds some truth, the unproven truths of the mystical child.

There is a similar, although less central, scene, in *Le Sabotage amoureux* when the five-year-old Amélie arrives in China, after having drunk a mug of strong tea: 'La théine est en train de provoquer des feux d'artifice dans mon crâne. Sans en rien laisser paraître je suis folle d'excitation. Tout me semble grandiose, à commencer par moi' (*SA* 18). It is significant that such exhilaration should arise from her coming into contact with China, a 'foreign' culture for a Belgian child who had been living so far in Japan. The underlying connection between the two scenes in *Métaphysique des tubes* and *Le Sabotage amoureux* is the protagonist's exploration of a national identity: what does it mean for Amélie Nothomb, born in Japan and bred in many foreign, far-eastern countries, to be Belgian. It comes as no surprise that Nothomb, daughter of a diplomat with a multitude of short-term postings, should be concerned with national identity. Her discovery of Europe at seventeen induced in her 'un malaise pathologique'.[14]

National identity is also a prevalent theme in Belgian literature. A case in point that is particularly telling for our study, is Jacques Lecarme's use of Belgian childhood tales to support the following analysis: 'Serait-ce alors une caractéristique culturelle que le désir de raffermir une appartenance culturelle toujours problématique en remontant aux sources du fleuve?'[15] Specific to Nothomb however are the exaggeration and humour she puts to good use in dealing with this core theme: the chocolate-induced revelation initiates a search for identity through language and, again as a 'metaphysical' child, she finds not her individual identity but a universal law. 'Pour moi, il n'y avait pas des langues, mais une seule et grande langue dont on pouvait choisir les variantes japonaises ou françaises, au gré de sa fantaisie' (*MT* 58). She accepts that East and West meet in her, a hybrid being. This is embodied in her choice of the best first words to utter, as obvious performative speech-acts: 'J'avais déjà donné leur nom à quatre personnes [maman, papa, aspirateur (sic) et ma sœur]; à chaque fois, cela les rendait si heureuses que je ne doutais plus de l'importance de la parole: elle prouvait aux individus qu'ils étaient là' (*MT* 49). Pastiche never being very far away, the chapter about speaking is articulated around Saussure's linguistic distinctions between 'langage' and 'parole'. It is also obvious that Nothomb is inverting other philosophers' theories of language: 'Barthes—mais aussi Foucault, Derrida et Lacan—[pensent que] le Moi n'est rien d'autre que le produit du langage, l'être n'existe que par l'énonciation'.[16] Our godlike protagonist, who had language at her disposal from day one, but would not utter any word aloud, scornful of even the need to communicate at all, is allowing *others* to come into existence by uttering their names. Language is indeed at the heart of all existences.

Language expression set in national hybridity is later dramatized in an episode where Amélie is drowning in the sea—a very 'Japanese' setting since 'la purification, l'absolution par l'eau, est une donnée culturelle du Japon'[17] as well as an amniotic-like liquid—and the seventh French word uttered by little Amélie (*MT* 78). This secular baptism forces her to call 'au secours', thereby confessing 'que je parlais la langue de mes parents' (*MT* 80). Yet something did drown in the Sea of Japan: her muteness in French and her preference for the Japanese language which she talked freely with her Japanese nanny. Reconciled now with her two national identities, she starts a series of many compromises with universal values. She has to separate the two 'varieties' of the mother language she imagined existed beyond all distinctions. Ultimately she will have to find a less provisional answer to her quest for identity: to be a hybrid leaves open the question of the respective dosages of the national influences. More importantly hybridity is an uncomfortable position to occupy as it threatens those people attached to unambiguous notions of nationhood. That is the reason why, in a reverse, ironical gesture of disappropriation, the narrator of *Stupeur et tremblements* will have to give up her Japanese language skills while working as an interpreter for a Japanese company: 'Comment nos partenaires [dit Monsieur Saito] auraient-ils pu se sentir en confiance, avec une Blanche qui comprenait leur langue? A partir de maintenant, vous ne parlez plus japonais' (*ST* 20). It is also revealing that the ending of *Stupeur et tremblements* would coincide with the birth of the writer—a French-speaking writer. Possibly because *Stupeur et tremblements* deals with Amélie as an adult, the question of national identity is treated, somewhat disappointingly, by way of simplified stereotypes (for instance, her comments on Japanese intolerance for Westerners' ways (*ST* 125)), whereas, in *Le Sabotage amoureux,* with its child protagonist, that question still makes up a polysemic dramatic element of the plot.

Le Sabotage amoureux, like *Métaphysique des tubes,* hails a 'heady celebration of childhood'[18] as the narrator's and the protagonist's minds seem again truly fused,[19] and the distance between adult author and younger self almost abolished as a manifestation of Nothomb's statement: 'Je suis une nostalgique à jamais de mon enfance'.[20] Despite a mock philosophical beginning (this time a reworking of Wittgenstein's theory on reality: 'Le monde est tout ce qui a lieu' (*SA* 11, 19)), *Le Sabotage amoureux* is a romanticized version of childhood, as a higher moral state than adulthood. The word 'romanticized' might seem exaggerated since Amélie, together with the children of many nations living in Beijing's diplomatic compound, are waging a war between themselves. Their war is presented, like Yves Robert's classic film *La guerre des boutons* (1962), as no less real in the minds of the children as an adult war, and certainly 'purer' in its objectives, and rules. It is based on honour, and nobody gets killed, just humiliated. National traits are ridiculed, with German, Italian, French, Korean, Cameroonese children of the 1970s trying to rectify World War Two's past alliances and errors: 'Le métier de nos parents consistait à réduire autant que possible les tensions internationales. Et nous, nous faisions juste le contraire. Ayez des enfants' (*SA* 146). Violent historical events—World War Two is also the backdrop to *Métaphysique des tubes,* with Nishio-san's horrific tales of her family being wiped out by accidents and by the bombing of Hiroshima—emphasize the notion that adulthood is a corrupt stage of human-kind, and how death and loss in fact underscore Amélie's happy childhood.

In effect, the divide between the world of adults and the world of children in *Le Sabotage amoureux* is as pronounced as in *Métaphysique des tubes,* with adults always slightly silly, inadequate, and certainly never bearers of truths. Compared with her godlike, all-knowing, haughty self, the adults surrounding Amélie (her parents, her Belgian grandmother, Kashima-san, called the 'Antechrist' (*MT* 73), Nishio-san, the doctors), are just like children, wide-eyed, incomprehending, over-whelmed by whatever situation they encounter.

Autobiographies are basically 'romans familiaux': Marthe Robert went as far as making 'le roman familial' the origin of all writings where 'le remplacement de ses parents par de plus intéressants implique leur suppression'.[21] In Nothomb's works, her parents occupy a limited space in the plot.[22] The mother figure seems to be vir-tually replaced by Amélie's two Japanese nannies, and the father, the Belgian Con-sul, is represented as a slightly ludicrous, likeable disciple of a tyrannical Nô mas-ter. It is as if a literary smokescreen shrouded the usual autobiographical exhibition of unresolved family dynamics.

In *Le Sabotage amoureux* adults are no more than a hindrance to the children's self-important manoeuvres; they must be 'surveillés' (*SA* 50) and contained. Grown-ups exemplify the absurdity of un-enlightened human beings who have warped views on true priorities. The dichotomy between children and adults is no-where better exemplified in *Le Sabotage amoureux* than in the love story between six-year-old Amélie and an Italian girl, Elena, a story which thematizes the forma-tion of gender identity, the third focal point of these texts.

As befits the metaphysical child, that love is of the purest kind as in a Greek tragedy—the parallels with Omer's *Iliad* are made explicit (*SA* 111–14) with Elena a substitute for Helen of Troy. It is not the first autobiographical text to contain a precocious love story, for instance, Romain Gary's *La Promesse de l'aube* and his pre-pubescent protagonist infatuated with cruel Valentine,[23] or Marcel Pagnol who, as an eleven-year-old, is subjugated by a poet's tyrannical daughter.[24] As Peter Härtling writes in *Ben est amoureux d'Anna:*

> Les adultes disent parfois aux enfants: 'Vous ne pouvez pas savoir ce qu'est l'amour. C'est une chose que l'on apprend quand on est grand'. Cela veut dire que les adultes ont oublié un tas de choses, qu'ils ne veulent pas vous parler ou qu'ils font les idiots. Je me souviens très bien qu'à l'âge de 7 ans, je suis tombé amoureux pour la première fois.[25]

In Elena, Nothomb too paints the 'éternel féminin': the beautiful, delicate, pretty, and crafty girl who is incapable of loving, but thrives on being loved, enjoying the power game and being made to exist through the lover's gaze, even if the 'lover' is only a tomboy. Elena's ultra-feminine behaviour challenges Amélie's views that 'l'humanité était divisée en trois catégories: les femmes, les petites filles et les ridicules' (*SA* 70). Amélie holds onto her conception regardless. Beyond the sheer intensity of discovering love for the first time and for someone who is incapable of reciprocating, the parallels with previous childhood tales stop here. In *Le Sabotage amoureux* unrequited love produces fantasies of cruelty and, following the advice of her mother, her only significant input in her daughter's life, Amélie calculatingly pretends indifference in order to win over Elena, all in vain. The protagonist learns many lessons about love and in particular that heroic actions (such as peeing over the 'enemy'. . . standing up like a boy) are not as efficient in love wars as making the loved one suffer, be it through jealousy, or feigned disdain. With her usual hyperbolic pen the narrator states at the very end of *Le Sabotage amoureux*: 'Merci à Elena, parce qu'elle m'a tout appris de l'amour' (*SA* 124). This final 'tout' is of the same ilk as the initial 'rien' of *Métaphysique des tubes,* it is all at once trivially and deeply true and false. The trivial tends to focus on an 'éducation sentimentale' of sorts, and turns the attention away from the more intimate theme of Amélie's gender identity formation, the real 'tout' of her learning.

This is after all a love between two little girls. In pre-sexual loves the gender of the 'lovers' is often irrelevant to the story, although this same-sex love can be analysed as an attempt at seducing the 'bad' mother. In *Métaphysique des tubes* Amélie's awareness of gender differences is framed by her avowed disgust for boys and men, 'les ridicules'. In Japan, the month of May is, unjustly in the protagonist's mind, dedicated to boys, through the worshipping of carps, 'emblème du sexe moche' (*MT* 99). Amélie's sickened fascination for water and carps leads her parents to give her three carps for her third birthday, a real fall from the 'divine age', and the beginning of a period of anguish and gender confusion, as if her parents wanted to endow her with a phallic attribute. It would be however simplistic to assume that carps, in the child's eyes, represent penises.[26] In effect with their open, greedy mouths they come to symbolize complementary masculine and feminine principles (maybe the impossible 'feminine phallus').[27] They fuel the anxiety that children entertain of being eaten alive, a universal fear of being annihilated, and returned to the life/death-giving womb.

In *Stupeur et tremblements* to a lesser extent, the same-sex sado-masochistic pattern played out between Elena and little Amélie is repeated between a twenty-year-old Amélie and Fubuki Mori. In a way, then, she has learnt 'rien' instead of 'tout'. The narrator, however, shows a rare hint of compassion for Fubuki, the epitome of the Japanese woman whose only alternative is suicide or abject submission to macho values (*ST* 86–95). Nothomb's commiseration for Japanese women tends to cancel out misogynistic pronouncements in her other works, as in *Hygiène de l'assassin*.[28] The author provocatively claimed in that text that the main protagonist's derogatory comments were her own.[29] It is also worth mentioning that Nothomb is a member of the 'Chiennes de garde', a vocal and sensationalistic movement against sexist statements made about female public figures.[30] Rather than try, on the basis of playful and provocative texts, to attribute to Nothomb gender definitions or sexual preferences (and much could be made of Amélie's macho ways of subjugating her enemies in *Le Sabotage amoureux*), it is more fruitful to note that the author leaves open and unresolved her quest for gender identity. Her proposition might be that this is what a search for identity is: never closed, never concluded.

In view of the three works' themes—the protagonist's metaphysical, national and gendered identities –, and their common tone—hyperbolic, ironic, provocative with a sustained foregrounding of their fictional and literary nature—would the reader be right in signing the autobiographical pact? We have to bear in mind that readers don't tie down autobiographers any more to a dogmatic generic pact, expecting rather aesthetic pleasure from overlaps and playful infringements of strict genre rules, working out for themselves each text's own mode of reading.

Notwithstanding her unsophisticated views of childhood memories and her provocative, self-assured, reversal of the tenets of autobiography, Nothomb does not spoil the modern-day trend that blurs the boundaries between fiction and autobiography. Nothomb belongs to a generation well aware of, and contributing to, changing horizons of expectations, and the new norms of compulsory aporia and contradictions regarding the various components that make up the writing of a life: self, truth, memories, etc. Contemporary writers are inclined simultaneously to exaggerate and deprecate the autobiographical labelling, and obscure any possible generic dichotomy between autobiography and novel, in particular with regards to truthtelling. The pendulum of truth oscillates between fiction and faction since André Gide's standoffish remark in a mere footnote to his own autobiography: 'Peut-être même approche-t-on de plus près la vérité dans le roman [que dans les mémoires]'[31] which is echoed by David Malouf's words: 'Maybe, in the end, even the lies we tell define us. And better, some of them, than our most earnest attempts to tell the truth'.[32] This has signalled the opening of the road towards intergenericity, of which two further signposts are worth mentioning. 'Tout ceci doit être considéré comme dit par un personnage de roman',[33] writes Roland Barthes in his own subversive autobiography; Serge Doubrovsky pursues and theorizes his series of autofictions, or fictions of his own self: 'Si j'essaie de me remémorer, je m'invente . . . JE SUIS UN ÊTRE FICTIF'.[34]

Although the events around which the three works are built are all based on true, verifiable facts of Amélie Nothomb's life, the autobiographer naturally selects, dramatizes, and ultimately mythifies them to form the framework of highly readable tales: a six-year-old girl experiencing an unrequited love affair in Beijing during the 1970s; a baby with the inflated ego of a God (or a Plant, depending on whom you believe) discovering its self by eating Belgian white chocolate and surviving two drownings; and finally, a one year job in a Japanese company turning into a sado-masochistic, mystical experience.

Despite the formal unity between author, narrator and character, despite the retrospective narration, despite the factual evidence and her own assertions, Nothomb discourages a strictly autobiographical reading by saying that '[*Le Sabotage amoureux*] est d'abord une écriture, donc un roman'.[35] Far from being provoked by such a comment about the opposition between life and writing, owing in particular to the theorization and successful practice of 'autofiction', modern readers do anticipate that 'Dans les souvenirs d'enfance, il ne faut pas chercher une biographie, mais un imaginaire'.[36]

Besides, in the same 1998 interview quoted at the outset, Amélie Nothomb claimed that 'Pour être bien claire, Tach, c'est moi. Je suis déguisée en mon contraire, en vieux bonhomme obèse, très célèbre et mourant, pour dire tout ce que je pensais'.[37] A thinly disguised (!) pastiche of Gustave Flaubert's pronouncement 'Madame Bovary, c'est moi' it implies that readers should don their autobiographical glasses at all times when dealing with her so-called fictional works.

Nonetheless, we have found a method in her autobiographical style: the systematic use of exaggeration, reversal, humour, and pieces of sophistry, suggesting that pastiche informs the three texts: pastiche of the book of genesis and educational treatises in *Métaphysique des tubes;* pastiche of tragedy and war stories (including a love war) in *Le Sabotage amoureux;* and finally a tangled pastiche of a sadomasochistic *roman d'éducation,* 'polar psychologique'[38] and 'rapport de stage'[39] in *Stupeur et tremblements.* Such a formula is also put to good use in her novels (see for instance *Péplum,* the pastiche of a futuristic novel, or *Mercure,* a reworking of 'Beauty and the Beast'). A question remains nonetheless with regards to the autobiographical works: what is the point of Nothomb's pastiches? There are obvious 'moral' lessons propounded by the confident narrator, very much as in a 'conte'. Nothomb's views on childhood are reminiscent specifically of the *Emperor's new clothes,* where children expose adults' flaws. In fairy tales it is quite acceptable to create a playful, magical atmosphere where archetypal adults (good, bad, cruel, saviours etc.) are secondary to the drama played out by resourceful children.

Nothomb in fact borrows from a specific type of 'conte', the 'conte philosophique'. Take for instance *Le Sabotage amoureux*'s allusions to *Candide,* with Voltairian sentences such as 'Nous le haïssions tous pour ces motifs excellents' (*SA* 47). 'Contes philosophiques' always volunteer moral lessons which in this case could be worded as follows: 'Urges such as violence and love are innate and atavistic. Educators should accept that' (*Le Sabotage amoureux*). 'Adults have to acknowledge and grieve for the lost spiritual, egotistical child in them' (*Métaphysique des tubes*); 'Sado-masochism is at the heart of the Japanese identity –and possibly all love affairs' (*Stupeur et tremblements*). Not everybody might agree that such crude wording does justice to the complexity of those multilayered, polysemic tales, but it is undeniable that all three books promote the view that there is no such thing as civilization: barbarism reigns supreme, in boys and girls, in childhood, in adulthood, in Japan, in China, in families, in love and war, in the past and the present. . .

Fairy-tale truths belong on a different plane to autobiographical truths, as they don't rely on accuracy or memory. They apply collectively to humankind, but do not disclose much about specific individuals. Now we can see the point of using the conventions of the 'conte'. On the side of the modern-day reader, the *self in fabula* makes for satisfactory reading because of its appeal to universality,[40] and because an autobiographical 'conte philosophique' is a first in literary history in France, I believe, and an outstanding accomplishment. For the writer too, it serves a purpose: not to reveal publicly Amélie Nothomb's personality of the flesh-and-blood person, one of the classical expectations of the genre of autobiography, but to add to the disguise by dressing herself in fantasy clothing.

Yet since writing one's autobiography is a golden opportunity for self-knowledge what did the autobiographer achieve for herself? Does it fulfil her 'devoir de mémoire', her early promise to herself? If we take the issue of national identity, in the end it seems that Amélie's search is diluted into nothingness by ironic generalizations: 'il est exact que nous sommes tous chinois. A divers degrés, certes: chacun a son taux de Chine en soi, comme chacun a son taux de cholestérol dans le sang ou de narcissisme dans le regard' (*SA* 81). The same goes for the other main themes: all babies are metaphysical beings, who later, as young children, turn into quasi-barbarians, and later again, as full-blown sadistic adults. Love is an exercise in sado-masochism. Nothomb's satire of a Japanese company obscures, rather than enlightens, the stereotypical, supposedly insurmountable exotica of far-eastern cultures. Yet, because of her ironic stance and exaggerations, Nothomb can't be pinned down to any 'theory' of national, gendered or spiritual identity, and therefore doesn't risk alienating any reader, or being fixed in lifeless, ossified self-portraits. However, it seems that she doesn't take the risk of self-revelation either. The narrator's position at once inside and outside the autobiographical pact allows her to remain uncommitted to truthtelling, even to herself. She stays in that very nothingness—in the last words of *Métaphysique des tubes,* 'entre deux eaux' (*MT* 171)—she facetiously praised. From there she entertains us with her grief in coming to terms with her lost metaphysical self, lost national identity, and lost illusions concerning love.

University of Western Australia

Notes

1. Marthe Robert, *Préface aux Contes de Grimm* (Paris: Gallimard, 1990), p. 20.
2. Interview d'Amélie Nothomb, Madeleine Tombeur, *Le Logographe,* 3 avril 1998, available online at http://www.multimania.com/fenrir/nothomb/logographe.htm (accessed 19 April 2001).
3. For a full discussion on memory, memories and reconstruction, see Julien Rouart, 'Souvenirs et fantasmes: de la remémoration aux constructions', *Revue française de psychanalyse* (2nd March 1971), 217–47.
4. *Métaphysique des tubes* (Paris: Albin Michel, 2000), p. 41. Subsequent references in the text will appear as *MT* followed by the page number.
5. *Cosmétique de l'ennemi* (Paris: Albin Michel, 2001). Subsequent references in the text will appear as *CE* followed by the page number.
6. *Stupeur et tremblements* (Paris: Albin Michel, 1999). Subsequent references in the text will appear as *ST* followed by the page number.

7. Marguerite Yourcenar, *Quoi? L'éternité* (Paris: Gallimard, Biblos, 1990), p. 813.
8. Richard N. Coe, *When the Grass was Taller, Autobiography and the Experience of Childhood* (New Haven & London: Yale University Press, 1984).
9. Michel Leiris, *L'Age d'homme* (Paris: Gallimard, 1973), p. 29.
10. Michel Picard, *La littérature et la mort* (Paris: Presses Universitaires de France, 1995), p. 60.
11. Op. cit., p. III.
12. Thierry Gandillot, 'Nô, carpes et chocolat', *L'Express,* available online at *www.l'express.fr* (accessed 9 June 2001).
13. For a psychoanalytical critique, see Anon. *Métaphysique des tubes,* available online at *http://www.multimania.com/fenrir/nothomb/tubes.htm* (accessed 9 June 2001).
14. Tombeur, op. cit. It should also be noted that Prétextat Tach said he 'died' aged seventeen, *Hygiène de l'assassin* (Paris: Albin Michel, 1992), p. 143.
15. Jacques Lecarme, 'La légitimation du genre', in *Le récit d'enfance en question, Cahiers de sémiotique textuelle,* 12, Université Paris 10 (1988), 21–39 (p. 34).
16. Mounir Laouyen, 'L'autofiction: une réception problématique', paper delivered at the Colloque Fabula, available online at Fabula.org, 1999, 4 (accessed 5 March 2000).
17. Frédéric Grolleau, 'La vie en tube', Paru.com, available online at *http://www.paru.com/redac/critiqueLitterature/axxxx687.htm* (accessed 6 September 2001).
18. M. A. Orthofer, 'Love in the Middle Kingdom: Amélie Nothomb's *Loving Sabotage*', *The Complete Review,* II, 2 (May 2001), available online at *http://www.complete-review.com/quarterly/vol2/issue2/nothomb.htm* (accessed 10 September 2001).
19. The blending of the two viewpoints, that of the adult narrator and the young protagonist is not seen as a quality by Ook Chung: 'les deux registres narratifs ont tendance à se télescoper et à confondre le lecteur', in 'Une enfance épique', *Liberté* 34, 3, 213 (Juin 1994), 220–226 (footnote 3, p. 221).
20. Quoted from an interview with Evelyne Wilwerth, 'Amélie Nothomb: sous le signe du cinglant', *La Revue générale,* 6–7 (1997), 45–51 (p. 47).
21. Marthe Robert, *Roman des origines et origines du roman* (Paris: Grasset, 1988), p. 76.
22. A critic suggested that the two nannies represent Mélanie Klein's concept of 'good' and 'bad' mothers, leaving the biological mother 'hors jeu', op. cit., available online at http://www.multmania.com/fenrir/nothomb/tubes.htm (accessed 10 May 2001).
23. Romain Gary, *La Promesse de l'aube* (Paris: Gallimard, 1960).
24. Marcel Pagnol, *Le Château de ma mère* (Paris: Julliard, 1958).
25. Peter Härtling, *Ben est amoureux d'Anna* (Paris: Bordas, 1981) (traduit de l'allemand, 1980), p. 71.
26. For a psychoanalytical analysis, see, Anon. op. cit.
27. See Picard, op. cit., pp. 119–38.
28. *Hygiène de l'assassin* (Paris: Albin Michel, 1992).
29. Tombeur, op. cit.
30. Annick Cojean, 'La rage des "chiennes de garde"', *Le Monde,* 12 février 2000, p. 13.
31. André Gide, *Si le grain ne meurt* (Paris: Gallimard, 1954), p. 545.
32. David Malouf, *Johnno: A Novel* (St. Lucia: University of Queensland Press, 1975).
33. Roland Barthes, *Roland Barthes par Roland Barthes* (Paris: Seuil, 1975), p. 5.
34. Serge Doubrovsky, *Le Livre brisé* (Paris: Grasset, 1989), p. 212.
35. Interview quoted by Jocelyne Hubert, *Amélie Nothomb, Le Sabotage amoureux* (Paris: Magnard, 2001), p. 6.
36. Danielle Deltel, 'Le meccano du souvenir: les doublets autobiographies chez Colette',

in *Le récit d'enfance en question, Cahiers de sémiotique textuelle,* 12, Université Paris 10 (1988) 137–153 (p. 150).

37. Entretien au centre culturel de La Botanique, 3 avril 1998, quoted in Hubert, op. cit., p. 6.

38. Hugo Marsan, 'Les dédicaces de France-Inter', *Le Monde,* 17 septembre 1999.

39. As was suggested by an anonymous reader to Alapage.com (accessed 30 August 2001).

40. As the quote heading this article implies.

APPENDIX

Date of publication	Title	Age of Amélie (as a character)	Age of narrator	Number of years covered
1993	*Le Sabotage amoureux* (2nd book published)	5 to 8 year-old	26 year-old	3 years
1999	*Stupeur et tremblements* (8th)	20 year-old	32 year-old	1 year
2000	*Métaphysique des tubes* (9th, penultimate)	0 to 3 year-old	33 year-old	3 years

Désirée Pries

PISCINA: GENDER IDENTITY IN
MÉTAPHYSIQUE DES TUBES

*Quel malheur que d'être femme! Et pourtant le pire malheur quand
on est femme est au fond de ne pas comprendre que c'en est un.*[1]

Puberty, or the Mind/Body Split

Amélie Nothomb's experience of puberty, and her transformation into
womanhood, was a revelation to her of her limitations: 'J'ai vécu la puberté comme un drame à de multiples niveaux, entre autres comme une limitation dans le regard d'autrui; c'était passer d'une identité totale (au sens du
"spectacle total") à une identité limitée dans laquelle je ne me suis jamais reconnue'.[2] Nothomb's first novel, *Hygiène de l'assassin,* sets the groundwork for the exploration of what she calls the feminine condition, and the crisis of puberty, seen
also in her later novels and autobiographies. Putatively fiction, *Hygiène de l'assassin* is highly suggestive of autobiography. Nothomb, who echoes Flaubert when
she claims 'Tach, c'est moi', speaks through this eighty-year-old man to express
dissatisfaction with, or rather outright disgust of, the feminine condition. The answer? 'Il faut supprimer les femmes'.[3] Prétextat Tach, Amélie Nothomb's surrogate in her first novel, proposes to obliterate women as a solution to the feminine
condition. Women are trapped in an existence which lies somewhere between life
and death, a non-life. Once a little girl reaches puberty, Tach explains, her life has
ended, and she enters into this non-life. Tach, with his cousin Léopoldine, attempts to stave off the onset of puberty through a particularly stringent regime
of self-starvation in *Hygiène de l'assassin,* in the belief that the answer to the feminine condition is to avoid adulthood and puberty, to remain pre-adolescents.

They are united in an unspoken pact, and wander the grounds of the Chateau of Saint-Sulpice, isolated as if in a Garden of Eden. Tach fails in his attempt to stay trapped in childhood, as Léopoldine does fatefully one day menstruate: she is strangled and her murder is re-narrated by her assassin-cousin as a drowning, a Hugo echo in her name, but more so a lost Ophelia, faithful to this literary icon. This adolescent Léopoldine-Ophelia of Nothomb's first novel is recuperated and saved in her third autobiographical novel of 2000, *Métaphysique des tubes,* in which young Amélie foresees being chased from her own Garden of Eden in Japan, and demonstrates that the awareness of gender difference and its social consequences comes at a much earlier age.

What does it mean to write as a woman? For Amélie Nothomb, it means to write, in part, about the feminine condition. This is consonant with the general scholarly conviction that gender, or the fact of femininity, is a shaping force in autobiographies written by women. Nancy K. Miller states in *Writing Fictions: Women's Autobiography in France* that 'the subject of women's autobiography is a self both occulted and overexposed by the fact of her femininity as a social reality'.[4] Michael Sheringham, in 'Changing the Script: Women Writers and the Rise of Autobiography', finds a similar pattern in canonical women's autobiography 'involving the struggle with social and cultural constructions of femininity [. . .] against the background of the biological realities of the female condition'.[5] Women perceive themselves as representing 'the fate of womanhood'. Where bodily experience (puberty, sexuality, or pregnancy) is invoked, it is often in ambivalent or negative terms. Such ambivalence characterizes Amélie Nothomb's works, where the body and the social construct of femininity are problematized.

Feminist theory tends to divide into the camps of essentialism (assigning inherent feminine traits to women) and constructivism (considering women as constructed entities, in the manner of Simone de Beauvoir that 'one is not born a woman, but becomes one'), although they are united in one respect: the problem of gender. The works of Amélie Nothomb deconstruct the notion of the feminine by utilizing both essentialist and constructivist discourses. The author insists that she is a humanitarian, not a feminist, in an effort perhaps to avoid this dichotomy,[6] and to deconstruct the social construct of gender. Nonetheless, as a woman writer, her focus is clearly on the formation of feminine identity. Susan Stanford Friedman claims that 'a [. . .] man has the luxury of forgetting his [. . .] sex. He can think of himself as an "individual". Women, reminded at every turn in the great cultural hall of mirrors of their sex [. . .] have no such luxury'.[7] Amélie Nothomb, looking into her autobiographical mirror, focuses on the importance of the female gender. Throughout Nothomb's texts, the role of women in a patriarchal society is re-evaluated and questioned. In *Stupeur et tremblements,* the Japanese woman is trapped within her own body.[8] Amélie-san finds herself confined in this society, and it is in fact a woman, Fubuki Mori, who arrests Amélies-san's ascent of the corporate ladder. Women are presented as victims in *Hygiène de l'assassin,* 'victimes particulièrement pernicieuses puisqu'elles sont avant tout victimes d'elles-mêmes, des autres femmes' (*HA* 67).

Childhood is presented as a problematic utopia, an escape from this victimization. In *Le Sabotage amoureux,* Nothomb defines her child self as a little girl, a third sex, separate from the other two sexes (male and female), and maintains a superiority of childhood for 'les petites filles', little girls. I use the term 'third sex', but Nothomb herself prefers a 'beyond sex', or 'au-delà des sexes', presumably to deconstruct gender, rather than add a third element to an already complex binary.[9] Interestingly, Cixous uses the German language in 'La Venue à l'écriture' to escape gender. Children, and more importantly for this thesis, little girls, are referred to with a neuter article, rather than a masculine or feminine article: *'das* Kind' and *'das* Mædchen'.[10] Nothomb exhibits a similar frustration with gendered articles when she uses a masculine form to refer to herself in *Le Sabotage amoureux:* 'Quand je serai gran*d,* je penserai à quand j'étais peti*t*' (my emphasis).[11] However, even the littlest girls do not ultimately escape the repressive gender binary, as is demonstrated in Nothomb's third autobiographical novel, *Métaphysique des tubes.* Between the ages of two and a half and three years, young Amélie first becomes aware of the consequences of gender difference and is revolted by, and revolts against, the feminine condition. If her earliest childhood constituted a utopian space, 'au-delà des sexes', the novel concludes with the sullen realization of normative feminine difference. The so-called autobiographical account of Nothomb's life from age zero to age three is in fact a metaphor for puberty and the trauma of the transformation of the body of a seemingly androgynous little girl.

Métaphysique des tubes presents a world where toddlers are demi-Gods and a baby girl is reassured of her place at the centre of the universe. Young Amélie has the impression of controlling her universe and the people surrounding her: with a word, she can give life and meaning, simply by naming an object. Her divine power brings her the adoration of her Japanese nanny and assures her of her supreme power. The beginning of the novel suggests a complete identity, such as that found in the womb, before the division of self and the creation of ego,[12] or for Nothomb, the onset of puberty. It is a Biblical wholeness, Oneness, possessed by God, ruler of the Christian world. The infant Amélie imagines herself to be a God, creating a fictive image of 'identité totale'. Yet, in this Garden of Eden which is childhood, even a divine ruler must fall. The first taste of evil comes in the form of a flag, brandished in honour of the month of boys.

Schizocarp: Carp as the Symbol of the Gender Binary and Identity Split

It is the month of May; Amélie is two months away from her third birthday. A scandal interrupts this earthly paradise when she discovers the first signs of gender difference, hoisted on a flagpole. The face of gender inequality is a fish. Her family lives in Osaka, Japan, and they follow Japanese tradition by raising a flag with a carp to honour each boy in the household during the month of May. She asks when the month of girls is celebrated, and is told that this does not exist. In Japan in 1970, there was no month to celebrate girls.[13] This is the first discovery of the social consequences of sexual differences. Although she had already noticed that there is a difference between genders (her mother and father, her brother and sister all provided examples), she realizes for the first time the injustice of this difference. Suddenly, the opposition between woman and man appears more important than all others (such as height, nationality, etc). She is puzzled about the superior place of males—why is there a flag and a month dedicated to masculinity, while not even a day is set aside to celebrate femininity?

> En quoi évoquait-elle davantage mon frère que moi? Et en quoi la masculinité était-elle si formidable qu'on lui consacrait un drapeau et un mois (. . .) Alors qu'à la féminité, on ne dédiait pas même un fanion, pas même un jour![14]

Amélie decides to study carps in order to unveil this mystery. Her parents interpret her curiosity as a 'passion ichytyologique' (*MT* 98) and later present her with a birthday gift of three fat, ever-hungry carps. However, Amélie's attraction for the carps is motivated by disgust. Initially, this disgust appears to be of the male body:

> C'était peut-être ça, le point commun à l'origine de cette symbolique: avoir quelque chose de vilain. Les filles n'eussent pas pu être représentées par un animal répugnant [. . .]. Les Japonais avaient eu raison de choisir cette bête pour emblème du sexe moche (*MT* 98–99).

An emblem of the 'ugly sex', a 'repugnant animal', the carp represents the difference between little boys and girls, that which little girls lack. In describing her disgust of the carps, young Amélie contrasts the outward physical realities of the male and female body, as seen through the eyes of a child:

> Les tuyaux ouverts avalent. Lorsqu'ils ont dégluti, ils en réclament de plus belle. Leur gorge est si béante qu'en se penchant un peu on y verrait jusqu'à leur estomac [. . .] *normalement, les créatures cachent l'intérieur de leur corps. Que se passerait-il si les gens exhibaient leurs entrailles?* (*MT* 157, my emphasis).

Female sex organs are neatly tucked away, hidden inside, while the male sex organs are external, readily exposed. Rather than exhibiting a Freudian penis-envy, she is revolted by a body that exposes its sexual characteristics on the outside.

The carps are a symbol for the masculine, and become a terrifying obsession. Forced, against her will, to feed the carps every day at noon, Amélie imagines herself overpowered by the carps, possessed by them:

> Sous mon oreiller, je pleurais d'horreur. L'autosuggestion était si forte que les gros corps écailleux et flexibles *me rejoignaient entre les draps, m'étreignaient*—et leur gueule lippue et froide me roulait des pelles. J'étais *l'impubère amante de fantasmes pisciformes* (*MT* 152, my emphasis).

She is the prepubescent lover of fish-like fantasy. Yet, just as she accepts unwillingly the gift of three carps from her well-meaning parents, she receives the kisses of these fish-dreams with horror. The carp scene, or rather her reliving of the carp scene in her bed at night, is presented as a rape in which she becomes the involuntary lover of carps:

> *Ce n'était pas son estomac qui me dégoûtait, mais sa bouche,* le mouvement de valvule de ses manibules qui me *violaient* les lèvres pendant des éternités nocturnes. À force de fréquenter des créatures dignes de Jérôme Bosch, mes insomnies naguère féeriques virèrent au *martyre* (*MT* 152, my emphasis).

'Violated' by their mouths, she is a 'martyr', a victim of their incessant hunger. Women are seen as food. This image is common in adolescent girls, who dream of their bodies being eaten alive during the transformations and turmoil of puberty. Amélie's own account of her fish dreams echoes this phenomenon documented in adolescent girls by psychologists such as Mary Pipher in *Reviving Ophelia: Saving the Selves of Adolescent Girls*.[15] The adolescent girl imagines herself to be eaten alive in the social restrictions of a Phallic economy.

Mirror: Fear of the Feminine

The image of the carp, however, cannot be reduced simply to the masculine. It is not the stomach that disgusts Amélie, but the mouth of the carp. The stomach, and by extension, the intestines, 'entrailles', as seen in the quotation above, are symbols of the masculine sex. In contrast, the gaping mouth of the carp represents the feminine sex. There is thus a slippage in the carp symbol from the masculine to the feminine. When Amélie claims, upon noting the useless and annoying nature of boys (and specifically older brothers), 'peut-être faudrait-il les exterminer' (*MT* 99), her disgust for the masculine gender echoes Prétextat Tach's own disgust of the adult feminine body in *Hygiène de l'assassin*. Tach imagines that the extermination of all women is the only solution to the feminine condition: ('il faut simplement exterminer les femmes . . . si les femmes n'existaient pas, les choses iraient enfin dans l'intérêt des femmes' (*HA* 145)).

The carps are evoked in remarkably feminine terms. They resemble 'Castafiore muettes, obèses et vêtues de fourrures chatoyantes' or 'épaisse silhouette de poissons-divas, de prêtresses surnourries de la pisciculture' (*MT* 97). Of course the word carp is feminine in the French language, yet Amélie goes beyond grammatical gender by using feminine nouns to describe the carps: 'divas' and 'prêtresses' and 'Castafiore'. There is a striking similarity between this description of carps, 'obèses et vêtues de fourrures chatoyantes', and Tach's description in *Hygiène de l'assassin* of girls when they mature sexually: 'les filles deviennent affreuses, boutonneuses, fessues, malodorantes, poilues, nichonneuses, hancheuses [. . .]—*femmes, en un mot*' (*HA* 145, my emphasis). The carp, symbol for the masculine sex, for the

Other, becomes the mirror in which Amélie sees herself, female, in opposition: 'unique spécificité individuelle [. . .]: dis-moi ce qui te dégoûte et je te dirai qui tu es. Nos personnalités sont nulles, nos inclinations plus banales les unes que les autres. Seules nos répulsions parlent vraiment de nous' (*MT* 150–151). If this transformed adage is true, Amélie is repulsed by her own femininity, and the place of woman in a Phallic order.

Young Amélie discovers herself in this mirror of the ever-hungry, never-satisfied mouths of carps, whose bodies are reduced to nothing but a digestive tube which eats, processes, expels waste, and asks for more: 'La bouche des carpes te rendrait-elle si malade si tu n'y voyais pas ton *miroir ignoble*? Souviens-toi que tu es tube et que tube tu redeviendras' (*MT* 158, my emphasis). A 'tube sorti d'un tube', the image of the carp reflects her existence as a female. Born of woman, she will become a woman. The carps are a mirror of her own sex, not her parents or whole family, but the female members of her family. 'Si ce spectacle t'obsède tellement, c'est peut-être parce que tu t'y reconnais. Crois-tu que ton espèce soit différente? Les miens mangent moins salement, mais ils mangent, et dans *ta mère,* dans *ta sœur,* c'est comme ça aussi' (*MT* 158, my emphasis). The use of 'les miens' in the masculine plural and the third person plural 'ils' grammatically includes both the masculine and the feminine. Yet the examples given further define the carps as a mirror of the feminine: 'les miens' are in fact 'les mien(ne)s', her mother and her sister (and not her father or brother). She is overcome by disgust with that which represents the feminine. The carp-tube is at once the male gender, which defines the feminine as the 'Other' or in Lacanian terms a 'lack', and the female gender, that which feels the hunger of this lack, expressed in the ever-open mouth of the hungry carp.

In her garden, Amélie sees a mirror of her decline, remarking for the first time the passage of spring to summer 'il y avait eu comme un automne au printemps. Une fraîcheur s'était fanée' (*MT* 95). It is her fall from grace, 'la fin de l'état divin' (*MT* 153), the biblical Fall from the Garden of Eden. Although young Amélie claims that 'Mai méritait bien d'être le mois des garçons: c'était un mois de declin' (*MT* 95), this fall is actually feminine. The passage of spring to summer is a metaphor not only for the recognition of sexual inequality, but also a foreshadowing of the passage of childhood to adulthood, or puberty.

The biblical metaphor is extended: baptized 'Jésus, Marie, et Joseph', the carps are associated with the transubstantiation she witnesses at midday. She imagines herself to be a 'prêtresse piscicole' (*MT* 148), crumbling and throwing the rice cake to the carps as if it were her own flesh: 'ceci est mon corps livré pour vous' (*MT* 148). In front of these 'sales gueules' she feels the transformation of her flesh as she watches the fish lips: 'lèvres poissonneuses qui me regardaient de leur regard de lèvres, ces lèvres saumâtres qui s'ouvraient et se refermaient avec un bruit obscène, ces bouches en formes de bouées qui bouffaient ma bouffe avant de me bouffer moi' (*MT* 149). The lips of the carps are obscene, nearly a *vagina dentate,* but without the need of teeth to consume. It is then she realizes that it is her own body, her female body, which feeds the carps, here a symbol for the feminine: 'j'avais de plus en plus l'impression que c'était ma propre chair qui nourrissait les carpes' (*MT* 151–2). She is 'that piece of bait named Ophelia'.[16]

Suicide: Fear of Feminine Death

In protest, Amélie begins to deprive her own body of nourishment. This is the onset of anorexia which will later plague both Nothomb and her sister in real life (the full onset at the age of thirteen and a half, the author often insists — the age of puberty): 'Je maigrissais. Après le déjeuner des poissons, on m'appelait à table: je ne pouvais rien avaler' (*MT* 152).[17] In order to control her body, she refuses to eat. Rather than nourish her flesh so that it in turn may nourish the carps, she fasts. Research on anorexia has shown that this disease is an attempt to remain in childhood (much like the unspoken pact in *Hygiène de l'assassin*). For example, 'Anorexia is [. . .] a complete suppression of sexuality, as well as a loss of secondary sexual characteristics; and a marked identification with the masculine and simultaneous rejection of the feminine'.[18] Amélie's true fear, in fact, is to become a woman. The 'fall' she fears is the transformation of her flesh, or puberty:

> Angoisse annexe: à trop subir les baisers poissonneux, n'allais-je pas changer d'espèce? N'allais-je pas devenir silure? Mes mains longeaient mon corps, guettant d'hallucinantes métamorphoses (*MT* 152).

Her hands trace along her body, imagining the round curves of womanhood. She wishes to stop this progression, this 'fall'. As is the case with documented cases of anorexia, the refusal to eat is 'an effort to make time stand still, not to grow but to go back to childhood size and functioning [. . .] a longing to re-create an old situation [. . .] *a lost Eden*'.[19] The terminology used in medical research on anorexia and found in both *Hygiène* and *Métaphysique des tube*s is strikingly similar.

Life, or the non-life of women, is represented as a continuous hunger and emptiness: 'la vie est ce tuyau qui avale et qui reste vide' (*MT* 159). In contemplation of this existence, Amélie asks herself: 'Entre la vie — des bouches des carpes qui déglutissent — et la mort — des végétaux en lente putréfaction —, qu'est-ce que tu choisis? Qu'est-ce qui te donne le moins envie de vomir? (*MT* 159). Which causes the least disgust, death or a life which is neither life nor death? Amélie answers her question by falling headfirst into the pond.

One must compare Amélie's own attempted suicide to the group suicide described earlier in *Métaphysique des tubes*. In 1945 at Okinawa, an island in the south of Japan, a group of Japanese threw themselves from a cliff, persuaded that the Americans were going to kill them. Not unlike the logic that incited the victims of the September 11, 2001 terrorist attack of the New York Twin Towers to take their destiny in their own hands and jump to their deaths, or the imagined 'défenestration' of *Stupeur et tremblements,* Amélie comments, 'La meilleure raison, pour se suicider, c'est la peur de la mort' (*MT* 165). In her garden, where she no-tices the change of seasons for the first time, the fading spring and the decadence of summer, Amélie imagines the life that awaits her, her oncoming puberty, and she refuses it. If the best reason to commit suicide is fear of death, it is the non-life of womanhood, the death that all woman know upon maturity that Tach ex-plains in *Hygiène de l'assassin,* which Amélie fears. The carps reflect to the little girl the woman she will become. In order to free herself, she chooses death. Her act is a way of regaining control. Margaret Higonnet, in 'Speaking Silences, Women's Suicide' states that suicide is motivated by the desire to control one's own life:

> To embrace death is at the same time to read one's own life. The act is a self-barred signature; its destructive narcissism seems to some particularly feminine. Some choose to die in order to shape their lives as a whole; others fragment life to generate the energy of fission or elision.[20]

This fission or elision is the search for a whole identity, not reducible to a gender binary.

Water: 'Eaux Sales' and 'Eaux Purificatrices'

It is not insignificant that Amélie's attempted suicide occurs in a pond. Engulfed in a text riddled with biblical allusions, this pond recalls the latin *Piscina,* which serves in a ritual of ablution, to cleanse the body. 'Suicide serves magically to purge the assaulted body'[21] from the metaphorical rape of the carp scene. Voluntary death is not merely a deathwish, 'but an incommunicable or impossible life-wish',[22] for the 'only way for a woman to attain a state of wholeness may be to move beyond the body'.[23] One way Nothomb distances herself from the body is to insist on the uto-pian nature of childhood, the near-androgynous little girl. The problematic notion of an androgynous little girl is found in the figure of Ophelia, Shakespeare's hero-ine destroyed by the conflicting pressures of society as she stood at the brink between childhood and adulthood. Pushed and pulled by the demands of her fa-ther, her brother, her uncle, and her lover, Ophelia is eventually driven to madness. Treated like a child by all of the male figures in her life, she is silenced and eventu-ally driven to madness and death. A girl struggling through the changes of pu-berty, her sexuality, her desire, is threatening. Her brother lectures her on chastity, her lover refuses her and suggests 'get thee to a nunnery'.[24] It is as if the world around her keeps her from developing into adulthood, despite the changes taking place in her body.

Like Ophelia, Amélie embraces suicide: 'délicieusement sereine, j'observe le ciel à travers la surface de l'étang' (*MT* 150). She repeats several times, as she is waiting for death: 'je me sens très bien' (*MT* 160). This scene recalls Ophelia's drowning in Shakespeare's *Hamlet* recounted by her surrogate mother (in-law):

> Queen [. . .] Her clothes spread wide,
>> And mermaidlike awhile they bore her up,
>> Which time she chanted snatches of old lauds,
>> As one incapable of her own distress,
>> Or like a creature native and endues
>> Unto that element.[25]

Léopoldine, the false *noyée* of *Hygiène de l'assassin,* is also reminiscent of Ophelia. Although the name Ophelia is not used in *Métaphysique des tubes,* there are many parallels between this character and Amélie. In the quote above, Ophelia is described as 'a creature native (to) that element', water. The narrator of *Métaphysique des tubes* also claims several times that water is her element. 'L'eau en dessous de moi, l'eau au-dessus de moi, l'eau en moi—l'eau, c'était moi. Ce n'était pas pour rien que mon prénom, en japonais, comportait la pluie' (*MT* 122). Just as the death of Ophelia is ambiguous, rewritten as an accident by the queen, or a suicide by the grave diggers who place her body in a cemetery, Amélie's protest is also silenced.[26] After being fished out of the pond by her nanny, her mother explains her death: 'Tu nourrissais les poissons, tu as glissé, tu es tombée dans le bassin' (*MT* 167). Amélie's choice (suicide), or protest, is rewritten as an accident.

Not only is her suicide covered up, Amélie also finds that she does not possess her own body. She continues to show evidence of her Ophelia-like insanity, 'ma propre folie' (*MT* 169), by trying to explore the wound that she has from her fall. 'Je veux entrer par le trou dans ma tête et explorer l'intérieur'. A nurse stops her and she cries bitterly 'on ne possède même pas son propre corps'. She asks for a mirror, but even this is refused: 'Je veux me regarder dans un miroir! Je veux voir le trou dans ma tête!'[27] The symbolism here is clear: Amélie is refused a *speculum* and is not allowed to explore her own body.[28] Her own sexual identity does not belong to her, but to the world around her.

The figure of Amélie-Ophelia is a metaphor for the fear of the feminine. Freudian hysteria, or insanity, is an unconscious revolt. This metaphorical death that occurs when the self is split in puberty (or in feminine terms, cleaved), is in fact a protest. Cixous also warns her reader of the death of a girl (and woman's desire):

> On tue une fille:
> Au commencement, j'ai désiré.
> – Qu'est-ce qu'elle veut?
> – Vivre. Rien que vivre. Et m'entendre dire le nom.
> – Horreur! Coupez-lui la langue!
> – Qu'est-ce qu'elle a?
> – Peut pas s'empêcher de voler!
> – En ce cas, nous avons des cages extra.[29]

Whereas Cixous's girl cannot stop flying, Amélie cannot stay out of the water, her element of choice. Swimming produces the weightlessness of flying. It is in the water that Amélie almost drowns twice, where her father is symbolically ridiculed in the sewer ('eaux sales'). It is also in water that young Amélie finds liberation, swimming in 'Le Petit Lac Vert' (*MT* 122), and recaptures her identity. In her beloved lake, swimming until she melts, the mind-body split is healed, and she reestablishes an identity unfettered by gender. Her nanny, and surrogate mother, fears for her and calls her back, but she has already found herself: '(*Nishio-san*) Sors du lac! Tu vas fondre! (*Amélie*) Trop tard. J'avais déjà fondu depuis longtemps' (*MT* 125). Rather than being split ('fendu') by a prescribed feminine identity, she has melted ('fondu') into her true self.

The writer Amélie establishes her identity through writing ('eaux purificatrices'). The fish dreams of *Métaphysique des tubes,* or 'fantasmes pisciformes' (previously cited) are a motivating theme in Nothomb's writing. These fish dreams recall Hélène Cixous's 'poissonges':

> Plus tard si je sors de mes eaux toute ruisselante de mes plaisirs, si je remonte le long de mes rives, si j'observe depuis mon bord les ébats de mes *poissonges,* je remarque les figures innombrables qu'ils produisent dans leur danse; ne suffit-il pas que coulent nos eaux de femmes pour que s'écrive sans calcul nos textes sauvages et populeux? Nous-même dans l'écriture *comme les poissons dans l'eau,* comme les sens dans nos langues et la transformation dans nos inconscients.[30]

Cixous suggests that women 'write through the body', in celebration of women's bodies, filling pages with milk-ink. Women and men alike are called upon to 'write through the body'. Using the biological realities of the female body symbolically (maternity and hence creativity, through mother's milk), Cixous exalts femininity as a source of inspiration.

Amélie Nothomb, in contrast, evokes the biological female body in disgust, yet redefines the body and her identity through the symbol of water in her writing. The feminine body is symbolic not for its creativity and possibility, but rather for the limitations placed upon it by a patriarchal society. Water is the cleansing element by which one can cleanse the body and start anew. Léopoldine-Ophelia dies and repeats the tragic legend in *Hygiène de l'assassin.* However, the twenty-year-old Amélie of *Stupeur et tremblements* survives subjugation by imagining a 'défenestration', and is finally liberated by the publication of her first novel. Rather than being silenced in a suicide/death, Ophelia speaks. Likewise, the Amélie-Ophelia of *Métaphysique des tubes* revives Ophelia, the saved self who shall overcome puberty. Tach's conviction that women must be assassinated at the start of adolescence, 'Il faut supprimer les femmes', should be understood as the necessity to destroy woman as a social construct, the feminine body as it is inscribed in language and history. Providing only unsatisfactory alternatives to the non-life of women (an abortive attempt to remain a child in *Hygiène de l'assassin),* encouraging the destruction of woman, Nothomb provocatively suggests an exploration outside the traditional associations with a woman's body, and the conception of an alternative feminine identity. The failed suicide attempt of Amélie-Ophelia in *Métaphysique des tubes* is a triumph. She finds her voice in water, 'tel un poisson dans l'eau'. A revived Ophelia, her voice is recaptured to describe the horror of puberty when a girl is transformed into a woman. Nothomb refuses to proselytize 'je n'essaie pas de donner des conseils aux autres. Je me contente d'envoyer mon itinéraire',[31] and *Métaphysique des tubes* closes with the provocative line 'Ensuite, il ne s'est plus rien passé' (*MT* 171). Not so: Ophelia speaks, re-narrates her own metaphorical death, and lives on.

Why this troubling final sentence (we know something happens later, we already have her biography from age five to seven in *Le Sabotage amoureux,* and at the age of twenty in *Stupeur et tremblements)*? Why does Nothomb refuse to be labelled a feminist, and prefer the term 'civisme' to 'féminisme'?[32] The answer can be found in the dual image of the carp. Just as the carp can be seen as either male or female, water is presented as a binary: it can either be stagnant or clean. The dirty water is rhetorically found in the womb, in menstruation, or by extension dish and laundry water, and all the biological and social realities of womanhood. Both men and women, born of woman, are fish swimming in this sea of gender difference (hence the double symbol of the carp, which is both masculine and feminine). Men do not escape the trap of gender, as is demonstrated when her father is trapped in the sewers in *Métaphysique des tubes.* Clean water (a metaphorical womb, an ideal of wholeness of total identity) can thus be a liberation for both men and women, not a feminist goal, but a civic goal, a humanitarian effort. Nothomb writes through her personal experience as a woman, but her individual drama felt during puberty is a universal phenomenon that touches both boys and girls, men and women. If we follow the hope found in Nothomb's texts, both Ophelia and Hamlet shall speak.

Indiana University

Notes

1. Kierkegaard, citation used as epigraph in Simone de Beauvoir's *Le Deuxième sexe, vol. II* (Paris: Gallimard, 1949).
2. Nothomb, cited from personal correspondence, dated from Paris 18.04.02.
3. *Hygiène de l'assassin* (Paris: Albin Michel, 1992), p. 145. Subsequent references in the text will appear as *HA* followed by the page number.
4. Nancy K. Miller, 'Writing Fictions: Women's Autobiography in France', in *Lifelines: Theorizing Women's Autobiography,* ed. by B. Brodzki & C. Schenck (Ithaca: Cornell UP, 1988), pp. . . . .
5. In *A History of Women's Writing in France,* ed. by S. Stephens (Cambridge: Cambridge UP, 2000), pp. 185–203 (p. 189).
6. Telephone interview with Amélie Nothomb on April 9, 2002.
7. Cited from *Autobiography and Questions of Gender,* ed. by Shirley Neuman (London: Frank Cass, 1991), p. 2.

8. Although both men and women must hide the physical realities of their bodies (for example, sweat), women take this to a higher level. For example, serving as Mme Pipi, Amélie-san discovers that Japanese women continually flush the toilet while using the facilities in order not to be heard. *Stupeur et tremblements* (Paris: Albin Michel, 1999), p. 89. Subsequent references to the text will appear as *ST* followed by the page number.
9. See note 6.
10. Hélène Cixous, 'La Venue à l'écriture', in *Entre l'écriture* (Paris: des femmes, 1986).
11. *Le Sabotage amoureux* (1993) (Paris: Albin Michel, Livre de poche, 2000), p. 55. Subsequent references to the text will appear as *LS* followed by the page number.
12. See Jacques Lacan, *Écrits* (Paris: Seuil, 1966) and Elizabeth Grosz, *Jacques Lacan: A Feminist Introduction* (London and New York: Routledge, 1990).
13. Girl's month in Japan is now the month of March, symbolized, unsurprisingly, by a doll.
14. *Métaphysique des tubes* (Paris: Albin Michel, 2000). Subsequent references in the text will appear as *MT* followed by the page number.
15. For research regarding the need to rediscover one's 'inner (girl) child', see Mary Pipher, *Reviving Ophelia: Saving the Selves of Adolescent Girls* (New York: Ballantine Books, 1995), specifically pages 31–32, and Emily Hancock, *The Girl Within: A Groundbreaking New Approach to Female Identity* (New York: Ballantine Books, 1989).
16. Jacques Lacan, 'Desire and the Interpretation of Desire in *Hamlet*', in *Literature and Psychoanalysis: The Question of Reading Otherwise,* ed. by Shoshana Felman (Baltimore: Johns Hopkins UP, 1982).
17. Nothomb, cited from personal correspondence, dated from Paris 18.04.02.
18. Leslie Heywood, *Dedication to Hunger: Anorexia Aesthetic in Modern Culture* (Berkeley: University of California Press, 1996), pp. 17–18.
19. Hilde Bruch, *The Golden Cage: The Enigma of Anorexia Nervosa* (Cambridge: Harvard UP, 1978), p. 70, my emphasis.
20. Margaret Higonnet, 'Speaking Silences, Women's Suicide,' in *The Female Body in Western Culture,* ed. by Susan Suleiman (Cambridge & London: Harvard UP, 1986), p. 69.
21. Ibid., p. 74.
22. Ibid., p. 81.
23. Ibid., p. 79.
24. William Shakespeare, *Hamlet,* ed. by David Benington (New York: Bantam, 1988), III: 1, p. 66.
25. *Hamlet,* IV. vii, pp. 176–82.
26. Much research has been done on the madness (hysteria) of Ophelia. See for example Gabrielle Dane, 'Reading Ophelia's Madness', *Exemplaria: A Journal of Theory in Medieval and Renaissance Studies,* 10, 2 (1998), 405–23.
27. All three preceding quotations are from *MT* 169.
28. L. Irigaray, *Speculum de l'autre femme* (Paris: Éditions de Minuit, 1974).
29. Cixous, op. cit., p. 17.
30. Ibid., p. 62, my emphasis.
31. See note 17.
32. See note 6.

REPRESENTATIONS OF THE BODY

Victoria B. Korzeniowska

BODIES, SPACE AND MEANING IN AMÉLIE NOTHOMB'S *STUPEUR ET TREMBLEMENTS*

Amélie Nothomb's *Stupeur et tremblements* was published to largely critical acclaim in 1999 and shared the 'Grand prix du roman de l'Académie Française' with François Taillandier's *Anielka*. The novel is, according to the author, an account of her experience working as a translator in Japan in 1990. Here, I will examine how the heroine in Nothomb's novel constructs her own personal reality. The theoretical basis for my discussion is derived from Mark Johnson's work *The Body in the Mind. The Bodily Basis of Meaning, Imagination, and Reason* in which Johnson stresses the importance of the body's physical relationship to space in the individual's conception and understanding of existence and of her or his place within it.[1]

'Virtually everyone agrees', Johnson notes, 'that human *experience* and *meaning* depend in some way upon the body, for it is our contact with the entire spatio-temporal world that surrounds us',[2] and he also argues that individual reality is shaped by 'the patterns of our bodily movement, the contours of our spatial and temporal orientation, and the forms of our interaction with objects'.[3] Embodied experience is thus fundamental to how we reason about our lives, and gives our existence structure. The central focus of Johnson's work is the 'image schema', which he views as a defining structure in human existence. He defines the image schema thus:

> in order for us to have meaningful, connected experiences that we can comprehend and reason about, there must be pattern and order to our actions, perceptions, and conceptions. *A schema is a recurrent pattern, shape, and regularity in, or of, these ongoing ordering activities.* These patterns emerge as meaningful structures for us chiefly at the level of our bodily movements through space, our manipulation of objects, and our perceptual interactions.[4]

Corporeal interaction with the spatial environment thus creates repeated patterns that contribute to our understanding of the world. However, these repeated patterns alone are not enough to complete our picture of our world and Johnson also foregrounds the importance of imagination as an ordering tool of human existence. Rejecting the definition of imagination that associates it solely with 'art, fantasy and creativity', he suggests that imagination should, in fact, be seen both as a creative force and also as 'a faculty that connects perception with reason'.[5] '"Imagination"', he suggests, 'is a basic image-schematic capacity for ordering our experience; it is not merely a wild, non-rule-governed faculty for fantasy and creativity'.[6]

Turning now to *Stupeur et tremblements,* it is immediately apparent that corporeality and imagination are central features of Amélie's experience of working for the Yumimoto company. The heroine's understanding of her world is shaped by a number of 'image schemata' which originate in the patterns of her body's movement through the spaces of the Yumimoto company, and also by her imagination which she uses both creatively and also as an ordering tool to rationalize what, at times, appears to be a surreal experience. The image schemata, which I will focus on in this discussion, are up-down and also in-out, and I will examine how the heroine uses her imagination to decode or, on occasion, subvert the messages from these image schemata. I should emphasize that Johnson's work includes a far greater range of image schemata than it is possible to study here and I have therefore selected those that are the dominant organizing features in *Stupeur et tremblements.*

The up-down or verticality image schema is, I suggest, the most powerful structure in *Stupeur et tremblements* and derives, according to Johnson, 'from our tendency to employ an UP-DOWN orientation in picking out meaningful structures of our experience'.[7] It is immediately established right at the beginning of the novel when Amélie talks about the Yumimoto company hierarchy and locates herself as an employee on a one-year contract within the physical pyramid of employees that is Yumimoto:

> Monsieur Haneda était le supérieur de monsieur Omochi, qui était le supérieur de monsieur Saito, qui était le supérieur de mademoiselle Mori, qui était ma supérieure. Et moi, je n'étais la supérieure de personne.
> On pourrait dire les choses autrement. J'étais aux ordres de mademoiselle Mori, qui était aux ordres de monsieur Saito, et ainsi de suite, avec cette précision que les ordres pouvaient, en aval, sauter les échelons hiérarchiques.
> Donc, dans la compagnie Yumimoto, j'étais aux ordres de tout le monde.[8]

This up-down structure is simultaneously accompanied by the other structuring schema in the novel, namely the in-out schema, and Amélie notes 'le 8 janvier 1990, l'ascenseur me cracha au dernier étage de l'immeuble Yumimoto' (*ST* 7). Spat out by the lift, she is immediately ingested by the insatiable Yumimoto company: a giant organism which swallows up its employees and devours their efforts in order to grow ever more powerful. Our recurring experience of 'in' and 'out' structures is, according to Johnson, one of the most powerful image schemata. 'Our encounter with containment and boundedness', he observes,

> is one of the most pervasive features of our bodily experience. [. . .] From the beginning, we experience constant physical containment in our surroundings (those things that envelop us). We move in and out of rooms, clothes, vehicles, and numerous kinds of bounded spaces. We manipulate objects, placing them in containers (cups, boxes, cans, bags, etc.). In each of these cases there are repeatable spatial and temporal organizations. In other words, there are typical schemata for physical containment.[9]

As the introductory paragraphs to *Stupeur et tremblements* seen above demonstrate, Amélie's initiation into the company, far from conveying reassurance and welcome is, instead, designed to emphasize her inferiority and insignificance. This is a company in which size matters and in which everything seems to be conceived to physically intimidate the individual and to promote feelings of inadequacy. For example, when Amélie first arrives and is shown round the offices by M. Saito, she is taken to 'une salle gigantesque dans laquelle travaillaient une quarantaine de personnes' (*ST* 9). The Yumimoto company itself, we learn,

> était l'une des plus grandes compagnies de l'univers. Monsieur Haneda en dirigeait la section Import-Export, qui achetait et vendait tout ce qui existait à travers la planète entière.
> Le catalogue Import-Export de Yumimoto était la version titanesque de celui de Prévert: [. . .]. L'argent, chez Yumimoto, dépassait l'entendement humain. A partir d'une certaine accumulation de zéros, les montants quittaient le domaine des nombres pour entrer dans celui de l'art abstrait (*ST* 15).

Within this titanic structure, offices are 'géants' (*ST* 26, 104), filing cabinets and the mail delivery trolley 'énormes' (*ST* 26, 65). Nothing is on a human scale, not even the Vice-President M. Omochi who is referred to as 'la montagne de chair' (*ST* 48) and 'l'obèse' (*ST* 108). On this grandiose scale of oversized office equipment and heavyweight management, the normal individual employee shrinks into insignificance. 'Les employés de Yumimoto', we learn, 'comme les zéros, ne prenaient leur valeur que derrière les autres chiffres. Tous, sauf moi, qui n'atteignais même pas le pouvoir du zéro' (*ST* 16).

Fortunately for Amélie, she has a highly active, or even hyperactive, imagination and, on her arrival at Yumimoto, she immediately spots what is to be the instrument of her salvation, the *baie vitrée*:

> La fenêtre, au bout du hall, m'aspira comme l'eût fait le hublot brisé d'un avion. Loin, très loin, il y avait la ville—si loin que je doutais d'y avoir jamais mis les pieds. Je ne songeai même pas qu'il eût fallu me présenter à la réception. En vérité, il n'y avait dans ma tête aucune pensée, rien que la fascination pour le vide, par la baie vitrée (*ST* 7–8).

Her fascination with this window punctuates the novel, and imaginary defenestration becomes a constructive political act designed to counteract the stifling conformism of the workplace. According to Kevin Hetherington, 'identity formation as a process of identification is a spatially situated process. It is, however, about creating symbolic spaces rather than always adopting established ones'.[10] In *Stupeur et tremblements*, Amélie rejects identification with the confining spaces and systematic domination of the Yumimoto company in favour of the sense of freedom and alternative values signified by the *baie vitrée*. Her elective identity thus lies elsewhere in a mental escape from reality: a transgressive act of resistance that creates an alternative ideology challenging that of her employer. This rejection of boundedness, and desire to situate herself on the 'out' side of the in-out schema also extends to Amélie's experience of the Yumimoto company hierarchy with its accompanying up-down or verticality image schema.

The up-down schema is not solely the product of the company's intimidating physical size; it is also amplified by a sadistic and misogynistic management style which is designed to further humiliate the individual employee. Physical intimidation, the feeling of not being able to measure up to the company's gargantuan structure is an everyday experience for the Yumimoto employee. Translated to an abstract level, this experientially based pattern builds up into a mental image which confirms the individual's lack of value and is an effective reinforcement of the up-down hierarchy which is the linchpin of the Japanese work ethic as presented in the novel. During what Hugo Marsan has called Amélie's 'expérience paroxystique de la soumission aberrante', she encounters the 'codes rigides d'une forteresse commerciale'[11] on a regular basis as she repeatedly commits serious errors of judgement and infringes the inflexible Japanese code of conduct. A number of her infractions result from ignorance of the strict etiquette which governs the Japanese work place, although her penchant for getting into trouble is also partly attributable to a detached irreverence and lack of respect for authority combined with an independence of spirit that does not go down well in this conformist society. As Dominique Bona indicated in her review in *Le Figaro*, 'la narratrice est une Désobéissante, une Nargueuse, une Insolente dans l'âme'.[12]

Even though Amélie begins her 'career' at what is ostensibly the bottom of this 'fourmilière de bureaucrates nippons',[13] her first steps are not auspicious as she dismally fails to write a satisfactory letter on behalf of M. Saito accepting a golfing invitation. This lack of success is characteristic of what is to follow as Amélie never, in fact, produces any work that meets with M. Saito's approval. A catalogue of errors ensues. Unfortunately, I do not have the space to go into a detailed analysis of all the different episodes here and I will therefore restrict myself to a number of the key milestones in Amélie's downward mobility.

Her inadequacy as an employee is further reinforced when she is severely reprimanded for being able to speak Japanese and for having done so when serving coffee to a visiting company. To the error of speaking Japanese is added the 'grave crime d'initiative' (*ST* 28) as Amélie decides to deliver the mail. After 'un savon mérité' (*ST* 29), she is allowed to advance people's calendars, but she once again gets into trouble for doing this in a humorous way. As punishment, she is given a thousand pages of M. Saito's golf club's annual report to photocopy, something which she, once again, fails to complete to M. Saito's satisfaction.

On each occasion Amélie finds herself subjected to a verbal assault by an inflexible, dictatorial management which treats her as an outsider, a foreigner and an incompetent. Her bosses never offer advice, help or praise; their role is to chastise, criticize and disgrace. Such behaviour is characteristic of the sadistic power relations within the company whereby superiors regularly humiliate those who work for them either to reinforce their own status within the organization or to force employees to internalize physical humiliation as professional humility. Amélie's imposed status as Other is, moreover, accompanied by regular encounters with management that result in bodily expulsion from their offices. Almost every time Amélie goes into one of the boss's offices, it results in her being chastised for doing something that is against company rules or established propriety. The 'in' action of going into offices thus has its corollary, the 'out' action of being physically expelled for some misdemeanour. This is most graphically illustrated when Amélie takes up M. Tenshi's offer to collaborate on a project, naively thinking that this will release her from her humiliating treatment to date: 'J'envisageai l'avenir avec confiance. Bientôt, c'en serait fini des brimades absurdes de monsieur Saito, de la photocopieuse et de l'interdiction de parler ma deuxième langue' (*ST* 41).

Her excessive optimism and fantasies about her future within the company are, however, rapidly cut short as her efforts are denounced by her superior Mlle Mori. As a result, Amélie and M. Tenshi receive a torrent of verbal abuse from the Vice-President who accuses them of being 'des traîtres, des nullités, des serpents, des fourbes et—sommet de l'injure—des individualistes' (*ST* 42) and who expels the recalcitrant Amélie from his office shouting 'Sortez! Je ne veux plus vous voir' (*ST* 46).

Amélie's experience of physical containment, of being swallowed up by the Yumimoto organism, of being suffocated by its rules and stifled by the rigid conventions of Japanese society, is thus offset by ejection from offices for various misdemeanours. Ingestion and expulsion, illusory elevation and subsequent relegation are recurring patterns which order Amélie's working life, confirming her status as a cultural and professional outsider. Not surprisingly, the narrator feels a sense of dislocation in this highly formalized environment peopled by Japanese functionaries. The workspace is an alien construct, a war zone with which the non-conformist heroine's self-constructed identity rejects any identification.

Our heroine's response, far from internalizing her subordination or exclusion, is to resist. The up-down and in-out schemata which are the mental product of her physical experience at Yumimoto are acknowledged, yet simultaneously refused. Amélie rationalizes her experience through using her imagination. 'Imagination', Johnson notes, 'is our capacity to organize mental representations (especially percepts, images, and image schemata) into meaningful, coherent unities. It thus includes our ability to generate novel order',[14] and he suggests that imagination is both a structuring tool which enables us to make sense of our physical experience of the world[15] and also a source of 'art, fantasy, and creativity'.[16] Imagination thus helps Amélie both to understand her experiences and to give order to them, yet her cultural and personal heritage as an individualistic Westerner also leads her to reject the ideology that the Yumimoto company would impose on her and to create an alternative meaning born of fantasy and a refusal to be constrained.

As I have already suggested, this counter-culture is primarily focused on the *baie vitrée* which Amélie spotted when she first entered the company. Whereas the management of Yumimoto wishes to coerce her into conformity whilst simultaneously emphasizing her exclusion and status as an outsider, Amélie turns this on its head and transforms the out schema into an act of her own volition which is a rejection of the company straightjacket. She therefore takes every opportunity available to go past the *baie vitrée,* creating a rhythm which punctuates her working day:

> Avec mon chariot, qui me donnait une contenance agréable, je ne cessais d'emprunter l'ascenseur. J'aimais cela car juste à côté, à l'endroit où je l'attendais, il y avait une immense baie vitrée. Je jouais alors à ce que j'appelais 'me jeter dans la rue'. Je collais mon nez à la fenêtre et me laissais tomber mentalement. La ville était si loin en dessous de moi: avant que je ne m'écrase sur le sol, il m'était loisible de regarder tant de choses (*ST* 27–28).

This fascination with the *baie vitrée* necessitates transgressive behaviour, as Amélie deliberately chooses paths that take her past the window whenever possible. The window becomes the focal point, encapsulating Amélie's feelings of containment and release, and has the quality of 'l'illimité dans le conscrit' that Jean Rousset identified in *Mme Bovary*.[17] 'La fenêtre', Rousset observes, 'unit la fermeture et l'ouverture, l'entrave et l'envol, la clôture dans la chambre et l'expansion au dehors [. . .] oscillant entre le reserrement et la dilation',[18] and for Flaubert's characters it thus becomes 'le site idéal de [leur] rêverie'.[19] For Amélie, like Emma Bovary, the window is the pivotal point between inside and outside, in which co-exist conflicting tensions of containment and release. It is the symbolic gateway to her other life outside work, the dynamic focus of imagined escape, and the height and panoramic vision afforded by the window enhance the feeling of potential freedom. Her mental defenestration is thus a defiant act of spatial subversion, an exercise in personal empowerment which offsets the humiliating reality of working for the Yumimoto company. Unfortunately for Amélie, this respite can only be a temporary interlude from the catalogue of misery that is work, and each fantasy of escape is inevitably followed by a descent back into reality.

To the crime of initiative is added incompetence as Amélie reveals herself to be totally incapable of completing the next tasks assigned to her, namely assisting with accounts and checking expenses claims. The accounts episode is a total fiasco but, refusing to admit defeat, Amélie spends several nights in the office vainly trying to verify expenses claims. Her ensuing tiredness results in delirium and she reverts to her childhood fantasy of being God:

Fubuki, je suis Dieu. Même si tu ne crois pas en moi, je suis Dieu. Tu commandes, ce qui n'est pas grand-chose. Moi, je règne. La puissance ne m'intéresse pas. Régner, c'est tellement plus beau. Tu n'a pas idée de ma gloire. C'est bon, la gloire. [. . .] Jamais je n'ai été aussi glorieuse que cette nuit. C'est grâce à toi. Si tu savais que tu travailles à ma gloire! Ponce Pilate ne savait pas non plus qu'il œuvrait pour le triomphe du Christ. Il y a eu le Christ aux oliviers, moi je suis le Christ aux ordinateurs (*ST* 77–78).

As this quotation confirms, Amélie sees her time at Yumimoto as a type of religious persecution and herself as a martyr. Fubuki, for whom she initially felt great affection, has revealed herself to be 'le pire bourreau de l'entreprise'[20] in the episode with M. Tenshi, subsequently taking what seems to be a sadistic delight in reminding Amélie of her inadequacies and the failings of Westerners in general. Amélie, however, rejects this daily ritual of humiliation, and instead views herself as one of the elect, whose suffering raises her above the everyday and into an alternative realm.

'Identity', Kevin Hetherington notes, 'is about correspondence and dissimilarity. Principally, identity is articulated through the relationship between belonging, recognition or identification and difference'.[21] In articulating her identity as an oppositional construct distinct from, rather than a member of the Yumimoto collective, in locating her identity within the symbolic space of freedom from constraint that is the *baie vitrée*, Amélie is, in fact, committing a highly subversive act. Rejecting the Yumimoto company's imposition of normative behaviour, Amélie further transgresses during her final night of calculating expenses when she climbs naked over the office furniture, does headstands and ends up tipping a waste paper basket over herself. Somewhat surprisingly, this extreme behaviour is treated more leniently than some of her more minor misdemeanours and Amélie concludes:

les systèmes les plus autoritaires suscitent dans les nations où ils sont d'application, les cas les plus hallucinants de déviance—et, par ce fait même, une relative tolérance à l'égard des bizarreries humaines les plus sidérantes (*ST* 83).

Firmly re-established at the bottom of the company hierarchy, Amélie sinks once more into blissful obscurity, serving tea and coffee interspersed with periodic visits to the *baie vitrée*. She thinks that everyone has forgotten about her and no longer seeks to challenge her lowly status through rash, inappropriate behaviour, concluding that she cannot sink any lower.

Such complacent serenity is, however, completely misguided and when Amélie tries to comfort Fubuki, who has just been violently chastised by the Vice-President, she once more finds herself in serious trouble:

Fubuki avait été humiliée de fond en comble sous les yeux de ses collègues. La seule chose qu'elle avait pu nous cacher, le dernier bastion de son honneur qu'elle avait pu préserver, c'étaient ses larmes. Elle avait eu la force de ne pas pleurer devant nous.
Et moi, futée, j'étais allée la regarder sangloter dans sa retraite. C'était comme si j'avais

cherché à consommer sa honte jusqu'à la lie. Jamais elle n'eût pu concevoir, croire, admettre que mon comportement relevât de la bonté, même de la sotte bonté (*ST* 118). Fubuki's physical humiliation by M. Omochi has dishonoured her in the eyes of her colleagues but, by concealing her tears, she at least maintained a degree of professional standing. The fact that Amélie has seen her cry has completely undermined this, and Fubuki sees Amélie's genuine concern as an act of vengeance for the fact that Fubuki mistreated her in the past.

Out of malice, Fubuki puts Amélie in charge of the toilets on the 44th floor, this being the nadir of our heroine's 'foudroyante chute sociale' (*ST* 123). Amélie sums up her career in the Yumimoto company thus:

> Récapitulons. Petite, je voulais devenir Dieu. Très vite, je compris que c'était trop demander et je mis un peu d'eau bénite dans mon vin de messe: je serais Jésus. J'eus rapidement conscience de mon excès d'ambition et acceptai de 'faire' martyre quand je serais grande.
> Adulte, je me résolus à être moins mégalomane et à travailler comme interprète dans une société japonaise. Hélas, c'était trop bien pour moi et je dus descendre un échelon pour devenir comptable. Mais il n'y avait pas de frein à ma foudroyante chute sociale. Je fus donc mutée au poste de rien du tout. Malheureusement—j'aurais dû m'en douter —, rien du tout, c'était encore trop bien pour moi. Et ce fut alors que je reçus mon affectation ultime: nettoyeuse de chiottes (*ST* 122–23).

Amélie's physical humiliation is now complete. Made to feel small and inconsequential on her arrival in the company, Amélie has endured progressive humiliations designed to undermine further any feeling of self-worth. Corporeal experience has confirmed her position at the very bottom of the Yumimoto pyramid, her position on the 'down' side of the up-down image schema and on the 'out' side of the in-out schema through her status as a foreigner and outsider. Much of what she experiences can, in fact, be rationalized in terms of cultural difference, whereby what Amélie sees as constraining or oppressive is accepted as an everyday fact of life by her Japanese colleagues.

Recognition of the structures which define her experience at Yumimoto do not, however, imply compliance or acceptance and Amélie remains a rebel right to the end. Fubuki may feel that by assigning Amélie to toilet duty, she has finally put her firmly in her place but, in reality, her tactic backfires since Amélie refuses to resign and spends the remaining seven months of her contract in the toilets. 'Mon retournement des valeurs', Amélie notes,

> n'était pas pur fantasme. Fubuki fut bel et bien humiliée par ce qu'elle interpréta sans doute comme une manifestation de ma force d'inertie. Il était clair qu'elle avait tablé sur ma démission. En restant, je lui jouais un bon tour. Le déshonneur lui revenait en pleine figure. Certes, cette défaite ne fut jamais consommée par des mots. J'en eus cependant des preuves (*ST* 128–29).

Working for Yumimoto is all a question of power games and of getting one up over someone else. Fubuki's final attempt to subjugate Amélie thus resonates with a double failure. Not only does Amélie stay, but she once again inverts the values and hierarchy of her host company and nation and interprets her position in her own individualistic way. What Fubuki sees as a lowering of status destined to humiliate Amélie, Amélie interprets as a promotion:

> Elle [Fubuki] avait d'autres subordonnés que moi. Je n'étais pas la seule personne qu'elle haïssait et méprisait. Elle eût pu martyriser d'autres que moi. Or, elle n'exerçait sa cruauté qu'envers moi. Ce devait être un privilège.
> Je décidai d'y voir une élection (*ST* 148).

In accordance with Japanese custom, Amélie (in tongue in cheek fashion) lays all the blame for her corporate misadventure on herself when she leaves Yumimoto. Fubuki cannot resist the chance to belittle Amélie yet again and agrees on the suitability of Amélie's humorous suggestion that she become a refuse collector. The final image of the novel as Amélie leaves the company, is of the *baie vitrée:*

> D'instinct, je marchai vers la fenêtre. Je collai mon front à la vitre et je sus que c'était cela qui me manquerait: il n'était pas donné à tout le monde de dominer la ville du haut du quarante-quatrième étage.
> La fenêtre était la frontière entre la lumière horrible et l'admirable obscurité, entre les cabinets et l'infini, entre l'hygiénique et l'impossible à laver, entre la chasse d'eau et le ciel. Aussi longtemps qu'il existerait des fenêtres, le moindre humain de la terre aurait sa part de liberté.
> Une ultime fois, je me jetai dans le vide. Je regardai mon corps tomber (*ST* 173–74).

The novel has come full circle as the window was the first thing that Amélie saw when she arrived at Yumimoto and it is now the last thing that she sees when she leaves. The gulf between Japanese and Western cultures identified at the beginning of the novel has not been attenuated and we do not have the impression that any greater understanding or flexibility has been achieved. The Japanese workplace and Japanese society are portrayed as places in which co-operation and consensus are alien concepts and in which individuals are expected to behave like automata. Amélie's year at Yumimoto is thus a source of disappointment which shatters her childhood illusions about the idyllic nature of Japanese society. On one level, she feels that she has been badly treated, but this is accompanied by a recognition that her colleagues' situation is not to be envied either. 'Mon calvaire', she notes, 'n'était pas pire que le leur. Il était seulement plus dégradant' (*ST* 151–52).

On a physical level, Amélie's bodily interaction with the spatial environment centres on a perception of humiliation, expulsion and ingestion by an oversized corporation. Boundedness and containment, subjection and oppression are the resulting ordering constructs determining her working life. Fortunately, for Amélie, her vivid imagination, as well as having the ability to rationalize her body's humiliating experiences, also has the capacity to creatively transform and assign unconventional meaning. When she is appointed to toilet duty she notes:

> j'entrai dans une dimension autre de l'existence: l'univers de la dérision pure et simple. J'imagine que j'y avais basculé par activité réflexe: pour supporter les sept mois que j'allais passer là, je devais changer de références, je devais inverser ce qui jusque-là m'avait tenu lieu de repères (*ST* 127).

This mental self-defence mechanism not only enables her to cope, but also transposes reality and applies a different set of values to those in operation at Yumimoto. Freedom from constraint is therefore created where none exists, while the *baie vitrée,* Amélie notes, 'avait pris dans mon univers une place colossale' (*ST* 140) since, 'ce qui m'a sauvé la vie, c'est la défenestration' (*ST* 150).

Following Mark Johnson's theory on the importance of the body and the imagination in the creation of meaning, I have endeavoured to show that meaning, in *Stupeur et tremblements,* is not a passive construct born of some pre-ordained rationality. Instead, it is a dynamic structure which is determined by a combination of corporeal interaction with space and also the creative potential of imagination. The heroine's repeated experience of containment, release, ingestion, expulsion, physical humiliation and imagined self-promotion thus establishes regular patterns in her life. The resulting image schemata create order and meaning out of a diverse range of experiences, enabling Amélie to make judgements and to understand her position within the Yumimoto organization. These judgements are, on occasion, supported by and, on occasion, contradicted by the power of her imagination which allows for a flexibility of interpretation and promotes resistance, subversion, transgression and free-thinking. These are the characteristics that are most in evidence in *Stupeur et tremblements,* in which the heroine's creativity and fantasy generate new and original order out of complex value-laden representations.

University of Surrey

Notes

1. My thanks to Professor Christopher Thompson from Warwick University whose seminar at the University of Surrey introduced me to Johnson's work.
2. Mark Johnson, *The Body in the Mind. The Bodily Basis of Meaning, Imagination, and Reason* (Chicago and London: The University of Chicago Press, 1987), p. xxi.
3. Ibid., p. xix.
4. Ibid., p. 29.
5. Ibid., p. 141.
6. Ibid., p. xx.
7. Ibid., p. xiv.

8. *Stupeur et tremblements* (Paris: Albin Michel, 1999), p. 7. Subsequent references in the text will appear as *ST* followed by the page number.

9. Johnson, op. cit., p. 21.

10. Kevin Hetherington, *Expressions of Identity. Space, Performance, Politics* (London, Thousand Oaks, New Delhi: Sage, 1998), p. 17.

11. Hugo Marsan, 'Au bonheur des larmes', *Le Monde*, 17 September 1999.

12. Dominique Bona, 'Les déboires d'une insolente', *Le Figaro*, 9 September 1999.

13. Bernard Le Saux, ' "*Stupeur et tremblements*" d'Amélie Nothomb', Dossier Amélie Nothomb, Bibliothèque Marguerite Durand, original source unknown.

14. Johnson, op. cit., p. 140.

15. Ibid., p. 168.

16. Ibid., p. 141.

17. Jean Rousset, *Forme et signification. Essais sur les structures littéraires de Corneille à Claudel* (Paris: José Corti, 1962), p. 123.

18. Ibid., p. 123.

19. Ibid., p. 123.

20. Nicolas Guerdin, Interview with Amélie Nothomb, available online at http://212.37.198.117/goncourt99/ auteurs/nothomb_itv.htm.

21. Hetherington, op. cit., p. 15.

Catherine Rodgers

NOTHOMB'S ANOREXIC BEAUTIES

As it was for Plato, for Nothomb beauty is an ideal we all desire, and her characters and narrators are unremittingly attracted to it. What precisely is the nature of this ideal in her works? What sensibility does it reveal? What are its consequences from feminist and literary standpoints?

Most of Nothomb's texts exhibit an intense fascination with beauty. Her characters turn to it above all else in their attempt to comprehend the world. In *Le Sabotage amoureux,* the narrator's mother weeps at her first sight of the ugliness of Beijing (*LS* 13).[1] For the narrator, the hideousness of this city is all the more striking because she has just left Japan where she had lived 'au cœur de la beauté' (*MT* 67). And for Nothomb herself, 'le Japon a apporté une vraie attirance pour la beauté' since 'peu de pays ont cultivé à ce point le souci de l'esthétisme'.[2] The words 'beau', 'beauté' and their opposites punctuate her writing, at times in unexpected ways. Tach says of *Voyage au bout de la nuit* that it is 'un grand livre de beauté' (*HA* 64). In *Métaphysique des tubes,* the God/Tube 'hurlait de plus belle et de plus laide' (*MT* 31). And when Kashima-san and Nishio-san discuss the changes brought about in Japan by the War, beauty is yet again both the principal point of reference and the most important currency:

> — Il ne suffit pas de parler de sa jeunesse pour que ce soit *beau*. Toi, si tu parlais de la tienne, ce serait misérable.
> — En effet. C'est parce que je suis pauvre. Avant-guerre, je l'aurais été aussi.
> — Avant, il y avait de la *beauté* pour tout le monde. Pour les riches et pour les pauvres. [. . .] Aujourd'hui, il n'y a plus de *beauté* pour personne (*MT* 131, my emphasis).

Not only are places, objects and ideas judged in terms of their beauty, but— most significantly—people too. Realistic novelists often, of course, introduce characters with a physical description, but in Nothomb's case the impact of physical appearance goes beyond this literary convention, and indeed verges on the obsessive. In *Stupeur et tremblements,* Fubuki Mori's breathtaking beauty is constantly restated, the narrator having been so subjugated by it that she is no longer able to listen to what Fubuki is telling her (*ST* 13). Fubuki is no exception. Ethel in *Attentat*; the young Prétextat Tach and his cousin in *Hygiène de l'assassin*; Hazel, Adèle and Françoise in *Mercure*; Elena in *Le Sabotage amoureux*; Kashima-san in *Métaphysique des tubes*—all are stunningly beautiful, and their beauty has an arresting effect both on the characters surrounding them and on the narrators. The reactions, for example, to the singular beauty of Elena (the little Italian girl with whom the narrator falls in love in *Le Sabotage amoureux*) are typical of the feeling beauty inspires in the dumbfounded onlookers. 'Elle [Elena] inspirait l'admiration, le respect, le ravissement et la peur' (*LS* 87), writes the narrator. When Françoise first sees Hazel's face, 'elle ressentit un choc d'une violence extrême' (*ME* 16)—not the shock which, at this point in the text, we as readers are expected to interpret as a reaction of horror to Hazel's disfigurement, but, as we discover much later, one caused by the sublime beauty of that face.

The face is a focal point of beauty in Nothomb's texts. It is no coincidence that in his fantasized torture of Lygie in *Attentat*, Epiphane Otos tramples on her body until her flesh is reduced to a pulp and her magnificent beauty driven up to her face; once the beauty is compacted, she is said to be at her most beautiful (*A* 32). But the real nature of Nothombian beauty resides in its thinness, its virginity and asexuality, its connotations of youth, adolescence and childhood, and its association with angels. The description of Elena is characteristic:

> Elena avait six ans. Elle était belle comme un *ange* qui poserait pour une photo d'art.
> Elle avait les yeux sombres, immenses et fixes, la peau couleur de sable mouillé.
> Ses cheveux d'un noir de bakélite brillaient comme si on les avait cirés un à un et n'en finissaient pas de lui dévaler le dos et les fesses.
> Son nez ravissant eût frappé Pascal d'amnésie.
> Ses joues dessinaient un ovale *céleste*, mais rien qu'à voir la perfection de sa bouche, on comprenait combien elle était méchante.
> Son corps résumait l'harmonie universelle, dense et délicat, *lisse* d'enfance, aux *contours anormalement nets*, comme si elle cherchait à se découper mieux que les autres sur l'écran du monde (*LS* 49, my emphasis).

Likewise the following passage refers to the young Tach and his cousin in *Hygiène de l'assassin* in similar terms:

> vous êtes tous les deux immenses, *maigres*, blafards, mais vos visages et vos longs corps sont parfaitement *enfantins*. Vous n'avez pas l'air normal, d'ailleurs: on dirait deux géants de douze ans. Le résultat est pourtant superbe: ces traits menus, ces yeux naïfs, ces faciès trop petits par rapport à leur crâne, surmontant des troncs puérils, des jambes grêles et interminables—vous étiez à peindre. [. . .] vous [Tach] avez gardé la même peau blanche, *lisse, imberbe* [. . .]. Vous étiez tellement beau, vous aviez les traits tellement purs, les membres tellement fins, et une complexion si *asexuée*—les *anges* ne doivent pas être bien différents (*HA* 135, my emphasis).

There is often a neat, self-contained exterior ('lisseté' is the word Nothomb creates (*LS* 107) to capture this attribute). With the exception of the young Tach, Nothombian beauties are all lissom girls or young women, a representation which is to some degree conventional in being not that dissimilar from the notion of beauty presented in advertisements, in women's magazines and by top fashion models; but it differs in its insistence on asexuality and childishness.

In order better to draw attention to the beauty of certain characters, Nothomb flanks them with hideous individuals. Epiphane in *Attentat* is presented as the incarnation of ugliness, the reincarnation of Quasimodo, a '*vomitorium* du regard' (*A* 53) whom Nothomb has self-evidently enjoyed creating:

> Mon visage ressemble à une oreille. Il est concave avec d'absurdes boursouflures de cartilages qui, dans les meilleurs des cas, correspondent à des zones où l'on attend un nez ou une arcade sourcilière, mais qui, le plus souvent, ne correspondent à aucun relief facial connu.
>
> À la place des yeux, je dispose de deux boutonnières flasques qui sont toujours en train de suppurer. Le blanc de mes globes oculaires est injecté de sang [. . .]. Des pupilles grisâtres y flottent, tels des poissons morts.
>
> Ma tignasse évoque ces carpettes en acrylique qui ont l'air sales même quand on vient de les laver. Je me raserais certainement le crâne s'il n'était recouvert d'eczéma. [. . .]
>
> Je suis maigre, ce qui peut être beau chez un homme; mais ma maigreur est vilaine. [. . .].
>
> À l'exemple des chiens sharpeïs, j'ai trop de peau. Mon ossature débile et ma pauvre chair flottent à l'intérieur de cet accoutrement qui, mal rempli, ne peut que pendouiller (*A* 10–12).

And, to cap it all, Epiphane's shoulders are covered with purulent acne (*A* 13). Being young and thin, he is atypical of the Nothombian repulsive character, but is representative in another respect: that of the breaking down of bodily boundaries. Nothing is firm in him, his skin with its many folds fails to contain him as it should, one part of his body runs into the next, some parts ooze out liquid—all characteristics, as Julia Kristeva has noted, of the abject body.[3]

There is a manifest revulsion in Nothomb's texts for the old, and especially for libidinous old men, such as the 'décati, chenu' Omer Loncours in *Mercure* (*ME* 121), who, at seventy-seven, forces himself on the young, lithe Hazel, or the Professor in *Les Combustibles* who has a sexual relationship with the young, thin, pretty Marina, reduced as she is to seeking the Professor's bodily warmth to counteract the bitter cold that tortures her. Herein lies the real pole of repulsion for Nothomb: the obese, elderly 'gentleman' (Bernardin in *Les Catilinaires,* Omochi in *Stupeur et tremblements,* Prétextat Tach in *Hygiène de l'assassin*). More than being merely old and ugly, these hideous characters inspire a disgust as a result of their propensity not only to consume large quantities of fatty, unsavoury food, but to strip their interlocutors of their dignity and humanity by devouring them too. They are modern ogres. Prétextat Tach, for example, is old, obese to the point of moving only with great difficulty, and with a smooth, hairless, white face and big cheeks resembling a backside (*HA* 19). As one journalist in the text puts it, Tach exposes to the world what normally remains hidden inside, and metaphorically ingests those around him:

> Un vrai viscère, ce type! Lisse comme un foie, gonflé comme son estomac doit l'être! Perfide comme une rate, amer comme une vésicule biliaire! Par son simple regard, je sentais qu'il me digérait, qu'il me dissolvait dans les sucs de son métabolisme totalitaire! (*HA* 25–26).

The journalist has to leave, 'la queue entre les jambes' (*HA* 25), while his colleague, equally incapable of enduring even the mention of the oily food Tach is gulping down, runs out to vomit on the pavement, 'terrassé' (*HA* 41).

The repulsiveness of such unappealing characters is not there solely as a foil to the grace of their attractive counterparts, in the way that Epiphane becomes a 'mannequin [. . .] repoussoir' (*A* 51): the ugly desire the beautiful. In this they are not alone, beauty being what most Nothombian creations, including the partly autobiographical narrators, yearn to possess and control by whatever means. Omer Loncours sequestrates Adèle, an attractive young virgin, in order to savour her beauty, making her believe she has been disfigured; and her suicide does not deter him from re-enacting the episode with Hazel, whom he sees as a re-embodiment of Adèle. Even the handsome Françoise, 'ange au sexe byzantin' (*ME* 177) succumbs, in the second ending of *Mercure,* to the temptation of keeping Hazel's beauty to herself: instead of revealing to Hazel the truth about her astounding beauty, she upholds the lie of disfigurement forged by Omer Loncours.

The desire itself for beauty often takes an oral form. The lover is said to devour with his/her eyes the beautiful beloved in both *Mercure* (*ME* 9) and *Le Sabotage amoureux* (*LS* 58). Françoise, as she eventually confesses to Hazel her monstrous lie, says to her: 'je n'ai pas perdu une miette de votre visage' (*ME* 188). Xavier sleeps with Ethel because she appears 'commestible' (*A* 119). And if beauty cannot be symbolically ingested by looking, a more extreme measure can be brought into play. In *Attentat,* when Epiphane finally realizes that Ethel rejects him, that there is no hope she will ever love him, he kills her while kissing her, thus eternalizing the illusion of love and his complete control over her, musing in his deranged mind: 'Je lui suis devenu indispensable: elle n'est vraiment rien sans moi' (*A* 153).

Nothomb is writing at the end of the twentieth century, thus at a moment when young women writers are strongly exerting their entitlement to write openly about sexuality, sometimes in explicit detail, yet her texts remain merely suggestive in this respect. Sexual encounters are there, such as those between Hazel and Loncours, or the Professor and Marina, or Ethel and Xavier, or Tach and his cousin, but they are only indirectly evoked. What is foregrounded is abstinence or virginity. Epiphane shelved any idea of a sexual relationship at the age of thirteen; Tach never experienced one after puberty. Even the characters who have been sexually active, like Hazel or Ethel, are described in somewhat virginal terms. Genital sexuality is constantly displaced into oral pleasure, especially in sado-masochistic relationships which often take the form of a verbal war. Controlling the Other, thus possessing her (or him), especially if she is beautiful, is the objective of most characters. The sadistic impulse in Epiphane is patent in the fantasy he creates when rewriting the end of *Quo Vadis,* where he takes on the role of the bull penetrating with his horns the naked body of the virginal Lygie, while his sadism meets Lygie's fantasized masochism. In *Hygiène de l'assassin,* both Tach and Nina want to see the other crawl in front of him/herself. The encounter is a verbal struggle during which Nina penetrates the intimacy of the fat old writer while he invades her very being. *Stupeur et tremblements* is a tale of a battle for humiliation between the beautiful, sadistic Fubuki and the sado-masochistic narrator, a battle in which each finds her *jouissance.*[4] The encounter had already been prefigured in *Le Sabotage amoureux,* where the narrator recalls her sado-masochistic relationship with Elena.[5]

Moreover, in Nothomb's fictional world, where there is often a meeting of extremes, the absorption of one character by another may not only be a means of controlling the Other, but also one of fusing beauty and ugliness, to the extent that the frontiers between Self and Other become blurred. Epiphane, by killing Ethel, incorporates his other half in him: beauty will be for ever dependent on ugliness, a fusion of opposites prepared for earlier in Epiphane's declaration of his love for Ethel: 'Nous sommes jumeaux, mon amour. Nous nous ressemblons comme le bien ressemble au mal, comme l'ange ressemble à la bête. Si mon corps s'unissait au tien, nous ne pourrions plus jamais nous dessouder' (*A* 141). In *Hygiène de l'assassin,* a kind of transmutation operates between Tach and Nina who at first are so opposed to each other—in their sex, their age, their appearance, their conception of the world. As the exchange between them takes place, Nina gradually takes on some of the characteristics of the old man: 'je vous vois devenir moi' (*HA* 194), says the latter; and at the end of the text it is difficult to decide whether Tach has reincarnated himself in Nina, or whether she has incorporated part of his personality. A transmutation of the same kind seems to take place between the narrator of *Le Sabotage amoureux* and Elena, and between Françoise and Loncours in the second ending of *Mercure.*

There also clearly emerges from Nothomb's works a desire to deconstruct stereotypical, simplistic ideas about beauty by drawing on legends and established characters of popular culture: *Beauty and the Beast, Notre-Dame de Paris, Cyrano de Bergerac* and diverse myths about ogres. Epiphane—who, on the question of beauty, is Nothomb's mouthpiece, as evidenced from her conversation with Pascal Bruckner[6] (author of *Les Voleurs de beauté*)—exposes the various intertexts within *Attentat* in his desire to disparage the conceptions of beauty they propose. Hugo's *Notre-Dame de Paris* is the most obviously discernible intertext, given Epiphane's nickname: Quasimodo. At the very beginning of his *récit,* he challenges the logic of Quasimodo's story:

Il y a quelque chose de mal digéré à propos de Quasimodo: les lecteurs ne peuvent que l'aimer, le pauvre—il est si horrible [. . .]. Quand il s'éprend d'Esméralda, on a envie de crier à la belle: « Aime-le! [. . .] Ne t'arrête pas à son aspect extérieur! » Tout cela est bien joli, mais pourquoi attendrait-on plus de justice de la part d'Esméralda que de Quasimodo? Qu'a-t-il fait d'autre, lui, que s'arrêter à l'aspect extérieur de la créature? *Il est censé nous montrer la supériorité de la beauté intérieure par rapport à la beauté visible*. En ce cas, il devrait tomber amoureux d'une vieille édentée: c'est alors qu'il serait crédible.

Or l'élue de son cœur est une superbe bohémienne [. . .]. Et l'on voudrait nous persuader que *ce bossu a l'âme pure*?

Moi, j'affirme qu'il l'a basse et corrompue (*A* 12–13, my emphasis).

Hugo's portrayal of Quasimodo is incontrovertibly subtler than is suggested in *Attentat*. Quasimodo is not simply a good soul, but, rather, an ambivalent character whose maliciousness is even pointed out by the narrator.[7] He is a bestial creature who relies on instincts and therefore a world apart from the sophisticated Epiphane, and it would be quite unjustified to see in Hugo's Quasimodo a symbol of interior beauty. Nothomb is plainly working from the popular, simplified perception of this character, the myth of Quasimodo as it were, and part of her narrative is intended to show the inconsistency of the myth. Through his sadistic sexual fantasy, then through his murder of Ethel, Epiphane is shown to be very far from a pure, beautiful soul concealed behind a hideous exterior, while Ethel, despite her beauty, gives the impression of being a perfectly average woman, neither angelic nor diabolic, and not as credulous as she at first appears in her relationship with Xavier. In fact, at the end of the text, just before she is murdered by Epiphane, she endorses his early critique of Quasimodo's tale: she does not see why she should be less interested in appearances than Epiphane. It is clear that Nothomb wishes to dislodge what she sees as the hypocritical view promoted by society that inner beauty is what counts. She has expressed herself quite forcibly on this question: 'La beauté de l'âme n'est rien. On dit tout le temps le contraire, mais ce n'est pas vrai. En amour comme ailleurs, on choisit le physique agréable; les autres, on les met de côté'.[8]

Again, if at one point Epiphane plays at being Cyrano de Bergerac in a slightly modified version of Rostand's tale of self-sacrifice and veiled expression of love, his self-effacement does not last long. Under the guise of transforming Xavier's loutish behaviour into declarations of love towards Ethel, he directly voices his love for her in a parody of the balcony scene in *Cyrano de Bergerac* (*A* 94–7), but discloses the whole stratagem in his faxes to Ethel (*A* 139–40), and lacks the moving and uplifting behaviour of Cyrano. Does Nothomb thus indicate, beyond the humour of the passage, that the type of self-sacrifice made by Cyrano is outmoded in a materialistic and egocentric society? Or is it simply that 'her' ugly man has no special generosity of spirit?

Attentat is also a very loose adaptation of *Beauty and the Beast*. Once more, Nothomb is working from a popular version of the story (as opposed to any standard published text), her main purpose being to demonstrate that although fairy tales—which she says she adores—'disent beaucoup de choses vraies sur l'être humain [. . .] ils n'avaient pas dit que la Bête n'était pas si gentille que ça, ni la Belle si méchante qu'on veut le faire croire'.[9] As Marina Warner has shown, there are many versions of the tale, from D'Aulney, to Villeneuve, to the better known version by Mme Leprince de Beaumont, to Cocteau's film and Walt Disney's cartoon, all differing significantly from each other.[10] None of them, however, develops the dichotomous view presented by Nothomb in the tale of a wicked Beauty and a kindly Beast. Having examined the evolution of the myth, Warner argues that in the twentieth century 'the Beast no longer needs to be disenchanted. Rather, Beauty has to learn to love the beast in him, in order to know the beast in herself'.[11] This certainly does not work out well for Nothomb's Beauty, who dies as a result of her encounter with the Beast. Nor can the Nothombian Beauty bear a confrontation with the Beast—perhaps a reflection of the fear of adult sexuality so noticeable in Nothomb's work. In fact, most of Nothomb's texts engage in an attempt to demonstrate that one cannot deduce anything from first impressions and physical appearances. In *Stupeur et tremblements,* Fubuki is built up by the narrator throughout the opening pages of the text as a gentle, soft, friendly presence. The narrator comes only slowly to understand her perfidy and her malice. In the same way, in *Hygiène de l'assassin,* Nina, who first appears as a helpless victim thrown into the ogre's cave for him to devour, turns out to be at least a match for Tach. And, in spite of her seraphic appearance, Marina in *Les Combustibles* reveals herself to be as much of a beast as the Professor. Nothomb presents us with beautiful, malevolent individuals, as well as beautiful, virtuous ones: physical beauty is no indication of character.

She also condemns the way in which one particular type of physical beauty is aggressively upheld in our society, that of the top fashion model and of beauty contests, a beauty determined by mere measurement. In *Attentat,* when Ethel goes to the modelling agency with Epiphane, she is subjected to a list of questions concerning her weight, her bust size and other statistics, questions judged 'pornographique[s]' (*A* 48) by Epiphane. She is advised to have silicone injected into her lips, an idea she rejects outright. Epiphane, as one of the judges in the Miss World competition—the epiphenomenon of the standardization of beauty which tyrannizes most developed countries, especially the United States—experiences an acute disgust for the spectacle which he perceives as 'dégueulasse' for its sheer hypocrisy; to him it is 'prostitution déguisée en vente de charité' (*A* 133). As Lipovetsky, amongst others, has noted, attention to appearance has become exacerbated in the postmodern era, part of this trend manifesting itself in the contemporary obsession with the body, which must be healthy, efficient, and eternally young and beautiful.[12] In *Péplum,* the degenerate civilization of the twenty-sixth century has created an aesthetic coefficient against which all individuals are assessed in order to determine whether they can become part of the oligarchy (*PE* 22). Nothomb has commented that in *Attentat* there are two different conceptions of beauty. The first is that of the super model, on whom she passes judgement via Epiphane, a threatening beauty she finds 'odieuse': 'Leur beauté est doublement menaçante. D'abord si vous ne les trouvez pas belles, vous avez mauvais goût—pour moi certaines ont une sale gueule, mais c'est mal vu de le dire. Ensuite si vous n'êtes pas comme elles, vous êtes moche'.[13] The other type of beauty, which she contrasts with that of the fashion model, is that of the beautiful female icon, one which society can admire. According to Nothomb, 'Toute société a besoin d'icônes à admirer', and 'Cette conception d'une beauté fédératrice est très positive car elle console le reste de l'humanité de ne pas être aussi belle'.[14] Nothomb does not explain, however, the distinction she draws between the fashion model and the icon, and it is hard to acknowledge that it is as clear-cut as she suggests. Are Claudia Schiffer, Kate Moss, and Naomi Campbell not in reality the modern icons of our society?

Whether or not one accepts Nothomb's distinction, it is worth examining the type of beauty offered by her icons (presumably Ethel, Hazel, Françoise, Elena, or Fubuki), a beauty which I see as stemming from an anorexic sensibility and which is arguably as complicit with patriarchy as the other type, as insensitive to women's feelings as the physical appearance of super models. All the characteristics of the developed, sexual, adult female body are rejected as more or less obscene in Nothomb's work. Needless to say, characters in fiction are not automatically to be identified with their authors, but when the same sensibility is carried across from text to text, one may at least infer that it is part of an author's vision. What is more, Nothomb has stated unequivocally that she is Tach,[15] the character who openly expresses the disgust for the female body lurking in most of Nothomb's texts: '[les femmes] sont laides [. . .] A-t-on idée d'avoir des seins, des hanches, et je vous épargne le reste?' (*HA* 67). He describes breasts as 'ces protubérances femelles' (*HA* 69). He fumes against the uterus ('toutes les saloperies de la vie viennent de l'utérus' (*HA* 144)) and against ovulation (*HA* 148). He kills his cousin on the day of the onset of her periods—according to him an act of love—to save her from the degradation of becoming a woman (*HA* 144).

Summarizing several accounts of anorexia, Barbara Brook stresses the 'revulsion [the anorexic feels] towards the adult female body, perceived as lacking boundaries, leaky and incomplete'.[16] Dieting enables the anorexic to reverse the maturation process: womanly fat is lost, periods are suspended. Unable to face the conflicting demands made on adult women in a patriarchal society, the anorexic regresses to pre-puberty. In *Le Sabotage amoureux,* Nothomb presents Elena as 'la beauté de l'humanité', adding: 'Seules les petites filles étaient parfaites. Rien ne saillait de leurs corps, ni appendice grotesque, ni protubérances risibles' (*MT* 106). In *Hygiène de l'assassin,* Tach reflects: '[elles] n'ont pas d'utérus, [. . .] ou si elles en ont un, c'est un jouet, une parodie d'utérus' (*HA* 144). Childhood is the ideal state, one that some of Nothomb's characters will attempt never to leave. Thus Tach invents, with some success, a whole programme of physical privations and constraints to maintain his cousin and himself in a state of permanent pre-adolescence. This includes sleeping and eating as little as possible, or eating indigestible food such as certain mushrooms, and spending as much time as possible in water (an attempt at the ultimate regression, to the waters of the womb?). In

Métaphysique des tubes, the narrator also spends much of her time in lakes and in the sea, twice coming close to death in her favourite element, each time the approach of death bringing plenitude. If, in *Hygiène de l'assassin,* Tach's attempt at arresting the ageing process finally fails, culminating in the murder of his cousin and his subsequent transformation into the opposite of his ideal (a 'montrueuse enflure' (*HA* 136)), in *Les Catilinaires* Juliette, the narrator's wife, appears to be suspended in a state of eternal childhood (*CA* 14): she is sixty-six but looks, we are told, as she did at the age of six. And if Juliette is able to maintain her childlike angelic appearance, it might be that her body is projected onto Bernadette, the monstrous, obese neighbour.[17] It is not surprising, then, that the ideal relationship is one which unites two children, such as Tach and his cousin, or, in their youth, Juliette and the narrator of *Les Catilinaires* who at one point reminisces about how he and his wife were already a couple at the age of six. There follows a memory/fantasy found again, slightly modified, in *Le Sabotage amoureux* (*LS* 114) and *Hygiène de l'assassin* (*HA* 158), involving extremely cold water, the nudity of the beloved and her pain, and the sadistic pleasure of the narrator.

The disgust at the adult female body, the absence of genital sexuality, the ideal of the thin, smooth and clearly contained childish body, even the need to control the Other and the absence of a clear boundary between self and other, all point to an anorexic sensibility.[18] *Métaphysique des tubes,* in disclosing the ambivalent role of food, shows us its construction, possibly in the life of Nothomb herself if this text is to be taken as in any way autobiographical. On the one hand, it is thanks to the discovery of the strong pleasure provided by white chocolate that the screaming monster the narrator once was becomes a subject able to say 'je' (*MT* 36), and a likeable little girl.[19] On the other hand, the feeding of the carps nearly causes her death. For the narrator, the carps are utterly abject: fat and overfed, they wallow in 'une durée adipeuse' (*MT* 98); the spectacle of their mouth turns her stomach:

> Le diamètre de leur orifice était presque égal au diamètre de leur corps, ce qui eût évoqué la section d'un tuyau, s'il n'y avait eu leurs lèvres poissonneuses qui me regardaient de leur regard de lèvres, ces lèvres saumâtres qui s'ouvraient et se refermaient avec un bruit obscène, des bouches en forme de bouées qui bouffaient ma bouffe avant de me bouffer moi! (*MT* 149).

She has a recurrent nightmare of the carps coming to her bed, embracing her, kissing her on the mouth (*MT* 152). Even without the nightmare, the sexual connotations are manifest. Besides, the narrator has told us that the carp in Japan is the symbol for the male sex; she cannot bear such connotations in the spectacle of the carps which unites male and female sex organs, and is repulsed by them because she can see right inside their body, into their digestive tube. They send her back an image of life, of living creatures, herself included, as tubes that must be filled (*MT* 158–59). 'Miroir ignoble', the carp shows her that she is 'un tube sorti d'un tube' (*MT* 158), an expression which further conflates the sexual and digestive associations. Nothomb's obese characters are variations on the carps, the fear and disgust they inspire stemming from what they reveal: that 'tout le monde a en soi un gros tas immobile' (*CA* 109). Accordingly, the narrator of *Les Catilinaires* is appalled by the sight of Bernadette, especially when she is drinking:

> Ce ne fut rien comparé à la répulsion qui me crispa les mâchoires quand le verre s'inséra dans sa bouche. L'orifice replia ce qui lui servait de lèvres et se mit à aspirer [. . .] chaque déglutition faisait le bruit d'une ventouse en caoutchouc en train de déboucher un évier.
> J'étais horrifié (*CA* 68)

or eating:

> c'était sa bouche qui faisait le travail du couteau. Elle portait jusqu'à l'orifice des morceaux énormes et l'espèce de bec-lèvres en prélevait une quantité. Le tentacule [son bras] redescendait [. . .] C'était ce que sa bouche fabriquait ensuite qui donnait envie de vomir (*CA* 72–73).

The narrator is nauseated by the spectacle, but is obliged to admit that Bernadette at least enjoys her food. The thought which is totally abhorrent to him, which he cannot withstand, is the idea of her sexual pleasure (*CA* 114). If oral pleasure is recognized, and ambivalently valued in Nothomb, sexual pleasure seems more difficult to accept. Conversely, the thin, beautiful, asexual characters are an idealized vision of an anorexic self. The ultimate desire is to become a tube, but a purified one, one that gives passage only to water. This is the fantasy of the narrator of *Métaphysique des tubes* as she sinks in the pool near the end of the text (*MT* 166).

By extension, the body of Nothomb's texts corresponds to the anorexic ideal: she privileges fast-moving narratives with a good measure of dialogue, and few introspective, digressive or descriptive passages. Her texts tend to be short and clipped, and her style is as slight as a lean, wiry body, as certain critics have pointed out: 'La vivacité d'une plume crissante';[20] (on *Les Catilinaires*) 'Une prose nerveuse, qui ricane et tape du pied [. . .] une espèce de méchanceté réjouissante';[21] (on *Péplum*) 'C'est vif, parfois agressif' or 'la fluidité, le claquement du dialogue, la relance nerveuse [. . .] Mlle Nothomb possède cela';[22] (on *Hygiène de l'Assassin*) 'Tendu, vif, il [*Hygiène de l'assassin*] s'approche de la cruauté' or 'Nothomb utilise, en guise de stylo, une lame. Elle écrit au couteau';[23] (on *Stupeur et Tremblements*) 'son style, acéré comme une griffe, cinglant comme un fouet, agit en antidote à tant de romans- somnifères' or 'l'histoire est bien contée, sobrement, avec vivacité'.[24]

There is, then, an anorexic sensibility present in Nothombian texts, in content and possibly in form, one which perhaps stems from Nothomb's own anorexia during her adolescence.[25] This sensibility is not without its inconveniences from a feminist standpoint. Writers on the subject of anorexia have oscillated in their interpretation of the phenomenon as either an act of obedience to patriarchal norms, within which women are required to be thin, delicate and self-denying, or one of rebellion in that a young girl refuses to take her place as an oppressed adult female in a patriarchal society. In the words of Noelle Caskey, 'Refusing to eat is supremely defiant and supremely obedient at the same time'.[26] The view that submission and revolt may coexist corresponds to Nothomb's own persona. Adored by the media and obviously playing their game, at the same time she imagines herself as *l'enfant terrible* of the literary world, declaring for example: 'Si l'on accepte que ce milieu de la mode est en partie une métaphore du milieu littéraire, alors oui, je suis Epiphane. Je ne peux pas revendiquer d'être un Quasimodo dans la vie de tous les jours. Mais du point de vue de l'écriture, oui!'.[27]

However, if there is ambiguity at the individual level as to the feminist value which can be afforded to anorexia, there seems little doubt that at a sociological level it can be seen as the product of patriarchal society. Morag MacSween's thesis is that anorexia is an attempt to negotiate its conflicting demands, namely that women are obliged to function as autonomous individuals in a bourgeois capitalist society whose ideal is the male subject, but also as dependent, submissive, females.[28] From a more militant perspective, Naomi Wolf also views anorexia as created by patriarchy.[29] For her, the ideal of beauty our contemporary society upholds — the thin, adolescent girl she calls the Iron Maid — is a means patriarchy has found to attempt to control the social, cultural and political march of women towards equality. It is a way of weakening strong, sexual, powerful women, by forcing them to diet, to become obsessed with food, to starve themselves, to lose their self-confidence, their physical strength and their sexual desire: 'Fat is portrayed in the literature of the myth as expendable female filth; virtually cancerous matter', while in fact 'Fat is sexual in women, [. . .] is not just fertility, but desire'.[30] 'The anorexic', she maintains, 'may begin her journey defiant, but from the point of view of a male-dominated society, she ends up as the perfect woman. She is weak, sexless, and voiceless [. . .] The woman has been killed off in her'.[31] From a feminist perspective, the problem with Nothomb's texts is that the ideal of beauty they promote corresponds to that of the Iron Maid, thus reinforcing the Beauty myth, and consequently patriarchal ideology. Nothomb does not offer her readers any sexually mature, well-developed beautiful women. And, except for fleeting mentions in *Métaphysique des tubes* and *Le Sabotage amoureux,* mothers are equally absent from her fictional world. Most of her female characters are from the same mould. The notable exception is Bernadette in *Les Catilinaires,* but is Bernadette still a woman? Not only is she more often evoked in terms which link her to the animal kingdom, but she is also referred to as the Cyst, making her cross both the animal/human and the gender divides. It is for this reason that she might better be understood as the projected body of Juliette. Nothomb's insistence on the beauty of the face is telling; hers is a cerebral notion of beauty, highly stylized, close to being disembodied.

Several factors may have influenced Nothomb's view of beauty and her denial of the female body. Her classical education may have reinforced a Platonic suspicion of the body; she does, after all, make an explicit reference in *Le Sabotage amoureux* (LS 107) to Plato and his interpretation of the body as a hindrance.[32]

More generally, the distrust of the body is a common trait in Western philosophy, as Susan Bordo reminds us:

> But what remains the constant element throughout historical variation is the *construction* of body as something apart from the true self (whether conceived as soul, mind, spirit, will, creativity, freedom. . .) and as undermining the best efforts of that self. That which is not-body is the highest, the best, the noblest, the closest to God; that which is body is the albatross, the heavy drag on self-realization.[33]

Nothomb may also have been influenced by the Japanese conception of beauty and the attitude towards the female body in Japanese culture. True, she points out that 'c'est à peine si [la Japonaise] a le droit d'avoir un corps, considéré comme dégoûtant',[34] and in *Stupeur et tremblements,* rages against the repression Japanese society enacts on women and their bodies. Nonetheless, these cultural constraints may have left their mark.

Whatever the cause of anorexia, it eventually turns against the person suffering from it, cutting her off from a grounded sense of self and the domain of adults, and locking her within a sterile universe. As the anorexic becomes more entangled in her illness, her ability to think and deal with the world diminishes, all her energy being channelled in her fight to control her hunger, where all her desires are condensed. This leads to physical and intellectual exhaustion. I am obviously not suggesting that this was the case with Nothomb's own anorexia, but the anorexic structure of her texts may nevertheless testify to a certain pernicious effect on creativity. Several critics have mentioned the repetitive nature of her writing. Pierre Marcelle, for example, writes in a review of *Stupeur et tremblements:* 'Tous procédés qui, ressassés de livre en livre avec trop d'aisance et de facilités, ressortissent de plus en plus à un catalogue de trucs'.[35] Bertrand de Saint Vincent in a review of *Attentat* writes: 'son roman sent la recette pour plat piquant'.[36] That she re-uses the same devices, the same ideas, is certainly a noticeable characteristic of her work when one follows a theme such as that of beauty. Can one justifiably draw a parallel here between the anorexic and Nothomb herself? By refusing to envisage the sexual, mature body, as well as life in its materiality, is she starving her texts? Are they getting too thin?

University of Wales, Swansea

Notes

1. References to Nothomb's texts are indicated within parentheses in the body of the article; the following editions and abbreviations have been used (Nothomb's publisher is Albin Michel, Paris): *Hygiène de l'assassin,* 1992 [*HA*]; *Le Sabotage amoureux,* 1993 [*LS*]; *Les Combustibles,* 1994 [*LC*]; *Les Catilinaires,* 1995 (edition used: Livre de Poche, 1999) [*CA*]; *Péplum,* 1996 [*PE*]; *Attentat,* 1997 (edition used: Livre de Poche, 2000) [*A*]; *Mercure,* 1998 (edition used: Livre de Poche, 2001) [*ME*]; *Stupeur et tremblements,* 1999 [*ST*]; *Métaphysique des tubes,* 2000 [*MT*].

2. www.soirillustre.be/3510amelie.html (interview with Amélie Nothomb by Corinne Le Brun, 'Amélie, Madame pipi des Nippons', reproduced on the Web site of *Le Soir Illustré*).

3. In *Pouvoirs de l'horreur. Essais sur l'abjection*, Julia Kristeva states: 'Ce [. . .] qui rend abject [est. . .] ce qui perturbe une identité, un système, un ordre. Ce qui ne respecte pas les limites, les places, les règles. L'entre-deux, l'ambigu, le mixte' (Paris: Seuil, 1980), p. 12.

4. If the narrator's masochism is most in evidence in the diegesis, she however takes her revenge on Fubuki by dominating and humiliating her in her tale, in showing her vulnerability to the European man's charms, by describing her metaphorical rape by her superior, her too easily induced jubilation over the narrator's humiliation, and finally her recognition of the narrator's mastery of Japanese and success as a writer.

5. Cf. Margaret-Anne Hutton's analysis of this relationship in ' "Personne n'est indispensable, sauf l'ennemi": l'œuvre conflictuelle d'Amélie Nothomb' in *Nouvelles écrivaines: nouvelles voix?*, ed. by Nathalie Morello and Catherine Rodgers (Amsterdam: Rodopi, 2002), pp. 111–27.

6. ' "La beauté, une malédiction", entretien croisé Pascal Bruckner-Amélie Nothomb', *Elle*, 15 septembre 1997, pp. 110–13.

7. Victor Hugo, *Notre-Dame de Paris* (Paris: Librairie Charpentier et Fasquelle, 1885), p. 80.

8. www.rdl.com.lb/1970/dedicace.htm (interview with Amélie Nothomb by Nicole El-Kareh).

9. Ibid.

10. Marina Warner, *From the Beast to the Blonde. On Fairy Tales and their Tellers* (London: Chatto & Windus, Vintage, 1994).

11. Ibid., p. 312.

12. Gilles Lipovetsky, *L'Ère du vide: essais sur l'individualisme contemporain* (Paris: Gallimard, 1983, Folio-essais, 1989), pp. 86–91.

13. 'La beauté, une malédiction', op. cit., p. 112.

14. Ibid.

15. 'Je suis totalement d'accord avec lui [Tach]. Il porte la moindre de mes idées à son comble [. . .]. Ce qu'il pense des femmes, je le pense aussi, même si j'en suis une. [. . .] Pour être bien claire, Tach, c'est moi. Je suis déguisée en mon contraire, un vieux bonhomme obèse, très célèbre et mourant, pour dire tout ce que je pensais' ('Le Logographe', www.multimania.com/fenrir/nothomb.htm, interview by Madeleine Tombeur, Gilles et Laurent).

16. Barbara Brook, *Feminist Perspectives on the Body* (London: Longman, 1999), p. 71.

17. The latest novel by Amélie Nothomb, *Cosmétique de l'ennemi* (Paris: Albin Michel, 2001) exposes a phenomenon, present although less noticeable in her previous texts: namely that characters are not always to be understood as discrete entities, but can be part-projections of each other.

18. Discussing H. Bruch's studies of anorexia, MacSween agrees with her analysis insofar as both consider control to be central in anorexia and that 'diffuse "ego boundaries" ' are 'significant' in the disease. Morag MacSween, *Anorexic Bodies: A Feminist and Sociological Perspective on Anorexia Nervosa* (London: Routledge, 1993), p. 45.

19. Chocolate initiates another existential climactic experience in *Stupeur et tremblements,* where the narrator, finally agreeing to eat the green chocolate that the ogre-like Omochi insistently offers her, discovers that it is good.

20. Armelle Heliot, 'Amélie Nothomb: le pur présent de l'enfance', *Le Figaro*, 11 octobre 1996.

21. '"Le diable à quatre heures". La chronique de Renaud Matignon', *Le Figaro*, 5 octobre 1995.

22. '"Amélie Nothomb: le temps en vadrouille". La chronique de Renaud Matignon', *Le Figaro*, 19 septembre 1996; Marc Lambron, 'L'Assomption d'Amélie', *Le Point*, 25 août 1996.

23. Alain Salles, 'L'art de la cruauté', *Le Monde*, 11 septembre 1992; '"Amélie Nothomb: une innocence meurtrière". La chronique de Renaud Matignon', *Le Figaro*, 20 novembre 1992.

24. Dominique Bona, 'Amélie Nothomb, les déboires d'une insolente', *Le Figaro*, 9 septembre 1999.

25. 'Ma sœur et moi nous avons été anorexiques en même temps. Ne pas quitter l'enfance était un bon moyen de rester ensemble à jamais, alors on a cessé de manger', interview by Nathalie Journo, 'Quasi modeste', *Libération*, 9 octobre 1997. Nothomb, when asked what her hobby was, apparently answered: 'vomir', Martine de Rabaudy, 'Les certitudes d'Amélie', *L'Express*, 24 août 1995, p. 101.

26. Noelle Caskey, 'Interpreting anorexia nervosa' in *The Female Body in Western Culture: Contemporary Perspectives,* ed. by Susan Rubin Suleiman (Cambridge (Massachussetts): Harvard University Press, 1985), pp. 175–189 (p. 181).

27. 'La beauté, une malédiction', op. cit., p. 113.

28. Morag MacSween, op. cit.

29. Naomi Wolf, *The Beauty Myth: How Images of Beauty Are Used against Women* (London: Vintage, 1990), p. 191.

30. Ibid., p. 192.

31. Ibid., p. 197.

32. Again Plato's thinking on the body and its relation to Beauty is more complex than Nothomb implies, since the body can certainly lead us to take what is transient for what is eternal, what are mere shadows for reality, but appreciation of physical beauty is the first step in a progression leading to the revelation of Beauty, even if, as one progresses, one is led to realize that physical beauty can be discarded in the light of its higher forms (Platon, *Le Banquet,* 209e-212a, Œuvres complètes, tome IV, 2ème partie, edited by Léon Robin (Paris: Les Belles Lettres, 1929)).

33. Susan Bordo, *Unbearable Weight: Feminism, Western Culture, and the Body* (Berkeley, Los Angeles & London: University of California Press, 1993), p. 5.

34. '"Amélie, Madame pipi des Nippons". Propos recueillis par Corinne Lebrun', available online at www.soirillustre.be, Web site of *Le Soir illustré.*

35. Pierre Marcelle, 'Deux professionnelles', *Libération*, 23 septembre 1999.

36. Bertrand de Saint Vincent, 'Attentat manqué', *Le Figaro Magazine,* 30 août 1997.

Lénaïk Le Garrec

BEASTLY BEAUTIES AND
BEAUTIFUL BEASTS

We know that Amélie Nothomb is not indifferent to her image, wearing as she does such eye-catching hats, those, as she puts it, 'lightning conductors which protect her', obsessed as she is by the encroaching of wrinkles on her face. Appearance naturally asserts itself in her works as a recurring theme. Beauty, whether explicitly revealed or hidden, is omnipresent and no texts escape this rule, even *Les Combustibles* and *Péplum,* which do not contain long descriptions of physical characteristics.[1] Inspiring both disgust and fascination, physical appearances steer Amélie Nothomb's novels. This article examines the representations of her male and female characters, and the key role played by the mirror in these explorations of appearance.

Feminine beauty is omnipresent; it haunts each page of Nothomb's work. In *Hygiène de l'assassin*[2] Léopoldine is 'belle comme le jour' (*HA* 132), and 'l'enfant la plus belle' (*HA* 112). In *Le Sabotage amoureux* Elena's cold beauty strikes the female narrator, who also presents herself as pretty.[3] In *Les Catilinaires* there is the example of Juliette Hazel, Émile's wife, but there is also Claire, his former student.[4] Similarly, there is a graceful student in *Les Combustibles,* Marina. In *Attentat,* Ethel, the actress, is the dreamlike ideal woman of the novel, even if a horde of models gravitate around Epiphane.[5] In *Mercure*[6] there are also two Venuses: Adèle and Hazel, 'Deux jeunes filles de 18 ans, orphelines, égales par la beauté et la grâce' (*ME* 127), but the nurse, Françoise Chavaigne, who is also undoubtedly attractive, must not be forgotten. In *Métaphysique des tubes* the female narrator is the beauty.[7] Her governess even says, '(. . .) qu'elle n'avait jamais vu une déesse au visage aussi admirable' (*MT* 68). Finally, the last beautiful girl of the summary is Textor Texel's wife in *Cosmétique de l'ennemi*.[8]

This exhaustive (perhaps rather off-putting) enumeration is an affirmation of the importance of physical appearance in Amélie Nothomb's work. Paradoxically, in spite of many descriptions of pretty girls, the narrator of *Cosmétique de l'ennemi*

maintains: 'Quoi de plus agaçant, dans les romans, que ces descriptions obligatoi-res de l'héroïne (. . .). Décrire la beauté d'un tel visage est aussi vain et stupide que tenter d'approcher, avec des mots, l'ineffable d'une sonate ou d'une cantate' (*CE* 50). It would appear, therefore, impossible to depict feminine beauty, to uncover its sparkle. Nevertheless, Amélie Nothomb makes countless attempts to represent it. One thing stands out among her portraits: an emphasis on whiteness, on pale and milky complexions as signs of purity and innocence. This is the case for Léo-poldine in *Hygiène de l'assassin* who is described as 'l'immense infante blanche et lis-se' (*HA* 142), and the same is true for Ethel in *Attentat* who is 'la pure svelte et bla-farde' (*A* 55). Elena in *Le Sabotage amoureux* is compared to an ermine, and even an ugly character like Prétextat Tach in *Hygiène de l'assassin* benefits from this charac-teristic, his skin described as follows:

> — Or, votre peau est très belle, blanche, nette, on devine qu'elle est douce au toucher.
> — Un teint d'eunuque, cher monsieur. Il y a quelque chose de grotesque à avoir une telle peau sur le visage (. . .) ma tête ressemble à une belle paire de fesses, lisses et mol-les (. . .) (*HA* 18).

Furthermore, the reference to whiteness is not just used with reference to skin colour, but can also concern other parts of the body. This is the case for Juliette's hair in *Les Catilinaires:* 'Les cheveux de Juliette étaient blancs (. . .) une couleur ra-vissante qui paraissait artificielle: la blancheur bleutée d'un tutu romantique (. . .) ce devait être cela, des cheveux d'ange' (*CA* 60).

This admiration for milkiness of skin could well be inspired by oriental women, following the example of Fubuki in *Stupeur et tremblements* who 'incarnait à la per-fection la beauté nippone' (*ST* 14). In this way, oriental women could well be seen as an ideal of beauty, and Amélie Nothomb has clearly been influenced by this aspect of Japanese culture which, as is well-known, attaches great value to appearance.[9]

In the enumeration of feminine beauties who inhabit Amélie Nothomb's work, the number of young and pretty girls is noticeable. This leads to the question whether beauty depends on age. This is, in any event, what Prétextat Tach, who in-vents a 'hygiène d'éternelle enfance' (*HA* 110), believes. He goes so far as to kill his cousin Léopoldine, in order to keep her forever young, pretty and pure. In accor-dance with Amélie Nothomb's archetype, to be beautiful one needs to look pale, be young, and ideally be slim, or indeed thin. Yet, if thinness is a model of beauty for women such as Léopoldine or Kashima-san, it is on the other hand a criterion of ugliness for men such as Textor Texel or Epiphane Otos. Are there handsome men in Amélie Nothomb's works?

The reader learns that Jérôme Angust in *Cosmétique de l'ennemi* has 'ce qu'on ap-pelle un physique avantageux' (*CE* 51), and that Celsius, the scientist of *Péplum*, has a high 'aesthetic coefficient'. However, masculine beauty is almost non-existent in an œuvre that is otherwise brimming with physical descriptions. Is beauty ex-clusively the reserve of women? The narrator of *Le Sabotage amoureux* seems to be-lieve in the superiority of womankind in this field:

Seules les petites filles étaient parfaites. Rien ne saillait de leur corps, ni appendices grotesques, ni protubérances risibles. Elles étaient conçues à merveille, profilées pour ne présenter aucune résistance à la vie (. . .), elles étaient la beauté de l'humanité—la vraie beauté, celle qui est pure aisance d'exister, celle ou rien ne gêne, où le corps n'est que bonheur des pieds à la tête (*LS* 70).

Beauty is presented largely as a female trait and one likely to spark conflicts, as is the case with Elena who is compared to Helen of Troy:

Existe-t-il histoire plus flatteuse pour une femme que l'*Iliade*? Deux civilisations s'étripent sans merci (. . .) tout ça pour quoi, pour qui? Pour une belle fille. On imagine volontiers la coquette se vantant auprès de ses amies:
— Oui, mes chéries, un génocide et des interventions divines pour moi toute seule! Et je n'ai rien fait pour ça. Que voulez-vous, je suis belle, je n'y puis rien (*LS* iii).

But how does Helen of Troy know that she is pretty? Of course, there is the attitude of the others towards her, but it is so subjective. In order to know for sure there is one indispensable element: the mirror. This reflective object, which is often presented as a magical element in fairytales, plays an essential role in many of Nothomb's novels: she does not use a magic wand but a mirror to transfigure reality. It is in the mirror that Ethel, the heroine of *Attentat,* finds satisfaction ('C'est parfait, sourit la belle, heureuse de son image dans le miroir' (*AT* 20)), whereas in *Hygiène de l'assassin,* Prétextat Tach resolves the problem posed by the mirror by eliminating the object that constantly reflects his own ugliness: 'la souffrance est pour les autres, pour ceux qui me voient. Moi, je ne me vois pas. Je ne me regarde jamais dans les miroirs' (*HA* 18). Not seeing oneself is, therefore, already a means of forgetting one's physical predicament.

In *Attentat,* Epiphane Otos had, on the contrary, decided to confront the mirror despite his unattractive features: 'La première fois que je me vis dans un miroir, je ris: je ne croyais pas que c'était moi. A présent, quand je regarde mon reflet, je ris: je sais que c'est moi' (*A* 9). This suggests an acceptance of his appearance; he is not afraid any more of it. Further on he states: 'Je me contemplais nu dans la grande glace (. . .). Ma laideur, pour extrême qu'elle fût, avait quelque chose d'équilibré dans sa distribution' (*A* 40). In the end, there seem to be varying degrees of ugliness, his tempered here by being evenly distributed.

If running away from mirrors allows one's own appearance to be forgotten, if temporarily, self-observation does not mean that our image or our appearances will stay forever fixed. This is what Amélie Nothomb reminds the reader in *Stupeur et tremblements:* 'Si tu admires ta propre joliesse dans le miroir, que ce soit dans la peur et non dans le plaisir: car ta beauté ne t'apportera rien d'autre que la terreur de la perdre' (*ST* 90). Beauty can fade away at any time, but equally it can return when it is revealed that life has not taken it from you.

This is one of the subjects of *Mercure.* Omer Loncours, the captain, had taken care to appoint a nurse who did not wear glasses, and removed all reflective surfaces from his castle to protect Hazel from her own image.[10] The antithesis of Narcissus, Hazel cannot gaze at herself. 'Amélie Nothomb', writes Jennifer Kouassi in *Le Magazine Littéraire*, 'transfigure le mythe de Narcisse, il devient le pendant du cogito: «Je me vois donc je suis»'.[11] If Hazel cannot see herself, she is not in love with herself. Besides, she does not really exist, she does not have her own life: she belongs to the captain, she is alive through him. If Narcissus is punished because he did not obey Nemesis, Hazel will be saved because she accepts the captain's authority. This situation persists until Hazel insists: 'Le jour de mon anniversaire, j'ai pleuré: n'était-il pas normal qu'une fille de 18 ans veuille voir son visage? Le capitaine (. . .) est allé chercher un miroir et me l'a tendu: C'est là que j'ai découvert l'horreur difforme qui me tient lieu de figure (. . .). J'ai ordonné que l'on détruise ce miroir (. . .)' (*ME* 29).

But the reader, and then the heroine, later hear of the deceptive nature of the mirror: '(. . .) j'allai chez un miroitier, avoua Omer Loncours, et lui demandai de me confectionner un miroir à main le plus déformant possible, pour faire une farce à un vieil ami' (*ME* 111). This mirror was Loncours's only hope: Hazel must think she is as hideous as Loncours in order for him to have a chance to own or to possess her. Hazel thought she was ugly because she could not see herself. By contrast, the captain finished by thinking he was handsome: 'Le manque de miroirs, lui fait remarquer l'infirmière, a eu sur vous une incidence comique: Vous vous croyez irrésistible. Puisse mon visage vous servir de reflet (. . .)' (*ME* 121). As such, it suffices to mentally imagine yourself as beautiful or ugly to have the impression that this is reality.

Thus far, beauty seems to be an exclusively feminine domain. It remains to be seen whether the same is true of ugliness. It seems to be the male characters who pronounce judgements on beauty and ugliness. For example, in *Hygiène de l'assassin*, Tach announces that he hates women: 'Je hais les femmes encore plus que les hommes (. . .). Pour mille raisons. D'abord parce qu'elles sont laides: Avez-vous déjà vu plus laid qu'une femme?' (*HA* 60). A few lines later we read: 'Les femmes, c'est de la sale viande. Parfois, on dit d'une femme particulièrement laide qu'elle est un boudin: la vérité, c'est que toutes les femmes sont des boudins' (*HA* 62). Epiphane Otos, alias Quasimodo, also describes women in terms of their unattractive physical features: '(. . .) le mâle horrible est moins comique à regarder que la femme repoussante. Cette dernière porte souvent des vêtements à grandes fleurs, des lunettes de star et des souliers étincelants. (. . .) sauf cas exceptionnels, elle n'a pas de barbe et ne peut donc pas dissimuler ses verrues ou son groin derrière un flot de poils' (*A* 76–77). These two male 'monsters' are merciless in their misogynistic diatribe. Do any of Nothomb's other characters also suffer from the indignity of ugliness?

Adèle and Hazel, who are told that they are ugly by the captain, are, in fact, pretty. In fact, only one heroine corresponds to this portrayal: Bernadette Bernardin in *Les Catilinaires*. In this text, worse than ugliness, is deformity: 'Bernadette ne possédait pas de nez; de vagues trous lui tenaient lieu de narines. De minces fentes situées plus haut comprenaient des globes oculaires (. . .). Ce qui m'intriguait le plus était sa bouche: On eût dit celle d'une pieuvre' (*CA* 67). There are a large number of descriptions of Bernadette and what is striking in the way that she is presented is that the Hazel couple who live next door, after the initial shock of seeing Bernadette, become fascinated by her, Émile especially taking pleasure in looking at her:

> En examinant ce qui lui tenait lieu de visage, je fus stupéfait d'y découvrir une véritable volupté. Je me souviens que, dans le couloir, j'avais assimilé ce bruit à un orgasme bestial: ce soupçon sexuel était une erreur, mais Bernadette éprouvait bel et bien du plaisir. Le sommeil la faisait jouir. J'en fus curieusement ému. Il y avait quelque chose de touchant dans la délectation de ce gros tas (*CA* 117).

This attraction to Bernadette's hideous body is surprising. Émile is as moved by Bernadette as he would have been if he had looked at a beautiful woman. But what of the unsightly male body?

Men are not exempt from representations of unsightliness, especially in *Hygiène de l'assassin* and *Attentat*. Prétextat Tach is a podgy, sedentary man who describes himself from the beginning of the novel in the following terms: 'Quatre mentons, des yeux de cochon, un nez comme une patate, pas plus de poils sur le crâne que sur les joues, la nuque plissée de bourrelets, les joues qui pendent et, par égard pour vous, je me limite au visage' (*HA* 18). Nothomb piles high the qualifying adjectives that describe this 'monstrueuse enflure' (*HA* 122). She goes even further, however, with Epiphane Otos, who, from the outset of the novel is nicknamed 'Quasimodo'.[12] The narrative pleasure taken by Amélie Nothomb is noticeable, as is her jubilation in describing at length, and in the minutest details, the physical appearances of these 'monsters', to such an extent that some scenes become amusing. Paradoxically, Epiphane's ugliness becomes his major asset and the foil of pretty girls: 'J'ai un physique d'exception qui produira deux effets prodigieux: le premier un choc émotionnel sans précédent qui permettra à vos défilés de ne pas sombrer dans l'oubli; le second consistera à multiplier par dix la beauté des filles que j'accompagne' (*A* 52). In this way, he turns his handicap into an advantage, thereby greatly inflating his vanity.

Amélie Nothomb skilfully mixes beauty and ugliness, juggling these two notions throughout her writings. Pretty girls can sometimes be portrayed as angels, or fairies, and monsters lose their humanity, sometimes resembling science fiction characters. This combination recalls *Beauty and The Beast,* a fairytale that can be applied to several of the novels, but especially to *Attentat,* in which Quasimodo falls in love with the beautiful Ethel, and not with Esméralda: 'Tu es la plus belle et moi le plus horrible au monde: c'est la preuve que nous sommes destinés l'un à l'autre. Personne autant que moi n'a besoin de la rédemption de ta beauté, personne autant que toi n'a besoin de l'ignominie de ma laideur' (*A* 140). The caricature is at its peak when the author, Amélie Nothomb, disrupts the established order, when Beauty is not so bad and the Beast is a pervert, confirmed by Ethel when she says: 'Tu attends de moi que je sois aveugle à ton physique et tu joues à la victime parce que je n'y consens pas. Alors que, si j'avais été moche, comme toi, tu ne m'aurais jamais regardé' (*A* 148–49). This proves to be too much for Epiphane who decides to kill his Beauty. It is as if, for beasts, love is only possible in crime. They know that love is impossible, so they kill their prey to make them immortal, and above all, avoid sharing their love, and it is Léopoldine and Ethel who pay the price.

Amélie Nothomb rejects the authority with which the norms of beauty are established and thrust upon us. She finishes by thinking, like Ethel, that '(. . .) les gens aiment ce qui n'est ni beau ni laid' (*A* 38). Nothomb puts our superficial society on trial, and even maintains in *Mercure* that it is difficult to be beautiful: 'La laideur, c'est rassurant; il n'y a aucun défi à relever, il suffit de s'abandonner à sa malchance, de s'en gargariser, c'est si confortable. La beauté, c'est une promesse; il faut pouvoir la tenir, il faut être à la hauteur (. . .)' (*A* 146–47). Nothomb here is close to the subject of Pascal Bruckner's novel, *Les voleurs de beauté,* which questions whether beauty is a crime.[13] Must beautiful creatures be punished for imposing their perfection on others? Is it more difficult to be beautiful than ugly?

Through *Péplum,* Amélie Nothomb also notes that aesthetic criteria are changing, that the attractive girl of 1995 may well be considered ugly in 2580. Canons of beauty are in perpetual evolution, as are means of thinking. Amélie Nothomb is a woman of the twentieth century, in tune with her times, or accepting to play the game of our times, and she claims as much in her novels with their contemporary subjects, and especially in her initiatory fairytales where the body is in turn hidden and flaunted. It is perhaps only natural that Dominique Viart should draw a parallel between Amélie Nothomb, Marie Darrieussecq and Christine Angot:

> (. . .) ces femmes de 30 ans proclament le corps féminin dans une parole autonome se situant à côté et non contre le discours masculin (. . .). C'est dans la froideur médicale qu'il est abordé (. . .) voire dans le plaisir de l'abjection (*Hygiène, Mercure*). Leurs romans passent ainsi par la violence d'un discours retourné d'abord contre soi-même: ils se déploient avec une radicale lucidité, sans complaisance à soi ni à la qualité stylistique.[14]

The image, through the media, reigns supreme in contemporary society, and these authors offer their readers a myriad of reflections of the male and female form. Here, contradictory images are reflected back to the reader in the wealth of physical descriptions, thanks to the power of Nothomb's writing to create, in vivid and all too physical detail, both beastly beauties and beautiful beasts.

Éditions Actes Sud, Arles

Notes

1. *Les Combustibles* (Paris: Albin Michel, 1994); *Péplum* (Paris: Albin Michel, Le Livre de Poche, 2001). Subsequent references in the text will appear as *LC* and *PE* respectively followed by the page number.

2. *Hygiène de l'assassin* (Paris: Albin Michel, Point Seuil, 1995). Subsequent references in the text will appear as *HA* followed by the page number.

3. *Le Sabotage amoureux* (Paris: Albin Michel, Le Livre de Poche, 2000). Subsequent references in the text will appear as *LS* followed by the page number.

4. *Les Catilinaires* (Paris: Albin Michel, Le Livre de Poche, 2001). Subsequent references in the text will appear as *CA* followed by the page number.

5. *Attentat* (Paris: Albin Michel, Le Livre de Poche, 2001). Subsequent references in the text will appear as *A* followed by the page number.

6. *Mercure* (Paris: Albin Michel, Le Livre de Poche, 2001). Subsequent references in the text will appear as *ME* followed by the page number.

7. *Métaphysique des tubes* (Paris: Albin Michel, France Loisirs, 2001). Subsequent references in the text will appear as *MT* followed by the page number.

8. *Cosmétique de l'ennemi* (Paris: Albin Michel, 2001). Subsequent references in the text will appear as *CE* followed by the page number.

9. She also writes, 'Toute beauté est poignante, mais la beauté japonaise est plus poignante encore. D'abord parce que ce teint de lys, ces yeux suaves, ce nez aux ailes inimitables, ces lèvres aux contours si dessinés, cette douceur compliquée des traits ont déjà de quoi éclipser les visages les plus réussis. Ensuite parce que ses manières la stylisent et font d'elle une œuvre d'art inaccessible à l'entendement' (*ST* 86–87).

10. 'Si ce n'étaient que les miroirs! Si ce n'étaient que les vitres! On ne me laisse jamais prendre un bain sans en avoir troublé l'eau à force d'huile parfumée. Pas le moindre meuble en marqueterie, pas l'ombre d'un objet en laque. A table, je bois dans un verre dépoli, je mange avec des couverts en métal écorché. Le thé que l'on me verse contient déjà du lait' (*ME* 31).

11. Jennifer Kouassi, *Le Magazine Littéraire,* 369, 1 October 1998, 83–84 (p. 84).

12. He describes himself as follows: 'Mon visage ressemble à une oreille. Il est concave avec d'absurdes boursouflures de cartilages (. . .). A la place des yeux, je dispose de deux boutonnières flasques qui sont toujours en train de suppurer. (. . .) ma tignasse évoque ces carpettes en acrylique qui ont l'air sale même quand on vient de les laver. Je me raserais certainement le crâne s'il n'était recouvert d'eczéma' (*A* 10–11).

13. Pascal Bruckner, *Les Voleurs de beauté* (Paris: Grasset, 1997).

14. Dominique Viart, *Histoire du roman français du 20ème siècle* (Paris: Hachette supérieur, 1999), p. 146.

Philippa Caine

'ENTRE-DEUX' INSCRIPTION OF FEMALE CORPOREALITY IN THE WRITING OF AMÉLIE NOTHOMB

Amélie Nothomb, 'l'enfant terrible de la littérature d'expression française',[1] with her elegant but offbeat gothic-geisha image and her much-publicized *bizarreries,* has, since 1992, published and promoted a string of hugely successful and entertaining books. Replete with references to vomiting, urinating, repulsive eating habits, and physical attractiveness or grossness, Nothomb's narratives consistently centre on the remarkable bodies and equally extra-ordinary bodily antics of her characters. Focusing primarily but not exclusively on *Hygiène de l'assassin, Le Sabotage amoureux,* and *Stupeur et tremblements,*[2] I propose to consider Nothomb's potentially deconstructive inscriptions of female corporeality within what I shall establish as her 'entre-deux' narratives. In the first part of this analysis I shall argue that her 'fantastical' tales, peopled by the ugly and the vile, the beautiful and the sublime, oscillate in a conceptual realm that flouts genre conventions, and challenges established (discursive) 'realities'. This argument will be central to my overall reading of Nothomb's confusion of commonplace conceptions of the 'monstrosity' of women's 'abject' corpo-reality and the comeliness of a sleek, slim, idealized feminine body.

I shall go on to discuss the admittedly disturbing traces of a Manichean association of thinness with virtue and of fatness with evil manifest throughout Nothomb's œuvre; on occasions, her narratives overtly idealize a *lisse,* pre-pubescent female form, as opposed to a cumbersome and repugnant, mature female body. With this in mind, I shall give consideration to Amélie Nothomb's ambiguous ('entre-deux') inscriptions of female corporeality in an attempt, finally, to discern whether her tales reiterate, or in fact cast doubt upon, perfidious associations of adult female corporeality with 'abject' menace. Is Amélie Nothomb guilty of reproducing an oppressive apprehension of female corporeality that permeates

(Western) discourse? Or do her 'monsters' discredit a phallocentric view of the threatening, 'swampy' female body?

The 'entre-deux'

Notwithstanding the aforementioned 'bodyish' quality and other characteristically Nothombian traits—such as the use of dialogue, erudite philosophical and literary allusions, and biting (if, at times, somewhat affected) wit, couched in structured and polished prose—Nothomb's œuvre cannot be homogenized or compartmentalized according to traditional literary genre conventions. Her numerous texts cleverly bring together features of (sub)genres as diverse as fairy-tale and *film d'épouvante*,[3] tragi-comedy and autofiction. Indeed, this latter mode is especially significant in Nothomb's writing, for the author frequently blends well-publicized, explicitly autobiographical, and invariably bizarre details from her own (embodied) experience into the extra-ordinary exploits of her characters. The resulting blurring of conceptual boundaries between extra-textual reality and sheer literary invention, and the overall 'métissage des genres',[4] encapsulate an overall 'narrative undecidability'[5] integral to Nothomb's 'entre-deux' writing, and central to her inscriptions of female corporeality such as I shall consider them here.

My conceptualization of 'entre-deux' textuality corresponds closely to the inscription of fantasy elucidated by Rosemary Jackson in *Fantasy: The Literature of Subversion*.[6] Her study extends Tzetan Todorov's insistence on the constituent hesitation between 'real' (rational, reasonable) and 'unreal' (supernatural, magical) explanations in the Fantastic proper,[7] to accentuate the subversive value in 'discovering' the 'unsaid and unseen of culture'. Jackson asserts that the fantastic 'takes the real and breaks it',[8] destroying from within the legitimized 'truths' recreated as part of a mimetic narrative frame, and that it 'transforms that "real" through this kind of dis-covery'.[9] I argue for a reading of Nothomb's 'entre-deux' inscriptions of female corporeality as potentially subversive of women's abject bodily reality as it is constructed in and by our androcentric culture and discourse.

Fantastical writing 'does not introduce novelty, so much as uncover all that needs to remain hidden if the world is to be comfortably "known"'.[10] From a feminist point of view, this dis-covery confuses reassuring cultural/discursive distinctions between, on the one hand, the threatening 'horrors' always safely removed from normalized androcentric 'reality' and, on the other hand, the comprehensible, controllable, and acceptable aspects of that 'normality'. Couched in a realistic narrative background, 'wondrous impossibilities', marginalized feminine perspectives, and the re-emergent repressed can no longer be dismissed as mere fabrication or horror and comfortably detached from our (patriarchal) worldly reality but, rather, they unsettle the values and constructs of that world when they (re)materialize from within it.[11] As Rosemary Jackson asserts in her study of the fantastic as a literature of subversion: 'the fantastic plays upon difficulties of interpreting events/things [. . .] thus disorientating the reader's categorization of the "real"'.[12]

In *Le Sabotage amoureux*, for example, the realistic backdrop of communist China, with its absurd melange of misery, ugliness, and idealized exoticism is altered, from within, by the callow *narratrice's* pre-eminent, 'non-realistic' perspective. The story begins with the bombastic little girl feverishly riding a two-wheeled *cheval*, and from there, the reader hesitates between the young *narratrice's* fanciful logic and the obfuscated background 'reality'. Her bicycle, for example, *is* a horse, an assertion referred to sympathetically by the adult narrative voice as a very real part of her childhood world: 'Je ne vivais aucune fantasmagorie puérile, je ne m'étais pas forgé une féerie de substitution. Ce vélo était un cheval, c'était comme ça' (*LS* 42).

Her childhood version of bodily 'reality' also confounds the supposed superiority of the penis/phallus which psychoanalytic theory regards as fundamental to subjectivity. The *narratrice* effectively invalidates a notion of the male organ as a symbol or sign of superiority—to her, it is something ridiculous. When she witnesses her beloved Elena according attention to a boy, she is perplexed by Elena's obvious ignorance of his 'chose grotesque' and her blindness to 'l'infirmité des garçons' (*LS* 71), but is certainly not in a position of 'penis envy': 'Se pouvait-il qu'Elena ne jugeât pas cet objet ridicule? [. . .] J'en conclus avec effroi que ma bien-aimée avait perdu la raison' (*LS* 74). And her tears later that night are not in lament of any physical or symbolic lack, wishing she had a penis/phallus, but rather they are the sign of bitter disappointment in Elena:

> Je compris qu'Elena était irrécupérable.
> Je passai la nuit à pleurer, non parce que je ne possédais pas cet engin, mais parce que ma bien-aimée avait mauvais goût (*LS* 75).

The equation of the penis with *l'infirmité*, the grotesque, and *mauvais goût* is quite the inverse of psychoanalytic discourse; attaching no value to the penis, the unworldly young *narratrice* persuasively counters the values of our phallocentric society: 'Je ne me posais pas la question de savoir ce que ce garçon avait de plus que moi' (*LS* 74). The young *narratrice's* indignation derives from an unalterable belief, which we shall discuss in more detail below, in the risible imperfection of all but the bodies of little girls.

In *Stupeur et tremblements* Nothomb also generates an 'entre-deux' narrative. The author herself has insisted that the events portrayed are neither invented nor exaggerated,[13] whence an ostensibly realistic backdrop to this autofictional *récit*, which begins with a description of the pecking order placing Amélie-san at the bottom of Yumimoto's hierarchical ladder. With typically sardonic humour, Nothomb blends the realistic and the unreal in *Stupeur et tremblements* to articulate a cogent critique of injustices inherent in an absurd and dehumanizing culture and power system. Most specifically, as we shall see in more detail below, the 'entre-deux' mixing of jocular fabulation with mordant reality permits a poignant critique of repressive dogma vis-à-vis the female body in ways that encourage the reader to rethink received ideas and 'realities' of female corporeality.

A disturbing example of an 'entre-deux' (re)presentation of female corporeality is evoked in Amélie-san's account of Omochi's 'violation' of Fubuki Mori. The obese Omochi severely reprimands Fubuki in front of the whole office, just metres from the speechless *narratrice,* for a fault undisclosed and in a manner that reduces the 'orgueilleuse et sublime' (*ST* 109) Nippon to a mortified, infantile underling. By means of the realistic backdrop to Nothomb's narrative, the reader is familiar with the power system which permits and perpetuates the meting out of such abuse, and cannot remain insensitive to the notion that superiors may exercise their power arbitrarily over their inferiors. Moreover, Nothomb is able deftly to (re)position the reader in order to perceive such abuse from an embodied, female point of view (rather than a commonly universalized, supposedly gender-neutral *male* gaze), in order to perceive how a young woman corporeally experiences such a violation. Taking the narrative beyond an ossified 'reality' of the scene, Nothomb significantly heightens it: exploiting the plural connotations of the verb 'violate', and actualizing the metaphorical dimension to the scenario, the theatrical dressing-down becomes Omochi's rape of Fubuki.

This propensity to actualize the metaphorical, shifting the narrative in-between the literal and the figurative, is a facet of most of Nothomb's writing. As Rosemary Jackson affirms, 'the fantastic does not introduce scenes *as if* they were real (except when it moves into allegory, dream vision, or the marvellous): it insists upon the *actuality* of the transformation (as in *Jekyll and Hyde* or in Kafka's *Metamorphosis*)'.[14] Beyond the first figurative layer, these 'entre-deux' texts accept the realness of the image, so that both are always available and the text always oscillates between possible interpretations, *in-between* alternative 'realities'. Omochi's violent admonishment of Fubuki Mori is, also, a monstrous scene of sexual abuse. More than merely elaborate allegory or metaphor with which to enhance a dramatic (if not banal, then certainly feasible) situation, Nothomb's 'entre-deux' writing goes beyond simple mimesis, beyond metaphor, to a hybrid literary mode in which she inscribes a fluid and unfixable, embodied experience:

> Je fus soudain frappée par l'idée que j'assistai à un épisode de la vie sexuelle du vice-président [. . .] il était en train de violer mademoiselle Mori, et s'il se livrait à ses plus bas instincts en présence de quarante personnes, c'était pour ajouter à sa jouissance la volupté de l'exhibitionnisme (*LS* 111).

> Si j'avais dû être l'interprète simultanée du discours de monsieur Omochi, voici ce que j'aurais traduit:
> —Oui, je pèse cent quarante kilos et toi cinquante, à nous deux nous pesons deux quintaux et ça m'excite. Ma graisse me gêne dans mes mouvements, j'aurais du mal à te faire jouir, mais grâce à ma masse je peux te renverser, t'écraser, et j'adore ça, surtout avec ces crétins qui nous regardent. J'adore que tu souffres dans ton orgueil, j'adore que tu n'aies pas le droit de te défendre, j'adore ce genre de viol! (*LS* 112).

No single textual reality wins over—neither the representation of everyday reality, nor the impalpable realm of perception, sensitivity, and phantasm. As a consequence the *récit* remains fluid and heterogeneous, oscillating in-between definitions and 'realities'.

Dis-embodiment and Defenestration

Besides Fubuki Mori's virtual *viol,* Amélie-san's ostensibly realistic narrative is infused with disorienting 'unreal' episodes such as Amélie-san's delirious nocturnal striptease where, deprived of sleep and high on caffeine, and cartwheeling naked around the deserted office, she 'becomes' God. Similarly, employed in a series of ever more inane activities—from turning pages on calendars to cleaning company toilets—she discovers an escape from the frustrating tedium in *la défenestration:*

> les toilettes pour dames de la compagnie étaient merveilleuses car elles étaient éclairées d'une baie vitrée. Cette dernière avait pris dans mon univers une place colossale: je passais des heures debout, le front collé au verre, à jouer à me jeter dans le vide. Je voyais mon corps tomber, je me pénétrais de cette chute jusqu'au vertige. Pour cette raison, j'affirme que je ne me suis jamais ennuyée une minute à mon poste (*ST* 140).

Amélie-san's experience is recounted both literally—'je me jetai dans le vide. Je regardai mon corps tomber' (*ST* 173–74)—and metaphorically—'je jouais alors à ce que j'appelais "me jeter dans la vue". Je collais mon nez à la fenêtre et me laissais tomber mentalement' (*ST* 27–28), so that it is both 'real' and 'unreal', always oscillating, 'entre-deux', between possible interpretations.

Amélie-san's defenestration presents the reader with a remarkable inscription of an experience of corporeality familiar to many women in contemporary Western society. Separating and 'freeing' her self/mind from her burdensome body at a time of considerable anguish—'j'étais libre. [. . .] Je défenestrai mon corps pour en être quitte' (*ST* 76)—she effectively exercises a manner of disembodiment paradigmatic of many women's painful attempts to separate themselves (their 'self') from and objectify a burdensome female body, deemed abject, volatile, too fleshy, too sexual . . . in/by phallocentric discourse. In her analysis of *Anorexic Bodies,* Morag MacSween speaks of (cosmetic) 'practices of objectification' that women (are encouraged to) adopt to control their 'hidden female bodily power',[15] while Sharlene Hesse-Biber refers to women's execution of 'self-imposed body practices and rituals'.[16] In a study of women who inflict often very drastic forms of self-harm on their alienated bodies, Marilee Strong explores many extreme examples of this kind of dis-embodiment or mind-body dissociation as a 'form of psychological escape' increasingly typical in young women.[17]

In *Le Sabotage amoureux,* the young *narratrice* also resorts to a dramatic form of disembodiment as a psychological 'way out'. No longer immersed in the plenitude of her idealized infancy in Japan, and now faced with the ugly 'reality' of China, initially she compensates by placing herself at the centre of her own 'marvellous' reality. But then the arrival of the aloof Elena provokes a vertiginous shift of focus in her world. Caught painfully in-between realities, she is now conscious of *impuissance*—because Elena remains totally unmoved by her admirer's ardour—and of suffering: negative (negating) states that had not previously undermined a blissful plenitude. Her only 'way out' is into an impossible, untenable *néant*, where her elated, subjective mind ostensibly transcends her *carcasse*. The paradoxical pleasure she gleans from self-instigated *sabotage amoureux* takes her to the very edge of nothingness—to the brink of death—as she pushes her asthmatic body to extremes, running round and round the playground at Elena's repeated command:

> Elle avait pensé à cette épreuve parce qu'elle me savait asthmatique; elle ignorait à quel point son choix était judicieux. L'asthme? Détail, *simple défaut technique de ma carcasse*. En vérité, ce qui comptait, c'était qu'elle me demandait de courir. Et la vitesse, c'était la vertu que j'honorais, c'était le blason de mon cheval—la pure vitesse, dont le but n'est pas de gagner du temps, mais d'échapper au temps et de toutes les glus que charrie la durée, au bourbier des pensées sans liesse, des corps tristes, des vies obèses et des ruminations poussives (*LS* 93, my emphasis).

This ecstasy of 'pureness' is to the detriment of her body, which, as for many women, constitutes a mere carcass to be transcended.

The endeavours of Nothomb's *narratrices* to attain oblivion (re)present an impossible, and a manifestly 'unreal' fantasy of returning to an untroubled, childlike state where they would be once more unperturbed by the frustrations and lacks occasioned by being in the (adult) world. The imperative for many women to return to an idealized filiform corpo-reality is closely associable with my reading of what her narratives expose as an *impossible* ideal. Adult women in Western society are constantly enjoined to overcome their recalcitrant bodies in order to re(at)tain the socially sanctioned completeness of a smooth, contained and youthful physique. Naomi Wolf in *The Beauty Myth*,[18] for example, elucidates a blatant discourse of 'battle' that has (been) evolved to this effect, and ubiquitous imagery of skeletal models of 'beauty' and 'health' provide a dangerous overstatement of this 'désir de rien'.[19] I argue that Nothomb's hyperbolic inscriptions of disembodiment may be read as representative, indeed paradigmatic of 'women's habitual separation of self from body'[20] in a way which, while it offers no (re)solution to the problem, certainly engages with and brings into play common contemporary experience of female corpo-reality.

This yearning for disembodiment both encapsulates and exceeds the (Western) valorization of mind over body. Much recent theory has considered how this obdurate Cartesian tendency of Western (phallocentric) thinking concurs with the vilification of corporeality.[21] In the tenaciously androcentric, resolutely Cartesian culture of Western society, where the masculine is commonly associated with the esteemed and valued mind, the feminine is identified with the dissolute and distrustful body. 'Woman' (a reductive label, highly charged with essentialism) is inexorably associated with an essentially 'swampy', mutable and uncontrollable, abject female body:[22] 'in dualistic logic, to be a body rather than a mind is to be outside culture, allied to "the abject" ':

> The abject is a realm outside culture and threatening to reduce culture to chaos: it is shapeless, monstrous, damp and slimy, boundless and beyond the outer limits. It is a realm associated primarily with the adult female body in its perceived fluidity and capacity to change, to bleed, to reproduce.[23]

Lacking the phallus, the female body purportedly lacks the wholeness of the 'normal', phallic body,[24] and is thereby perceived as inconsistent, and distinctly other. And 'otherness', as Rosemary Jackson expounds, 'is all that threatens "this" world, this "real" world, with dissolution'.[25]

The perplexing interstice always seething somewhere in-between discursive 'reality' and its defused 'fictions', 'ideals', and even 'non-ideals', is the site of all that is (only ever provisionally) repressed by and for our (phallocentric) society in order to establish and maintain its edicts.[26] This 'entre-deux'—'qui ne respecte pas les limites, les places, les règles'[27]—is the very essence of what is identified with, and most apprehended in, the 'abject' and the abjected female body.

'Monsters' and 'Beauties'

Disembodied, non-abject models of 'femininity' have become increasingly valorized and coveted, and a correlative denigration of corpulence has become ever more virulent in contemporary Western (consumer) society. Amélie Nothomb's texts, admittedly, do bear traces of just such an ethic: her beautiful heroines are often svelte and ethereal; her contemptible 'monsters' are often corpulent and brutish. But I argue that, by dint of her confusing 'entre-deux' inscriptions of 'monstrosity', Nothomb vitiates rather than reiterates such associations of fatness with evil, and thinness with virtue—for while her 'monsters' are despicable, they turn out, at the same time, to possess certain endearing traits. Likewise, the potential equation of Nothomb's 'beautiful', graceful and slight characters with rectitude and loveliness is attenuated by the gradual dis-covery of their appalling attributes. Consequently, there is an irresolvable ambiguity in Nothomb's tales as to who the 'monster' is, and what constitutes the indubitably monstrous deed.

Nothomb's most despicable *personnages* exaggerate, and ultimately distort, an extra-ordinary array of unpleasant characteristics.[28] Her monsters and beauties are, at first glance, the very stuff of horror stories and fairy tales. However, a wholly offensive character, like a purely beauteous one, would belong safely to a wholly fictive realm, disengaged from the prosaic nitty-gritty of the reader's world. And I argue that this disengagement might foreclose any querying of the potentially reductive associations reproduced in the text. The theatrical 'monstrosity' of Nothomb's characters, however, piled on thick and then mitigated by estimable or endearing traits, produces a disquieting effect of both recognition and repulsion, identification and rejection. These overblown and equivocated 'monsters' and 'beauties' exaggerate, contaminate, and thereby dis-cover the delimitative nature of prevailing preconceptions—most particularly associations of physical beauty with virtue and social value, and of corpulence with vileness and social menace.

Bernardin Palamède of *Les Catilinaires*[29] is a gross, surly, outwardly 'monstrous' character, and the revolted narrator refers to the elephantine Madame Palamède in terms much less than human. But by the end of the text the gentle, cultivated, cerebral narrator has strangled the forlorn Palamède, and the hideous Madame Palamède, who ultimately has a certain 'sympathique' and 'charmant' quality about her,[30] has become the *meilleure amie* of the narrator's wife. This aporetic ending generates the unresolved question of who, of what, is indubitably 'monstrous'. In a particularly graphic embodiment of the ambivalent attraction/repulsion of these equivocal monsters, the prodigiously unsightly Epiphane Otos, 'le monstre à face hirsute' of *Attentat*,[31] paradoxically becomes a fashion model, and proves capable of the most eloquently articulated love for the beautiful, candid Ethel. When, in the end, he murders her, he insists on having done so for love, and in order to save her from the insensitive *oubli* of the superficial people around her. Prétextat Tach, the 'monstre d'obésité et de misanthropie' (*HA*, back cover) who insists emphatically on the purely amorous motive behind the murder of his *cousine* is also extravagantly, yet inconclusively abominable. There is a paradoxically engaging side to this highly intelligent, perceptive, titanesque monster.[32] Nothomb's ugly characters do not embody *le mal:* their monstrosity is always attenuated by traces of merit.

At the same time, it frequently becomes clear in Nothomb's novels that her outwardly *exquisite* characters are in fact quite loathsome. The radiant Elena of *Le Sabotage amoureux* is in effect toying with her infatuated devotee, much as Fubuki Mori manipulates the ardent Amélie-san. In the same way, the estimable Françoise (potentially) perpetuates the seclusive deceit of Hazel in *Mercure*,[33] and the respectable Nina's interview, in the end, constitutes the torturous mortification of Prétextat Tach. Again and again conventional criteria of 'monstrosity'—especially ugliness and corpulence—are confounded in Nothomb's 'entre-deux' texts, so that the reader is always uncertain as to who and what is virtuous, and as to who and what is truly vile.

In *Stupeur et tremblements,* Fubuki Mori's sublime beauty and 'monstrous' behaviour are particularly at odds, as she vindictively instigates Amélie-san's vertiginous descent through the lower echelons of the company. Amélie-san, always oscillating between being enamoured of and disaffected by her Japanese *tortionnaires,* does not ever assuage narrative undecidability as to whether Mori is more beautiful or beastly. And Mori's malicious conduct is effectively mitigated by Amélie-san's lucid observations concerning the constrictive social system, and its inhibitive discourse, which doom (Japanese) women to a desolate existence:

Ce qui est asséné à la Nippone à travers ces dogmes incongrus, c'est qu'il ne faut rien espérer de beau. N'espère pas jouir, car ton plaisir t'anéantirait. N'espère pas être

amoureuse, car tu n'en vaux pas la peine: ceux qui t'aimeraient t'aimeraient pour tes
mirages, jamais pour ta vérité. [. . .]
Espère travailler. Il y a peu de chances, vu ton sexe, que tu t'élèves beaucoup, mais espère servir ton entreprise (*ST* 88).

Clearly this prompts Mori to assert rigorously what little power she has over her
inferior, fiercely to defend what little she has been able (as a woman) to achieve.[34]
Her behaviour, in this light, is altogether less heinous than the malefic 'dogmes incongrus' compelling her to act in this way. Nothomb's other narrators also, on occasion, openly inveigh against oppressive features of patriarchal society. In *Hygiène de l'assassin,* for example, Nina argues vehemently against Tach's misogynistic
propos, and the beautiful Ethel of *Attentat* candidly slates the world of fashion
modelling. Amélie-san's is a particularly impassioned invective against the 'corsets
physiques et mentaux' of the social system that contrives to suppress and subdue
Japanese women. Her first-person narrative slips ironically into a 'voice of
authority', wryly rendering explicit the incongruous tenets of a discourse of the
inherently 'swampy' female body which must be transcended:

> "Si à vingt-cinq ans tu n'es pas mariée, tu auras de bonnes raisons d'avoir honte", "si
> tu ris, tu ne seras pas distinguée", "si ton visage exprime un sentiment, tu es vulgai-
> re", "si tu mentionnes l'existence d'un poil sur ton corps, tu es immonde", "si un gar-
> çon t'embrasse sur la joue en public, tu es une putain", "si tu manges avec plaisir, tu es
> une truie", "si tu éprouves du plaisir à dormir, tu es une vache", etc. Ces préceptes se-
> raient anecdotiques s'ils ne s'en prenaient pas à l'esprit (*ST* 87–88).

> Tu as faim? Mange à peine, car tu dois rester mince, non pas pour le plaisir de voir les
> gens se retourner sur ta silhouette dans la rue—ils ne le feront pas—, mais parce qu'il
> est honteux d'avoir des rondeurs (*ST* 90).

Amélie-san's denigration of the acute oppression levelled at the female form accen-
tuates, and thereby calls our attention to, the insidious discourse of the always potentially boundless, abject female body as a menace to be controlled—a discourse
equally prevalent in the West.

La lisseté

Nonetheless, it is clear that Nothomb's narratives repeatedly privilege a beautiful,
slight, non-abject female form over 'cumbersome' and boundless adult (female)
corporeality, and for this aspect of her writing Nothomb could understandably
be the target of (feminist) criticism. Her inscriptions of female corporeality—as
either pre-pubescent, thin, 'lisse' and splendid, or adult, swampy and 'encombrant'—might be read as reiterating pervasive ideologies which endeavour to suppress and control women's bodies. But I contend that, while Nothomb offers no

tenable alternative, her inscriptions both embody and exceed such negating attitudes. For the seven-year-old *narratrice* of *Le Sabotage amoureux,* for example, the little girl's body incarnates bliss, gratification—in short, perfection:

> Il faut avoir été une fille pour savoir combien il peut être exquis d'avoir un corps.
> Que devrait être le corps? Un objet de pur plaisir et de pure liesse.
> Dès que le corps présente quelque chose de gênant—dès que le corps encombre –, c'est fichu.
> [. . .] Platon qualifie le corps d'écran, de prison, et je lui donne cent fois raison, sauf pour les petites filles (*LS* 70–71).

The binary attitude suggested by Nothomb's use of the term *corps encombrant,* further reiterated by reference to Plato's idea of the body as a prison, is one that feminists have long criticized as particularly tenacious in Western thinking.[35] In a culture that has come to identify women with the (undisciplined) body, and men with the (disciplining) mind, this amounts to endorsing and reiterating ideas of the female/corporeal as constituting the inferior domain to be transcended. But in Nothomb's texts the sleekness of the immature female form, the comfortable child-like, 'amniotic' plenitude, constitute an impossible ideal in contrast with, and as unreal as, the boundless 'monsters', so that one can regard her writing as a manner of bitter-sweet, nightmarish wish-fulfilment. Both extremes are a-social and untenable. In this way, she exposes and engages with the impossible cultural (non-)-ideals of female corporeality.

The gluttonous Madame Bernardin of *Les Catilinaires* is the only truly physically monstrous female character in Nothomb's œuvre—the articulate narrator dubs her 'le kyste', effectively evoking the invasive, ambivalent nature of the abject: *le kyste* at once terrifies, repulses, and fascinates the narrator. Her flesh spilling over each side of her chair, she effectively embodies and exceeds, horrifically and humorously, an apprehensive discourse of engulfing and wholly appetitive female corporeality: 'Madame Bernardin n'était autre qu'un énorme organe digestif' (*CA* 76).

This is the very discourse to which Prétextat Tach subscribes in *Hygiène* when he describes the abjection of mature female corporeality:

> —[. . .] Ignorez-vous que les filles meurent le jour de puberté? Pire, elles meurent sans disparaître. Elles quittent la vie non pour rejoindre les beaux rivages de la mort, mais pour entamer la pénible et ridicule conjugaison d'un verbe trivial et immonde, et elles ne cessent de la conjuguer à tous les temps et à tous les modes, le décomposant, le surcomposant, n'y échappant jamais.
> —Quel est donc ce verbe?
> —Quelque chose comme reproduire, au sens bien sale du terme—ovuler, si vous préférez. Ce n'est ni la mort, ni la vie, ni un état d'entre-deux. Ça ne s'appelle pas autrement que femme: sans doute le vocabulaire, avec sa mauvaise foi coutumière, a-t-il voulu éviter de nommer une pareille abjection (*HA* 133–34).

And this is precisely the status from which he endeavoured to spare his young *cousine* by imposing '[de] délirants préceptes d'hygiène' (*HA* 121), then by remorselessly killing her on the very day she started menstruating:

> les filles deviennent affreuses, boutonneuses, fessues, malodorantes, poilues, nichonneuses, hancheuses, intellectuelles, hargneuses, stupides—femmes en un mot [. . .].
> Grâce à moi, celle que j'aimais aura évité le calvaire de devenir une femme (*HA* 112).

In strangling Léopoldine, Tach claims in fact to have saved her from the 'fate' of abject womanhood. In this fantastical tale, oscillating between the realistic and the incredible, Tach extravagantly encapsulates prevalent (Western) attitudes towards the female form: for women, the only means to attain the non-abject ideal of 'contained' 'femininity' is never to age, always to remain youthful—the very jargon of the multi-million pound cosmetics and diet industries. For Tach's cousin—as for many tortured anorexics—this impossible ideal is achievable only in death.

A question essential to this study is whether Nothomb condones or confounds such an attitude—I argue for the latter. Throughout her corpus, Nothomb's hyperbolic, 'beautifully monstrous' inscriptions of female being-in-the-body incarnate but variously *exceed* phallocentric fears of Woman's 'swampiness' and go beyond the idealization of its contained, filiform counterpart. I have argued that Nothomb effectively exploits a phallocentric fear and abhorrence of the 'fleshy' female body lucidly to expose the oppressive nature of prevalent body discourse and body practices. The safely contained 'smoothness' of the girlish body is an in-credible and impossible ideal for the living, breathing, desiring woman whose adult body will inevitably surpass this constrictive paragon, and will, within this discourse, always be experienced as 'swampy' and monstrous. Nothomb offers no (re)solution to this corporeal quandary, but her excessive female bodies dis-cover and bring into question an ambivalence towards the female body familiar to countless women in the (Western) world—including the author herself. 'After all', says Susan Bordo, 'what woman, growing up in a sexist culture, is *not* ambivalent about her "femaleness"?'.[36]

Nothomb's narrative mixing-up of virtue with vileness, of beauty with ugliness, and of allure with repulsion, effectively 'blows-up' common dualisms and, with them, the negative connotations of corpulence and abjection, and the positive connotations of slenderness and beauty. Engaging with the atrocity of cultural fantasies of corporeality that impel women to disregard their bodies, to 'disembody' and to starve themselves, her characters incarnate these bodily (non-)ideals to obviously un-real extremes. This exposes such absolute extremes, whether revered or repudiated, as actually implausible and untenable. The graciousness of the girlish body and the blissful plenitude of youth are ideals as unrealistic as her repulsive monsters. I conclude that, without offering any comforting, comfortable alternative, my reading of Amélie Nothomb's 'entre-deux' texts opens up an opportunity to move on, beyond and between restrictive dualisms. Her hyperbolic inscriptions of women's being-in-the-body as always either the horrific 'swampy' nightmare or the fantasy of *lisseté* do not reiterate but exceed damaging associations of adult female corporeality with monstrous menace, ultimately to dis-cover the prospect of a potentially fulfilling, 'entre-deux' female corpo-reality.

University of Stirling

Notes

1. 'Amélie Nothomb, Métaphysique des tubes', *Communauté française de Belgique*, 22 May 2001, available online at *http://www.cfwb.be/lyceens/nothombo1.htm* (accessed 10 May 2002).
2. Amélie Nothomb, *Hygiène de l'assassin* (Paris: Albin Michel, Points Seuil, 1992); Amélie Nothomb, *Le Sabotage amoureux* (Paris: Albin Michel, Livre de poche, 1993); Amélie Nothomb, *Stupeur et tremblements* (Paris: Albin Michel, 1999). Subsequent references in the text will appear as *HA, LS* and *ST* followed by the page number.
3. Renaud Matignon, 'Amélie Nothomb: une innocence meurtrière', *Le Figaro*, 20 November 1992.
4. Yolande Helm, 'Amélie Nothomb: "l'enfant terrible" des Lettres belges de langue française', *Études Francophones*, II (1996), 113–120 (p. 118).
5. Alex Hughes, *Heterographies: Sexual Difference in French Autobiography* (Oxford, New York: Berg, 1999), p. 3.
6. Rosemary Jackson, *Fantasy: The Literature of Subversion* (London & New York: Routledge, 1981).
7. See for example, Tzvetan Todorov, *Introduction à la littérature fantastique* (Paris: Seuil, 1970).
8. Jackson, op. cit., pages 4 and 20 respectively.
9. Ibid., p. 65.
10. Ibid.
11. It is in the *pure* marvellous that 'wondrous impossibilities' constitute mere fabrication 'accepted as normal within an imagined world clearly separated from our own reality' (see Chris Baldick, *The Oxford Concise Dictionary of Literary Terms* [Oxford & New York: Oxford University Press, 1990], p.129). This severance from 'our own reality', I am arguing, is not valid here.
12. Jackson, op. cit., p. 20.
13. Amélie Nothomb, personal appearance, Librairie Kléber, Strasbourg, 6 October 1999.
14. Jackson, op. cit., p. 85.
15. Morag MacSween, *Anorexic Bodies: A Feminist and Sociological Perspective on Anorexia Nervosa* (London & New York: Routledge, 1993), p. 180.
16. Sharlene Hesse-Biber, *Am I Thin Enough Yet?: The Cult of Thinness and the Commercialization of Identity* (New York & Oxford: Oxford University Press, 1996), p. 23.
17. Marilee Strong, *A Bright Red Scream: Self Mutilation and the Language of Pain* (London: Virago, 1998), p. 8.
18. Naomi Wolf, *The Beauty Myth* (London: Vintage, 1990).
19. In a book of the same name—*Désir de rien* (Paris: Aubier, 1990)—Christiane Balaise employs this expression to describe the double-edged endeavour of the anorectic: s/he does not want (to eat) anything *and* s/he desires nothingness (*néant*, or oblivion).

20. Barbara Brook, *Feminist Perspectives on the Body* (London & New York: Longman, 1999), p. 31.

21. See for example David Le Breton, *L'adieu au corps* (Paris: Éditions Métailié, 2001).

22. Even for Simone de Beauvoir, whose commitment to essentially 'feminist' reflection is undeniable, women had to 'conquer the *"swampy"* female body and give the self to the mind' (Brook, op. cit., p. 15); 'de Beauvoir's expressed revulsion for the physicality of an adult, reproductive female body echoes the terms of Jean-Paul Sartre's description of the female sex as "obscenity", in common with other things that "gape open". The association of adult female bodies with the jungles, swamp, etc. has a long history; it is taken up at a psychical level by Freud with his description of woman as "the dark continent" ' (Brook., p. 42, note 1).

23. Brook, op. cit., p. 14.

24. Here I am evoking the strain of binary opposites and resultant hierarchized dualisms widely critiqued by feminist theorists, whereby Woman has historically been identified with a devalued and deficient pole *in relation to* a full and centralized (phallocentric) masculine pole. The poles constitute not two 'opposite-but-equal' ends of a spectrum, but rather universal(ized) male, and female "other": 'The full, phallic, masculine body necessarily assumes its antithesis: the lacking, castrated [female] body' (Moira Gatens, *Imaginary Bodies: Ethics, Power and Responsibility* [London: Routledge, 1996], p. 38).

25. Jackson, op. cit., p. 57.

26. In psychoanalytic terms, repression is a mechanism that attempts *in vain* to efface that which is unacceptable within the sphere of the reality principle, but which is never suppressed and always persists, making its presence felt in 'le retour du refoulé': 'Le refoulement du désir n'est pas sa suppression' (See Evelyne Caralp & A. Gallo, *Le Dico de la Psychanalyse et de la Psychologie* [Paris: Milan, 1999], p. 165); 'Ce qui est refoulé [. . .] persiste'; 'Ce qui est refoulé ne l'est pas une fois pour toutes' (See Alain Vanier, *Éléments d'introduction à la psychanalyse* [Paris: Nathan, 1996], p. 72).

27. Julia Kristeva, *Pouvoirs de l'horreur* (Paris: Seuil, 1980 [Points Essais N°152]), p. 12. All subsequent references will be to the Points Essais edition.

28. The author herself has acknowledged a taste for extremes, admitting that she's 'attracted by extreme beauty and extreme ugliness' but that 'it's easier to describe extreme ugliness.' Amélie Nothomb in Paul Ames, 'Diplomat's Daughter rocks French literary scene with dark novels', *Canoe.ca* web page, available online at http://www.canoe.ca / JamBooksFeature/nothomb_amelie.html (accessed 1 Nov 2001).

29. Amélie Nothomb, *Les Catilinaires* (Paris: Albin Michel, Livre de poche, 1995). Subsequent references in the text will appear as *CA* followed by the page number.

30. My observation about the surprisingly endearing qualities of the outwardly 'monstrous' Madame Palamède was substantiated in a telephone interview with Nothomb (10 October 2001) about the 'entre-deux' nature of her writing. Here I am quoting Nothomb's own words.

31. Amélie Nothomb, *Attentat* (Paris: Albin Michel, Livre de poche, 1996).

32. Again, my own interpretation was corroborated in my telephone conversation with the author (10 Oct 2001).

33. Amélie Nothomb, *Mercure* (Paris: Albin Michel, 1998).

34. See *Stupeur et tremblements,* for example when Fubuki Mori defends the fact that she denounced Amélie-san to the vice-president for 'jumping rank': J'ai vingt-neuf ans, vous en avez vingt-deux. J'occupe mon poste depuis l'an passé. Je me suis battue pendant des

années pour l'avoir. Et vous, vous imaginez que vous allez obtenir un grade équivalent en quelques semaines?' (*ST* 53).

35. See, for example, Hesse-Biber (op. cit.), particularly Chapter 2, 'Men and Women: Mind and Body' (pp. 17–30), and Susan Bordo, *Unbearable Weight: Feminism, Western Culture, and the Body* (Berkeley, LA & London: University of California Press, 1993), particularly the section entitled 'The Dualist Axis' (pp. 144–48), where Bordo elucidates the influences inherent in the Western view of human existence as 'bodily and the material, on the one hand, [and] mental or spiritual, on the other' (ibid., p. 144), of Plato's philosophy of the body as '*alien,* the not-self, the not-me', as '*confinement and limitation:* a "prison," a "swamp" [. . .] from which the soul, will, or mind struggles to escape', and as '*the enemy* [and] the source of obscurity and confusion in our thinking' (ibid., pp. 144–45; my emphasis).

36. Susan Bordo, ibid., p. 37.

Jean-Marc Terrasse

DOES MONSTROSITY EXIST IN THE FEMININE? A READING OF AMÉLIE NOTHOMB'S ANGELS AND MONSTERS

It would be difficult to read one of Amélie Nothomb's novels without stumbling upon a monster. Monsters, whether discreet or self-proclaimed, are on every page of each one of her adventures. Heroes or secondary characters, they are often the very subject of the narration, the obstacles which it encounters and the material on which it feeds. But what is a monster? How should we define it? How define a being which resembles a monster? And, besides, is it at all possible to resemble a monster? Of course not, says Jacques Derrida, for a monster is by definition unique. Derrida comes to this conclusion because he tackles the question of how to define a monster in reverse: he does not use the term 'monster' in the sense of a figure, such as it is for instance used by Homer when he describes Polyphemus as a monster, but, rather, from a narrative point of view. He states: 'un événement n'advient que si son irruption interrompt le cours du possible et surprend toute prévisibilité'.[1] In a way, one can say that every event is itself akin to this concept of the monster, a unique being, 'une forme conceptuelle in-ouïe car elle est au delà de la pensée qui se pense, de la pensée pensée'.[2]

This idea of the monster, which Derrida later, in direct relation to guilt, excuse and accusation[3]—a relationship to which I shall return—, defines as a 'machine événementielle', is omnipresent in Amélie Nothomb's novels. None of her texts is without a character who is either presented as a monster or suspected to be one by the author, a character whose monstrosity is always anterior to the story, but which only comes to the fore as the narrative unfolds, in the guise of an apparently inno-cent appearance (what Yves Bonnefoy, in his lectures on Baudelaire at the Collège de France, has likened to an experience of epiphany, as the manifestation of a seemingly divine presence),[4] an appearance which is at once rendered moving through its *mise-en-scène* and harmless through its entrance onto the narrative stage. The beautiful Elena of *Le Sabotage amoureux* is an example *par excellence* of this: 'Le centre du monde habitait à quarante mètres de chez moi. Le centre du monde était de nationalité italienne et s'appelait Elena'.[5]

We are facing a type of monster here which, according to usual criteria, would not qualify as such, but which, following Derrida's definition above, I shall call a 'monstre événementiel'. The person whom the narrator, throughout *Le Sabotage amoureux,* calls her 'bien-aimée', is such a 'monstre événementiel'. This girl will make her suffer for more than one hundred pages (minus the thirty-two at the beginning and even that is not all that clear-cut). This monstrosity thus does not refer to Elena as an individual, the 'individual little girl'; rather it refers to the monstrosity of a love that is performed, but not shared, love as an event that has happened to someone who seeks to inflict it on the other. This monstrosity, although described in minute detail, is denied as such by the first-person female narrator.[6] And so, by contagion, everything in the text becomes monstrous: China, the country in which this one-sided love story is set, and rather than China, Beijing, and rather than Beijing, a no man's land reserved for foreign diplomats, and rather than this no man's land, an even more self-contained world which is that of the diplomats' children who are meticulously described, like a social machinery full of secret machinations.

In this monstrous world, the old myth of the beauty and the beast is reinterpreted, not to say reversed. At first reading, the beauty is definitely the Italian girl whose objective criteria of seduction come straight out of a fairy tale. The beast, by simple deduction, is the one who wants to come closer to beauty and hurts itself in her contact. This does, of course, imply that the heroine has an unattractive physique.[7] The apparent alternation between the roles of beauty and beast continues to operate and to make us tumble from one camp into the other until the final unveiling eventually takes place, until we finally know what to make of the sex of angels and that of monsters.

The word 'angel' in Nothomb is opposed to 'monster' and not to 'demon': 'Là, c'était précisément ma lutte avec l'ange, et j'avais l'impression de m'en tirer aussi bien que Jacob. Je ne cillais pas et mon regard ne trahissait rien' (*LS* 118). At this moment, the child (the female narrator, the little Amélie) affronts the object of her love: the other child, the girl Elena. She does not blink, she keeps quiet, she is silent as only children can be. She is an *infans,* that is to say, according to its etymological meaning, one who does not speak. This silence accompanied by the silence of her eyes, which give nothing away either, is a victory. Amélie listens to Elena's silent response, she listens to Elena's confessions, and her silence is confession and these confessions are her victory: 'Elle baissa les yeux. C'était une défaite beaucoup plus forte que ciller. Elle baissa carrément la tête comme souligner qu'elle avait perdu' (*LS* 118).

The narrator managed to keep silent for a few days, she managed to give the impression that her love was gone, to pretend that she no longer was in love. And so Elena finally yields, and her silence says that she does not understand, that she wants, that she expects, that she needs, that she, in turn, is ready for enslavement, that is to say for the enslavement of words. The angel is defeated. But the narrator should be careful and yet she is not, for this defeat of the other is unbearable to her because the angel cannot yield to this demon who faces the angel and who is all the more demonic because she says that she lies, that she has lied, that she has only feigned that she doesn't love, that all this is a hatched plot. And the young Amélie should be careful because angels are always silent. Only 'deux cascades silencieuses qui déferlent sur ses joues' (*LS* 118) speak of the alleged defeat. But what remains mute does not lose entirely. Only words can bring about the angel's downfall and these words are not spoken. And so the other, the one who faces the angel, the demon, that is to say Amélie, confesses to the defeated angel that she is lying. She confesses her monstrosity which is not only manifest in her lie, but, worse, in the fact that she has remained silent, that she has said nothing, that she has stopped declaring her love, that she has simply stopped speaking—and looking. All these weeks without speaking and without looking:

> Je t'aime, je n'ai pas arrêté de t'aimer. Je ne te regardais plus à cause de la consigne. Mais je te regardais quand même en cachette parce que je ne peux pas m'empêcher de te regarder parce que tu es la plus belle et parce que je t'aime (*LS* 119).

In one single moment all has changed. The word kills reality at the very moment when it is spoken, it curses reality. The demon is once again a demon and the angel becomes an angel again. Roles are reversed: the angel once again holds the natural power of the one who does not love over the one who loves, of the one who is silent over the one who speaks. Elena crushes the narrator, humiliates her for ever, arrogantly claims that she has only been playing to make Amélie confess her love, that it is she who pulls the strings, who worms information out of her, who extracts poems from her soul and avowals from her stomach. It was even worse, Amélie tells us: 'Elena ne disait rien et me regardait avec un intérêt médical. Je m'en rendais compte'. Then, grudgingly and from a distance: 'C'est tout ce que je voulais savoir'(*LS* 120).[8] Amélie is dead, destroyed, once and for all mute in the face of love which, whilst revealing itself to her ('elle m'a tout appris de l'amour'), reveals her for what she is: a monster, a monster facing love, a monster facing the feminine angel. For, as can we see and as we have already understood, the angel in this novel is a girl.

We are confronted here with a novel of apprenticeship, as is revealed from the book's ending:

> Au détour d'une lettre distraite de mon père, j'appris qu'Elena était devenue une beauté fatale. Elle étudiait à Rome, où d'innombrables malheureux parlaient de se suicider pour elle, si ce n'était déjà fait. Cette nouvelle me mit d'excellente humeur. Merci à Elena parce qu'elle m'a tout appris de l'amour. Et merci, merci à Elena parce qu'elle est restée fidèle à sa légende (*LS* 124).[9]

This, however, is not just any kind of apprenticeship; what is at stake here is the total experience of love, the experience of total love: 'elle m'a tout appris de l'amour'. Nothing more can be said about it. The legend of love is not only written by Amélie Nothomb who, thanks to this singular experience has become a writer, it is also invented by her. For if Elena has remained faithful to her legend, what legend is it, if not the one created by little Amélie, first Amélie the child and then Amélie the writer? It is the legend of the beautiful little girl, for Elena is still entirely a girl (one is reminded of the famous phrase: 'Wanting to give an idea of perfection, God created the little girl'). In her outward behaviour, Elena, in an almost parodying fashion, shows all the signs of femininity. She represents the unbearable seduction of femininity just like Amélie Nothomb's other heroines: the Japanese mademoiselle Fubuki in *Stupeurs et tremblements,* Hazel, the young girl in *Mercure* who believes that she is a monster because she has never seen herself in a mirror, Marina the student who is anxious of everything except her own body in *Les Combustibles,* Claire the uncertain visitor, the fugitive student of *Les Catilinaires* and all the others.[10] And each time, facing this adopted femininity, this almost ontological product of its own essence, the female narrator almost literally stops breathing, remains in blissful contemplation, like a fish with an open mouth and half-closed eyelids, as she herself explains to us in *Métaphysique des tubes.*[11] She loses all strength, sinks into a painful powerlessness, and believes that she will instantly become aware of her own monstrosity.

In order to attempt to get closer to the transformations of angels and monsters, I would like to refer to *Les Catilinaires.* The narrator Émile Hazel is a man approaching the age of sixty-five. Everything makes him appear feminine: his whiteness which is even mentioned in the text's final page ('quand fond la neige où va le blanc? demandait Shakespeare', and further down, 'ma blancheur a fondu et personne ne s'en est aperçu' (*CA* 151)); his weak reactions and lack of masculinity when he is face to face with the neighbours; even his surname 'Hazel' which is the first name of the girl in *Mercure,* a novel published two years later, but which may well have been written first. But, above all, the fact that he presents himself as inseparable from his wife Juliette 'aux cheveux d'ange' whom he has known and loved since his childhood.

In the story of Hazel and Juliette, childhood is once again the source of real love, of love considered as total fusion between two beings. This fusion in childhood gives rise to the only erotic scene in all of Amélie Nothomb's books, a silent scene under the shower where the two children press their bodies against each other under the water like twins in the maternal placenta. These two children, who speak little to one another and strive towards yet more silence, build for themselves an ideal silence, an isolated house, the ultimate incarnation of their fusion and their isolation from the world, and a place where they can finish their lives in the delight of being together and alone. But a neighbour disturbs them, breaks their silence, not with words, but, on the contrary, with an even greater silence. And this neighbour who, because of this very silence and contrary to any reason, is revealed as a monster, walks through the door for a courtesy visit as if it were the most obvious thing in the world.

His monstrosity is slowly built up, and it has a cause which will be unveiled in two steps: first, behind the pseudo-monster appears another monster, whose appearance is far more monstrous than that of the neighbour: his wife Bernadette.

> Un kyste, cette chose était un kyste. Eve fut tirée d'une côte d'Adam. Madame Bernardin avait sans doute poussé comme un kyste dans le ventre de notre tortionnaire. Parfois, on opère des malades d'un kyste qui pèse le double, voir le triple de leur poids: Palamède avait épousé l'amoncellement de chair dont on l'avait libéré (*CA* 66).

This description should warn us. It irremediably links Palamède[12] with Bernadette, presents them as made from the same flesh, a monstrous reflection of the angelic couple Émile and Juliette. What we have here is more than a monster; it is a growth, a couple torn from *one* whole being rather than being made up of *two* beings which, through fusion, become one. Angelic nature is the fusion of two beings into one, monstrosity is the tearing apart of one being into two. Prétextat Tach, the monster in *Hygiène de l'assassin,*[13] who is first an angel, becomes a monster when he kills Léopoldine, not because of his crime as such, but because this crime separates him from her. He has been fighting the wrong battle: it was not a matter of, as he believed, fighting against old age — and the couple Émile and Juliette prove this –, but of fighting against being torn apart into two beings. Yet this is a battle he cannot fight, thus condemning himself to monstrosity but also to writing. And the greater his fall from angel to monster, the greater his glory as a writer will be, since, ironically, he is awarded the Nobel Prize.

The second unveiling of Bernadette's monstrosity is, in fact, a reversal of the situation. The characters realize, or more precisely, Juliette realizes, that Bernadette is not what she seems to be. Gradually, the disgust she inspires fades, soon even her monstrosity fascinates. At this point, Juliette offers Bernadette chocolate, which the latter swallows with such great pleasure, that she quite literally seems to have an orgasm. This pleasure is unbearable to Palamède, but Juliette insists and gives her more chocolate. In *Métaphysique des tubes,* we learn of the initiatory role of (Belgian) chocolate which quite literally saves little Amélie's life by making her discover physical pleasure. Chocolate is the antidote to the devouring tubes, to the Japanese carps. It is soothing plenitude in the face of emptiness, in the face of the 'metaphysical' tube of the title. It is childhood. Bernadette who does not speak, becomes a child again, becomes the little girl again she never ceased to be, that is to say, the angel. She is not a monster. The real monster is Palamède.

On one side, there are the angels Juliette and Bernadette, her 'best friend'. On the other, there are Émile and Palamède, united in a crime they both desire and accomplish together. This is a crime which Émile does not mention to Juliette, namely that he literally stopped Palamède's breathing (he suffocated him with a pillow) and thus joined him to become a monster himself. Once he has become a monster, he can begin to write: 'je ne sais plus rien de moi'. This last sentence of the book refers back to the first one: 'On ne sait rien de soi'. He thought he was forever to be in unison with Juliette, until he discovered another truth and threw himself into writing, an act which symbolizes the end of innocence.

This age of innocence represents a life where words are not yet given to the child: this is paradise.[14] The end of innocence then is resolved in writing, in the text.[15] We only write because we have lost original silence, we write in the impossible search of this, in the search of lost silence.

Bibliothèque nationale de France
Translated by Marion Schmid

Notes

1. In *Papier machine: le ruban de machine à écrire et autres réponses* (Paris: Galilée, 2001): 'Mais peut-on ressembler à un monstre? Non, bien sûr, la ressemblance et la monstruosité s'excluent. Il nous faut donc déjà corriger cette formulation: la nouvelle figure d'un événement-machine ne serait même plus une figure. Elle ne ressemblerait pas, elle ne ressemblerait à rien, pas même à ce que nous appelons encore familièrement un monstre. Mais cela serait donc, par cette nouveauté même, un événement, le seul et le premier événement possible car im-possible. C'est pourquoi je me suis risqué à dire que cette pensée ne pouvait qu'appartenir à l'avenir—et même rendre l'avenir possible. Un événement n'advient que si son irruption interrompt le cours du possible et, comme l'impossible même, surprend toute prévisibilité', p. 36.
2. Ibid., p. 36.
3. 'He who excuses himself, accuses himself' [Qui s'excuse, s'accuse], as the saying goes.
4. *Cours 2001–2002*, to be published by Gallimard in 2003.
5. *Le Sabotage amoureux* (Paris: Folio, 1993), p. 32. Subsequent references in the text will appear as *LS* followed by the page number.
6. It can be assumed that this first-person narrator is Amélie herself as a child.
7. However there are no other hints as to this in the text.
8. This reminds me of a sentence by Kafka: 'henceforth the sirens possess a weapon even more horrible than their song: silence', in 'Das Schweigen der Sirenen', *Sämtliche Erzählungen* (Frankfurt: Fischer, 1970) (author's translation).
9. I shall not insist here on the typical Nothombian double register of humour and pathos, of which this quotation is a clear example.
10. *Stupeurs et tremblements* (Paris: Albin Michel, 1999); *Mercure* (Paris: Albin Michel, 1998); *Les Combustibles* (Paris: Albin Michel, 1994); *Les Catilinaires* (Paris: Folio, 1995). Subsequent references in the text will appear as *CA* followed by the page number.
11. *Métaphysique des tubes* (Paris: Albin Michel, 2000).
12. This very unusual name is identical to the first name of the Baron de Charlus in Proust's *A la recherche du temps perdu*.
13. *Hygiène de l'assassin* (Paris: Albin Michel, 1991).
14. For Amélie Nothomb paradise is represented by Japan, the Japan she knew before words came into her conscience.
15. The relation between text and pre-text is symbolized by the name of one of Nothomb's heroes, the protagonist of *Hygiène de l'assassin*, Prétextat Tach. The pre-text is that which comes before the text. The pre-text attaches or attacks, depending on the pronunciation of the family name Tach.

NARRATIVE PRACTICE

Shirley Ann Jordan

AMÉLIE NOTHOMB'S COMBATIVE DIALOGUES: ERUDITION, WIT AND WEAPONRY

> — *Quel manque d'imagination pour une romancière!*
> — *J'étais surtout dialoguiste.*[1]

I interpret this exchange from *Péplum* between the twenty-sixth century scientist and sage Celsius and the twentieth-century author referred to as 'A.N.' as a clear declaration of Amélie Nothomb's temperamental affinity with dialogue rather than with narrative forms. My aim in this essay is to pursue that affinity and to put forward some ideas about the uses and the specificity of dialogue in Nothomb's writing project. I should point out at this early stage that my essay will refer to four kinds, or levels, of dialogue. The first is the dialogue form proper—the classical literary/philosophical form consisting almost entirely of debate between two interlocutors which finds its earliest expression in the Socratic dialogues and which Nothomb adopts and adapts. The second concerns the extensive passages of dialogue in novels which are not dialogues proper but whose interchanges share the same qualities. The third is to be found in the complex dialogue *about* Nothomb and her work which the author cleverly conducts with the reader and with the literary establishment, and the fourth and final level of dialogue is constituted by the intra-psychic conflicts within Nothomb herself, conflicts which are the very wellspring of the dialogic imperative in her writing.

Dialogue, then, plays a central role in all Nothomb's texts, with third- or first-person narration taking up only a tiny percentage of a number of them and often serving mainly to set the scene for gripping interchanges between protagonists. Dialogic performance is not only responsible for much of the intellectual interest of her work but also for producing a very distinctive brand of dramatic intensity which makes her association with the theatre—in the form of her play *Les Combus-tibles*[2] and the eventual staging of *Hygiène de l'assassin*[3]—feel almost inevitable. Nothomb specializes in one-to-one jousts of extraordinary virtuosity and tension where the stakes involved for the dialecticians are high and the outcomes surprising. One way of characterizing her work, in fact, is as a sustained meditation on the interpersonal dynamics of power and from her first novel onward, extended dialogues have been a staple feature of this project.

In this essay I propose to draw on examples from just three texts. The first, in chronological terms, is *Hygiène de l'assassin* in which four mini dialogues and one extended dialogue pit the wits—and ultimately the survival—of the Nobel Prize winning author Prétextat Tach against a number of journalists. This is of particular interest to the latter part of my argument given its focus on narrative practice, the literary world and the figure of the author. The second, *Les Catilinaires* is not a dialogue proper but offers an interesting slant on the functions of dialogue in Nothomb whilst also illustrating the themes of erudition, wit and weaponry.[4] The story of the sabotage of Juliette and Émile Hazel's dream retreat to the countryside, it is also the story of the sabotage of dialogue and the defeat of oratory by the silence of an ever-present neighbour, Palamède Bernardin. The third, *Péplum,* is a close partner to *Hygiène de l'assassin* in terms of its construction and the tenor of its repartee. Set within a futuristic science fiction framework, this dialogue dramatizes an intellectual conflict and a fight for survival between the powerful Celsius and the writer A.N. who seeks the arguments which will result in her being allowed to return to her own century.

I will begin with some general observations about the dialogue as Nothomb practises it, considering the traditions within which her use of it may be placed. I will then examine some functions of erudition and wit, the sharpest of the panoply of weapons drawn upon by Nothomb's invented interlocutors. Finally my essay will return to the figure of the author and to the combative dialogue Nothomb herself conducts through her texts with those who would consume her.

Situating the Nothombian Dialogue

In Nothomb's fictional universe people do not say things like 'pass the salt'. They do not chat about everyday banalities in a loose and meandering fashion as you or I or characters in a realist novel might do, and 'chewing the fat' can only be envisaged, as readers of *Hygiène de l'assassin* will know, in a literal sense.[5] Instead there is a sense of purpose, a sense that fundamental principles are at stake, that one set of values is being pitted against another and that an individual's utterances are part of a strategy for dominance. Interlocutors do not speak for long without challenging each other; they bring forth apparently spontaneous reflections which are polished, penetrating, cleverly ironic, sometimes formulaic or lapidary, and which, as part of an ongoing intellectual enquiry, demand a response.

This brings us to the first of the predecessors on which Nothomb draws: the dialogues much favoured in ancient Greek and Latin literature and used for satirical purposes (*Hygiène de l'assassin* comes to mind here for its satire of literary journalists) or for didactic purposes. I have already suggested that Nothomb's dialogues proper are clearly composed with reference to the most influential of these, Plato's Socratic dialogues of the fourth century BC. The Socratic method, as we know, attributed positions to characters and gave them voice in order better to explain philosophical concepts through a dialectical process of question and answer. There is certainly something of this procedure at work in Nothomb, since dialogue is usually between just two people and is intensively focused. Issues raised in her dialogues include large perennial questions—questions about moral choices and responsibilities, about the uses of literature, the nature of language and about abstract concepts we can capitalize such as Truth, Power, Beauty and so on. Debates about the relative importance of 'le Bien' and 'le Beau' (*PE* 40) and about power and democracy (*PE* 71) are two examples among many. There are also some variations on old favourites redolent of student debating societies, such as who one should eject from a plummeting balloon and in what order, and in fact the very plot of *Les Combustibles* is an adaptation of this idea.[6] The sense of philosophical debate, then, is strong.

Both the notion of dialogue as conflict rather than collaboration and the notion of the adaptation of pre-existing genres place Nothomb in the framework of a Bakhtinian endeavour. Whereas Merleau-Ponty's definition of dialogue stresses common ground, collaboration and co-existence,[7] Mikhail Bakhtin stresses the struggle against the other.[8] In fact, for Bakhtin every utterance is a dialogic struggle since every utterance involves language and language involves the appropriation of words which have been given layers of meaning by previous owners. Bakhtin speaks of words being 'saturated' or 'contaminated', and this perception of re-appropriation applies not only to language but also to traditional literary genres. These too are permeable, porous and susceptible to 'carnivalization' or 'contamination' by the popular.[9] Clearly Nothomb's dialogues can be placed in such a perspective, and equally clearly, the contaminating factors are numerous.

For example, Nothomb's overriding purpose is less to explore philosophical concepts than to generate entertaining and intellectually impressive confrontations. Arm wrestling often seems to be more important than any arrival at the 'truth' of a proposition; power games, humiliating the opponent and the imposition of will seem to be what really matter. The dialogues are not seriously or usefully polemical, and the sustained didactic apparatus of the classical dialogue keeps dissolving. There may be some trivial sniping, some petty jibes which interrupt and dilute the deductive reasoning. A.N. is referred to by her adversary as 'le Petit chaperon rouge' and in turn labels him 'un jean-foutre!' (*PE* 50); the status of *Péplum* has in fact been described by one critic as 'entre scène de ménage et dialogue platonicien'.[10] In addition, the dialogue paradigm is usually overlaid with borrowings from other lesson-imparting genres such as the fable, the allegory, the satire, the fairy tale or the science fiction fantasy.

A further interruption comes from the sheer stature of the interlocutors. Many of them are so much larger than life, with fantastic or almost mythical dimensions, that our interest in the individual takes over from the subject under debate. Finally, it is very clear in Nothomb's universe that reason is, in the last analysis, secondary to the body and to the physical world. The failure of the intellect before overwhelming bodily imperatives is conspicuous as protagonists succumb to visceral reactions of disgust or to violent physical action. In *Hygiène de l'assassin* journalists vomit, shake and exude 'fear' hormones after their encounter with Tach and in the end rhetorical weapons give way to blows. Similarly, Celsius assaults A.N. after the warning: 'C'est des coups que vous voulez?' (*PE* 62), whilst Celsius's reasoning about the necessity of war and poverty is met by A.N.'s threat to vomit in response (*PE* 94; *PE* 114).[11] Physicality is always near the surface in Nothomb, threatening to submerge the intellect, and this is another of the distinguishing features of her dialogues.

This modification of the Socratic dialogue by the injection of physicality, theatricality and larger-than-life character brings us forward in time to other literary points of reference for situating Nothomb's dialogues. Figures such as Prétextat Tach, Palamède Bernardin (the obtuse and gruff saboteur of dialogue in *Les Catilinaires*) and, to a lesser extent, Celsius, are among Nothomb's ever expanding cast of grotesques. They evoke two notable predecessors: Rameau's nephew, the compellingly disturbing 'grain de levain' of Diderot's wonderfully digressive late eighteenth-century dialogue *Le Neveu de Rameau*,[12] and the dangerous figure of Jean-Baptiste Clamence in Camus's mid-twentieth-century implied dialogue *La Chute*.[13] Both these monstrous ancestors provide cynical commentaries on and dubious alternatives to the accepted moral order and received ideas of their day. Both fascinate us because of their deeply corrosive potential and both generate dialogues with great emotional involvement. Rameau, a provocative force for change, galvanizes the right-thinking *philosophe* to try to reconfigure his own world view in order to fit this new and troubling energy within it. The sardonic Clamence lurks in a darkened Amsterdam bar like a spider just as Tach, the diseased ogre figure, lurks in the obscurity of his flat. The arch manipulator, he is determined to justify his own morally ambiguous stance by cornering others and reasoning them into sharing it. Celsius too puts us in mind of Clamence as he challenges A.N.'s assumption of her own innocence in the genocide referred to as 'l'anéantissement du Sud'.[14] These vividly portrayed brothers meet across the centuries, united by their determination to destroy purity, to jam the machinery of our habitual understandings and to root out and satirize what they view as the hypocrisies of their age. *Péplum* and *Hygiène de l'assassin* certainly share this satirical function, and Jean Fabre's comment that *Le Neveu de Rameau* 'trouve son unité non dans une thèse, mais dans une présence' could be applied to all Nothomb's dialogues.[15]

A further step in drawing out the characteristics of Nothomb's dialogues is to look at the constraints within which they take place, or rather at what we might call the Nothombian situation. Like the authors of *Le Neveu de Rameau* and *La Chute,* Nothomb injects suspense into her dialogues, creating ingenious dramatic situations, placing within them a small number of characters and observing the unities of time, place and sometimes action. Sequestration is a constant and A.N.'s futuristic cell, Tach's obscure and sinister lair, M. Hazel's rural retreat-cum-prison are complemented by the confinement on the island of Mortes-Frontières in *Mercure*,[16] the Kafkaesque interior of the Yumimoto building in *Stupeur et tremblements*[17] and other examples. Nothomb elects characters calculated to irritate, wound, provoke or torture each other, characters who are as intent on seeking out each other's weak spots as Sartre's relentless and eternal trio, Inès, Estelle and Garcin. *Huis Clos* springs to mind quite often, in fact, particularly in *Péplum* where A.N. threatens to torture Celsius until the end of time, reminding him that physical violence against her is futile since she is already dead.[18] Perhaps the Nothombian situation is best defined, then, as one of dangerous intimacy. The dialogic relationships in which protagonists become enmeshed go beyond the mere exercise of reason and because they tend, ultimately, towards the destruction of one party by another, they remind us of our existential dependency on our interlocutors.

A further feature, and the final one I shall mention here, is the way in which protagonists devise rules, stakes and tactics for their combat as they go along. 'Je propose que l'enjeu soit identique pour nous deux', suggests Nina in the last of what have been referred to as the 'entretiens-jeux de massacre'[19] of *Hygiène de l'assassin;* 'si je craque, c'est moi qui rampe à vos pieds, mais si vous craquez, c'est à vous de ramper à mes pieds' (*HA* 99). The metaphors which spring to mind for such dialogues are those of competitive sports such as fencing, of strategic games such as chess (a trope also running through Diderot's *Neveu de Rameau*) and of warfare.

To take just one example to conclude this section, let us look at how metaphors of war and games do indeed underpin the conception of one text: *Les Catilinaires*. Here the siege and the conspiracy—both 'behind-the-scenes', unpredictable forms of attack which make it difficult to assess the potential of the adversary—lurk eruditely and wittily behind the scenes of the novel. The tactics of the impenetrable and infuriating Palamède Bernardin are suggested by his name: Palamède was the Greek hero who participated in the siege of Troy. Not only is this a humorous reference to Palamède's determination to 'sit it out' passively and on his own terms, it also accounts for M. Hazel's erroneous assumption that his home, referred to by the almost generic 'la Maison', is his fortress. In addition, Palamède the Greek is credited with inventing the game of dice during the siege, and with devising other games such as chess and draughts as well. Such inventions are associated with intensive interaction, with getting somewhere through turn taking, and as such they are figures for dialogue. Palamède's surname, however, is in direct contradiction with his forename since the fifteenth-century Saint Bernardin is associated with the proscription of games: 'Saint Bernardin se montra un jour si éloquent, si entraînant, dans un sermon contre le jeu, que ses auditeurs convaincus brisèrent à l'envi tables de jeu et jetons'.[20]

Les Catilinaires is in fact notable, as I have already suggested, for the thwarting of the dialogic project, brought about by the sapping silence of Palamède Bernardin, and the disturbing autism of his wife. It is characterized by utterances of increasing frustration on the part of M. Hazel, which culminate in an all-out verbal attack via one of the 'catilinaires' of the novel's title. This term applies to Cicero's four violently hostile orations of 62 BC attacking Catalinus for leading a conspiracy against Rome and the famous opening lines of the first catilinaire are entirely appropriate as an expression of M. Hazel's exasperation: '«Jusques à quand, Catilina, abuseras-tu de notre patience? Combien de temps encore servirons-nous de jouet à ta fureur? Quel sera le terme de cette audace effrénée. . .?»'[21] M. Hazel's 'catilinaire', like Cicero's, is a retaliatory measure, although in this most morally ambiguous and disturbing fable it is not the orator but the silent man who steals a victory.

It would be interesting to establish a complete taxonomy of Nothombian rhetorical weaponry, but there is not space here to enumerate all the arms she and her interlocutors employ. I intend therefore to limit my observations to some examples of erudition and wit.

Erudition and Wit

Nothomb's protagonists delight in the rarefied. The wealth of often obscure references they bring to the arena of the dialogue is a source of pleasure to them and a confirmation of their own singularity, and displaying erudition is clearly a form of point scoring. It is invariably an implicit challenge to which the interlocutor must rise by demonstrating familiarity with the reference.

Participants in the dialogues display a breadth of cultural knowledge allowing them to back up their arguments by making detailed references to figures as diverse as Roland Barthes, Einstein and the town-planners of antiquity (PE 7–8). Their literary knowledge is extensive and they demonstrate an easy familiarity with even the more obscure protagonists and episodes from Greek mythology. Their erudition manifests itself on the linguistic level with some choice lexical items, a heightened awareness of rhetorical skills, and a broader philosophical consideration of the relationship between language, self and world: 'C'est le langage qui m'a toujours manipulée', claims A.N. (PE 73), or 'Nommer les choses, c'est leur enlever leur danger' (PE 109).

Protagonists are also seasoned practitioners and analysts of debate, accusing each other of sophistry (PE 5, 51, 141) and constantly judging the quality of each other's questions and responses as they spar. 'Vous vous trompez de débat' (PE 6), or 'Vous posez les mauvaises questions' (PE 102), says Celsius, frustrated by what he sees as A.N.'s inadequate lines of inquiry. Sometimes protagonists will express mock surprise that their interlocutor cannot wield a certain weapon, and will score points through erudition alone. Usually, though, erudition is made more crushing by being at the service of wit, and all Nothomb's good dialogists are witty.

The term 'wit', as the Oxford English Dictionary reminds us, is understood nowadays as the '(Power of giving sudden intellectual pleasure by) unexpected combining or contrasting of previously unconnected ideas or expressions.' It implies a quick inventiveness, the pleasure such inventiveness procures, and the power it confers on the inventor—particularly the inventor of the unexpected punch line. Thus Celsius scores points by replying to A.N.'s enquiry, 'La préhistoire, cela n'existe plus?' with the existentially unsettling: 'La préhistoire, c'est vous' (*PE* 7). Thus, in the midst of the struggle between Tach and Nina, the aged author steals a point through a supremely bathetic moment of pedantry:

> — Mais je suis déjà déchu! Je n'ai fait que déchoir depuis soixante-cinq années et demie.
> — En ce cas, je veux vous voir déchoir davantage. Allez-y, déchoyez.
> — Vous ne pouvez pas dire ça, c'est un verbe défectif (*HA* 185).

A particularly rewarding example of erudition and wit is to be found in a wonderfully combative episode of *Les Catilinaires*. In a twelve-page tour de force, the mild-mannered narrator and his wife Juliette become unusually barbed and malicious and enjoy planning and executing a campaign designed to crack Palamède Bernardin's impassivity, to humiliate and wound him and ultimately to discourage him from perpetuating his siege. Their weaponry involves laughter ('Désormais, nous rirons de monsieur Bernardin'(*CA* 63)), hyperbolically over-zealous hospitality and above all a dazzling display of erudition in the form of a protracted disquisition on ancient taxonomies and anthropological relativity ('Je résolus', says M. Hazel, 'd'être accablant' (*CA* 65)).

The passage begins with the couple disrupting the norms of hospitality, as of course Palamède Bernardin himself has persisted in doing. Whereas his behaviour is a flat refusal to engage with the norms, they over-egg the pudding and treat him as a dear friend. They feign surprise at his regular 4 o'clock arrival ('Quelle surprise!' 'Le docteur? Ça alors!' (*CA* 63)), squeeze his hand, appear excited to see him and invite him to accept something from an extensive list of mouth-watering desserts—none of which they have ever actually had in their kitchen. With the opening gambit '– Mon cher Palamède, que pensez-vous de la taxonomie chinoise?' (*CA* 65), M. Hazel breaks the rules of conversational appropriateness and of turn taking by introducing a topic so obscure that it is most unlikely to elicit a response; it is designed to be unpalatable for his non-interlocutor, who covets silence, and to make him conscious of his intellectual inferiority (he is a man of science: has he not heard of this particular passage from Borge's *Enquêtes,* a passage which is apparently 'si connu'?) the monologue is punctuated with thirteen questions, the question form itself being, of course, a weapon when the adversary is Palamède Bernardin. Some of these are rhetorical questions, an integral part of any orator's skill ('D'où vient que l'homme a eu besoin de classifier le réel?' (*CA* 67) and 'où Tachandre range-t-il les insectes, les crustacés?' (*CA* 69)), but they nevertheless solicit the doctor at every turn, purporting to draw him in by the use of 'vous' and feigning to believe in his interest ('Savez-vous à qui et à quand remonte la première classification ternaire?' (*CA* 67); 'Avez-vous songé à ce qui s'est passé dans la tête de Tachandre?' (*CA* 68)). Others are direct questions soliciting a reply and therefore reinforcing the doctor's inaptitude in the role of guest ('que pensez-vous de la taxonomie chinoise?'; 'Qu'en pensez-vous, Palamède?' (*CA* 65)). The monologue's zenith comes when, musing on a classification of birds in the 1994 edition of Bordas's *Les Oiseaux du monde*, M. Hazel remarks on the peculiar technique of classifying something by firstly saying what it is not, and goes on with Juliette to apply this technique, with ironic and cruel wit, to his guest:

> — Par exemple, on pourrait dire que le docteur n'est pas un animal à plumes!
> — En effet. Et il n'est pas un emmerdeur, ni un rustre, ni un idiot (*CA* 72).

In this instance, however, it is not erudition and wit but the strategy of silence which wins the battle of wills, as M. Hazel continues to hold forth about 'Dieu sait quel présocratique' (*CA* 74) long after he realizes that he is losing ground.

It is testimony to Nothomb's fascination with the power of language and the existential project of dialogue that she invents a situation which plunges her principal protagonist into enforced monologism. The awful figure of Palamède Bernardin represents the short-circuiting of dialogue, the denial of the other, who emerges from the encounter not with enhanced self-knowledge (the expected position of dialogic partners at the end of the game) but with reduced self-knowledge. 'Je ne sais plus rien de moi' (*CA* 210) is the closing line of *Les Catilinaires*.

Hide and Seek

All the combatants in Nothomb's dialogues are of course drawing from one repository of erudition, wit and intellectual agility: the author herself, the holder of all the cards. Her indifference to differentiation of voice throughout her work allows us to characterize the whole as an exercise in extended ventriloquism and to view this corpus as a polished showcase for her ingenuity. Everything in her texts points us back to her own astonishing and precocious cleverness, including the very choice of the dialogue form for some of her works, since this is an unusual choice and a form requiring great skill if its intensity is to be sustained.

In this final part of my essay I shall consider the notion that the various struggles for dominance or survival through dialogue which Nothomb invents are subsumed within the master dialogue she is conducting, about *herself*, with readers and critics. Despite the gaily disingenuous disclaimer in *Péplum* that 'Toute ressemblance ou homonymie avec des personnes existant ou ayant existé serait fortuite et involontaire' (*PE* 4), Nothomb's writing is auto-centric: she does not disappear behind the folds of the text but persistently draws our attention to her. Like Diderot in *Le Neveu de Rameau* she is constantly donning masks, her playful theatricality epitomized by the image of the anachronistic peplum she wears in the dialogue of that name, but she is always there and any work is always, ultimately, about her own conflictual relationship with the world. If she is not present as autobiographical subject (*Stupeur et tremblements*, *Métaphysique des tubes*, *Le Sabotage*

amoureux)[22] she sneaks in like Hitchcock (for example in *Mercure* where she is referred to in passing as the lightly disguised lady Amelia Northumb, writer of Eliz-
abethan tales (*ME* 161)). Nothomb, it has been suggested, '[sacrifie] ses intrigues à
son ego'[23] as she replays over and over the same dramas about corporeal unease,
the passage from childhood to adulthood and the fear of rejection. Having 'choisi
d'être sa propre tortionnaire'[24] she is never without a dialogic partner, as the following extended quotation about her enemy within reveals: 'Je me demande si
nous n'avons pas tous cet ennemi, mais comment l'affronter? Pour moi, l'écriture
est le moment du combat, le seul où je me sens assez forte. Entre lui et moi, c'est
un dialogue, et ce n'est pas un hasard s'il y a tant de dialogues dans mes livres. Je
suis rarement en paix'.[25]

Just as Tach plays on the insecurities of journalists whose professional reputation is at stake, so Nothomb is a 'grain de levain' challenging critics to contend
with 'la comédie Nothomb'.[26] 'Who am I?', she seems to ask, and also 'am I a literary colossus, or a dilettante—a mere flash in the pan?' It seems to me that she
writes from a position of sustained awareness of the brutally invasive machinery of
the contemporary literary world in which the author's self is at stake, and that she
anticipates and toys with its demands with combative verve.

Her presence as writer is especially strong in *Hygiène de l'assassin* and *Péplum*,
both of which deliberately bring into play gender dynamics and the questions of
authority and power by pitting a young woman against a much older, more experienced male figure. In fact, it is young women like Nothomb—strong, resourceful
and with considerable *culot*—who often prove the better and more interesting rea-
soners. So it is tempting to posit a feminist reading of these combats, seeking in
them a series of comments about the place of women in the male-dominated literary establishment. The story of Sollers' rejection of the manuscript of *Hygiène de
l'assassin* which he interpreted as a hoax is by now well known.

Ultimately, however, one wonders whether Nothomb's alter ego is to be found
in the spirited Nina or in the misogynistic Prétextat Tach, given that her ludic triumph is to have made of herself a phenomenon every bit as self-absorbed and
monstrous as this literary giant whose very name is indicative of theatricality.[27]
Both her intra- and her extra-textual appearances reveal that she shares his cultiva-
tion of the exceptional, his prolixity, his single-minded commitment to writing,
his idiosyncratic eating habits, his clear-sightedness about the literary circus and his
clever manipulation of it. Like him she has strewn throughout her writing numerous teasing self-referential clues. What is quite amazing is that a mature assessment
of a writer's dialogue with the media should be the subject of her *first* published
work; that she should *begin* her literary career with a clear-sighted satire on the vo-
racity and the hypocrisies of literary journalism.

Nothomb challenges those who sit in judgement on her work by incorporating
self-referential comments on its status. These alternate wittily between self-
aggrandizement and self-deprecation, especially in *Péplum* where she devises op-
portunities to indulge in praise of her own inventiveness as the quotation with
which I began my essay illustrates. Here, Celsius takes A.N. to task for the lack of

imagination she has demonstrated in hypothesizing about world developments during the three centuries of history she has just jumped. The facts that Nothomb should have him do so in a work which is so patently, so pyrotechnically imaginative on this score and that Celsius, the agent of criticism, is in any case her own creation, provide a neat example of Nothombian wit. The relationship between writer, critic and reader is foregrounded in this text too. Here the question of A.N.'s posterity comes into play, and although the all-powerful *Tyran* is impressed by the fact that she is a writer, Celsius does not perpetuate the French tradition of veneration for literature: 'votre qualification d'écrivain lui jetait une telle poudre aux yeux!' (*PE* 57) he comments disappointedly of his superior.

A.N.'s own observations about her writing include the difficulty of classifying it in generic terms, and the fact that the literary establishment of the late twentieth century accorded her no gravitas: 'Lisez les critiques de mon temps', she comments, 'on ne me prenait pas au sérieux' (*PE* 26). Surely the staple literary framework of the philosophical dialogue is a pointer telling us that the author is involved in an earnest endeavour which *should* be taken seriously? Later on in the text, however, A.N. appears to condemn to absurdity any attempt at earnest critical analysis of her work by describing it as frivolous nonsense: 'j'adorais les pitreries et j'en remplissais mes bouquins à longueur de pages' (*PE* 66). This suggests her writing is just an examplar of post-modern showmanship.

Despite the weighty issues upon which they touch, then, are we to see dialogues in her texts as pale simulacra of philosophical dialogues proper, burrowing into a borrowed shell like the hermit crab but lacking any seriousness of purpose? Can we say that they are true to the humanist tradition of the philosophical dialogue in attempting to make erudition accessible, to be 'the midwife of men's thoughts',[28] to affirm the possibility and the value of human self-development? When Diderot began writing *Le Neveu de Rameau* he was experimenting with the creation of a character who would give expression to aspects of his own nature and who would challenge the larger part of himself. A similarly self-questioning motivation lay behind Camus's creation of Clamence. Both works were integral to protracted processes of serious philosophical enquiry. By comparison, Nothomb's writing appears to be merely a self-indulgent stage for her own psycho-dramas. The explosive bursts of creativity with which she lights up the sky of the literary *rentrée* are enormously erudite, enormously witty, enormously inventive, but there is little substance in them other than their function as a sign of our post-literary times.

There is, however, undoubtedly much pleasure for readers as we are drawn into Nothomb's self-absorbed dialogic games. The writing is of the highest quality, the wit and inventiveness are a delight and the game of hide-and-seek conducted with the literary establishment remains tremendous fun. As Nina says to the elusive Prétextat Tach: 'Passer sans cesse de la bonne à la mauvaise foi, c'est d'une malhonnêteté géniale' (*HA* 105).

Oxford Brookes University

Notes

1. *Péplum* (Paris: Albin Michel, Livre de poche, 1996), p. 95. Subsequent references in the text will appear as PE followed by the page number.
2. *Les Combustibles* (Paris: Albin Michel, Livre de Poche, 1994).
3. *Hygiène de l'assassin* (Paris: Albin Michel, 1992). Subsequent references in the text will appear as *HA* followed by the page number. The novel was adapted for the theatre by Pascal Lissilour with Jean-Claude Dreyfus in the role of Tach. It had its première in the *Petit Théâtre de Paris* on 6 November 1999.
4. *Les Catilinaires* (Paris: Albin Michel, 1995). Subsequent references in the text will appear as *CA* followed by the page number.
5. The obese protagonist Prétextat Tach consumes large quantities of fat.
6. During a siege in a war-torn, wintry landscape the protagonists progressively burn the library of a Professor of literature in order to keep warm and exchange views on the value and uses of literature as they determine the order in which the books should be burned.
7. 'In the experience of dialogue, there is constituted between the other person and myself a common ground; my thought and his are interwoven into a single fabric, my words and those of my interlocutor are called forth by the state of the discussion, and they are inserted into a shared operation of which neither of us is the creator. We have here a dual being, where the other is for me no longer a mere bit of behaviour in my transcendental field, nor I in his; we are collaborators for each other in consummate reciprocity. Our perspectives merge into each other and we co-exist through a common world'. Maurice Merleau-Ponty, *Phenomenology of Perception*, Smith, Colin (trans.) (London: Routledge, 1962), p. 354.
8. See Mikhael Bakhtin, *The Dialogic Imagination: Four Essays*, Holquist, Michael (ed), Emerson, Caryl and Holquist, Michael (trans.) (Austin: University of Texas, 1981).
9. Ibid.
10. Renaud Matignon, 'Amélie Nothomb: le temps en vadrouille', *Le Figaro*, 19 septembre 1996.
11. Vomiting is frequently used in Nothomb as a metaphor for rejection. Provocatively, she refers to vomiting as her 'hobby' (see Fabrice Pliskin, 'A.N. L'Incendiaire', *Le Nouvel Observateur*, 1 septembre 1994).
12. This term is used by Diderot in *Le Neveu de Rameau* to refer to his eponymous 'anti-hero' (see *Le Neveu de Rameau* (Paris: Éditions Sociales, 1972)), p. 91.
13. *La Chute* (Paris: Gallimard, 1956).
14. 'Êtes-vous inconsciente à ce point? Je vais vous apprendre quelque chose à votre sujet: c'est que vous vous en fichez éperdument, de l'anéantissement du Sud! La mort de cinquante milliards de personnes, vous vous en battez l'œil' (*PE* 141).
15. 'Diderot dialoguiste', in *Le Neveu de Rameau*, op. cit., pp. 5–18 (p. 11).
16. *Mercure* (Paris: Albin Michel, 1998). Subsequent references in the text will appear as *ME* followed by the page number.
17. *Stupeur et tremblements* (Paris: Albin Michel, 1999).
18. 'Notre sort n'aura donc pas d'échappatoire. Vous et moi, Celsius, nous sommes ensemble pour l'éternité. L'éternité, Celsius! Le mariage cauchemardesque et sans résiliation possible. Chaque matin, quand vous vous réveillerez—pour autant qu'après l'apocalypse le sommeil soit encore accordé—vous vous retrouverez face à face avec mon visage' (*PE* 135).

19. Alain Salles, 'L'Art de la cruauté', *Le Monde,* 11 septembre 1992.

20. Larousse, Grand dictionnaire universel du vingtième siècle.

21. Ibid.

22. *Métaphysique des tubes* (Paris: Albin Michel, 2000); *Le Sabotage amoureux* (Paris: Albin Michel, 1993).

23. Pierre Marcelle, 'Face aux piles', *Libération,* 17 septembre 1998.

24. Martine de Rabaudy, 'Occupons-nous d'Amélie', *L'Express,* 28 octobre 1999.

25. 'J'ai un ennemi en moi', available online at http://www.multimania.com/fenrir/nothomb/ psychologies.htm, 17 octobre 2000.

26. Micheal Abescat, 'Amélie Nothomb: chapeau bas', *Télérama,* 6 septembre 2000.

27. The *praetextae* were dramas in which actors impersonated those who wore the *praetexta* (dresses embroidered in the front, worn by Roman magistrates, priests and children of the aristocracy). Hence persons who pretended to be what they were not. See *Brewer's Dictionary of Phrase and Fable* (London: Cassell, 2000), p. 939.

28. Socrates referred thus to the function of his dialogues.

Claire Gorrara

L'ASSASSINAT DE L'ÉCRITURE: AMÉLIE NOTHOMB'S *LES COMBUSTIBLES*

*'N'y a-t-il pas lieu de se réjouir qu'il y ait autant
de lectures qu'il y a de lecteurs?'*[1]

Amélie Nothomb's meteoric rise to fame in the early 1990s with her first publication, *Hygiène de l'assassin,* set the tone for her subsequent career and literary reputation. In this text, a dying author, Prétextat Tach, ridicules the opinions of a whole host of journalist-critics who have come to interview him about his Nobel Prize-winning novels. After dismissing close textual readings, psychoanalysis and other interpretative frames, his bad faith as an author is revealed by a female journalist, Nina, who forces him to acknowledge the murderous secret at the heart of his work.

Like the monstrous Tach, Nothomb too has puzzled, challenged and irritated the critical establishment. Her first accepted manuscript, *Hygiène de l'assassin* was believed to be a hoax by one member of the Gallimard reading panel, whilst another critic, Françoise Xénakis, speculated that a well-known personality was hidden behind this apparently 'new talent'.[2] As a media darling and queen of self-promotion, Nothomb began as and remains a contentious figure in the francophone literary world.

This literary notoriety has fed Nothomb's reception as a cult author with websites and fan clubs devoted to her work. Her novels are often to be found on bestseller lists and her fiction is marketed for a general readership with suggestive covers where author, character and life history are confounded.[3] This popular status has also to be put alongside a sparkling prose style that demonstrates a sophisticated appreciation of structure, form and literary history. In many of Nothomb's fictions, the status of literature and the relationship between reader and text are pivotal to plot development, while provocative intertextual links with both classical and popular literary traditions open up her novel to multiple interpretations.[4] With her highly playful sense of cross-referencing and intercultural exchange, Nothomb invites the reader to dissolve the barriers between 'high' and 'low' culture and engage with hybrid texts that draw on a variety of sources.

This essay will explore representations of literature and the figure of the reader in Nothomb's third published text, *Les Combustibles* (1994). Written in the form of a play, *Les Combustibles* has been adapted for the stage in France and abroad and has also been performed as an opera.[5] What distinguishes this text from others in Nothomb's œuvre is its sustained meditation on the nature of literature. Set in an unknown Eastern city under siege, *Les Combustibles* sets forth the exchanges between three protagonists, the Professor, Daniel and Marina, who take refuge in the Professor's library as the city is destroyed by bombings. All three struggle to survive the siege in the freezing cold for a second winter and, to keep warm, they slowly burn all two thousand books in the Professor's library.

In this bleak and minimalist setting, the text questions the function of literature when a country is surrounded by the horrors of war. Amélie Nothomb was apparently inspired to write *Les Combustibles* on reading a newspaper report about the siege of Sarajevo.[6] A man who had escaped the war was interviewed about living conditions and had replied that it was so cold people burnt their books to survive. This is the major premise of Nothomb's text. In such an extreme situation, 'quels livres auriez-vous le moins de scruples à détruire?'.[7] Which books to burn and in which order constitutes another facet of the war for the protagonists as they argue amongst themselves over the intrinsic value of the books they consign to the flames. As an exercise in literary evaluation and destruction, *Les Combustibles* also gives the reader insight into Nothomb's own attitudes towards literature and the role of the writer. The prospect of eliminating the literary heritage of a nation and culture—*l'assassinat de l'écriture*—brings the characters in *Les Combustibles* to consider the impact of literature on readers and their perceptions of the world.

Dialogic Encounters

Les Combustibles is a hybrid text in many respects, fusing diverse literary forms, genres and influences. As Nothomb's only play to date, it takes to its logical extension Nothomb's fascination with dialogic encounters. Here, as in other texts such as *Péplum* and *Hygiène de l'assassin*, Nothomb experiments with dialectical forms of writing which privilege the speaking voice. In a pattern familiar to readers of Nothomb's fiction, a young female interlocutor (Marina) challenges the authority of an older male figure (the Professor) with devastating consequences.[8] These dialogic encounters between individual characters are also framed in encounters of another sort, as different styles and modes of writing are juxtaposed for dramatic effect. *Les Combustibles* draws on a number of literary influences and intertexts. It employs the classical unities of Aristotelian tragedy (time, action and place) in a tightly woven structure where characters seem ineluctably driven towards death. Yet, for an educated reader, its battling three characters also recall the infernal triangle of Sartre's *Huis Clos*. With its reworking of classical and contemporary forms, *Les Combustibles* could perhaps best be described as a play of voices, well suited to a medium, such as radio, and the imaginative resources of a listening public.[9]

This dialectical form functions as an ideal structure for the fictional universe of *Les Combustibles*. The battle of words between the three protagonists reflects the conflict that rages outside the claustrophobic space they inhabit. Marina sadly reflects that war has contaminated all of their relations: 'Professeur, nous n'allons pas nous faire la guerre n'est-ce pas? Il y a assez de guerre comme ça à l'extérieur' (*LC* 31). As conditions worsen, so the verbal exchanges between them intensify and their words translate into violent actions that even come close to rape as Marina initially repels the Professor's advances. All physical contact appears to be a struggle or combat between two beings for domination and even dancing degenerates into 'un tango de boxe' (*LC* 42). Throughout these linguistic skirmishes, the nature and purpose of literature is a recurrent theme. Books and authors are evaluated, discussed and compared as the Professor, Daniel and Marina select books for the fire.

Contesting the Canon

As Yolande Helm has commented insightfully, Nothomb's writing project 'est avant tout une enterprise de désacralisation de l'écriture, de la lecture et des mythes'.[10] *Les Combustibles* is no exception and can be read as a sustained attack on the Western literary canon and the hierarchies it creates. In a spirit of mockery and derision, Nothomb targets the literary establishment and its prescriptive approach to literature. The mouthpiece for such views is the Professor of literature, never named, who epitomizes some of the worst aspects of the academic system and is eventually exposed as a fraud and coward. After years spent lecturing his students on which books they should read, he admits to preferring above all else a saccharine teenage romance, *Le Bal de l'observatoire* by Blatek, rejoicing that 'brûler ces bouquins que j'ai décortiqués pendant dix ans puis encensés pendant vingt ans, ça me fait rigoler' (*LC* 64).

In *Les Combustibles,* Nothomb ridicules the activities of academia as a factory for producing PhD theses. The Professor and his assistant, Daniel, spend hours comparing the relative merits of books to throw on the fire. Yet the reader is deliberately distanced and disengaged from their conversations and can have no opinion on the qualities and reputations of the authors they discuss. For despite passing references to biblical and classical culture, as well as to a sprinkling of French authors,[11] Nothomb invents both authors and titles. Names, such as Blatek, Kleinbettingen, Sterpenich and Faterniss, have a vaguely baroque ring to them, while their novels seem to come from the annals of popular fiction with kitsch titles such as *La Poupée parle* or *Le Mythe du sultan*. With such absurd and unlikely titles, the contemporary reader is encouraged to laugh at the futility of creating a literary canon and to enjoy the irony of burning a book entitled *Le Liquide*. The result is that the intense and often childish battles between the Professor and his teaching assistant over literary worth (Professor: 'Et je vous rappelle que le chef, c'est moi' (*LC* 67)) remain a purely formal exercise of little interest. Such games of literary one-upmanship highlight how subjective and biased the canon can be, based on no surer foundations than personal taste and preference. In *Les Combustibles,* these debates are designed to alienate ordinary readers and to show up how the academy excludes none but the privileged few from its club of respected opinion-makers.

If Nothomb accuses academia of being the elitist gatekeeper of literary culture, she also attacks a slavish devotion to critical theories. As a teacher-philosopher in the mode of Socrates, the Professor could be expected to teach his students how to approach the study of literary texts in the 'testing procedure' or dialectical model pioneered in Plato's Socratic dialogues.[12] Instead, he appears as one of Nothomb's more monstrous characters, the lone figure who entraps the students in his library like a spider in his web of deceit and lies. He betrays their dreams and aspirations and is the catalyst for their deaths as he taunts them with the last book left in the library. In many ways, he resembles Prétextat Tach, the grotesque parody of the great, dead, white, male author in *Hygiène de l'assassin*. Both satirize established critical theories and reduce the literary text to a literal truth that denies the validity of others' readings. In the Professor's case, after years spent denouncing Blatek's novel as 'petit bourgeois', he projects his own personal fantasies onto Blatek's unexceptional love story between a fifty-year-old man and a teenage girl. For this book, it transpires, parodies his own frustrated affair with the young student, Marina. Naïve identification with fictional characters ultimately overwhelms any sophisticated literary-critical frame as the Professor grafts a romanticized version of his own life history into a popular romance.

Nothomb's merciless parody of literary criticism and the canon begs the question of her own place in that system. For while she carefully avoids invoking the names of authors living or dead in the debates between the Professor and Daniel, the reader is called to ponder on where Nothomb herself might be positioned in this fictive canon. On one level, this would seem to be on the margins for, although the gender of the writers under discussion is indeterminate, it would seem that the literary universe of *Les Combustibles* is resolutely masculine. Men act as the judges of literature in the text with Marina's views very much undermined and contested by the two male characters. Questions of gender and gender relations in the books under discussion are also singularly absent and female characters are reduced to romantic lovelorn heroines, such as Larissa in *Le Bal de l'observatoire*. Yet in a playful act of self-parody, one of the recurrent images from Nothomb's own œuvre is preserved as the abiding symbol of literary perfection—the encounter between a young woman and an older man. In *Le Bal de l'observatoire,* it is the dance between Larissa and her fifty-year-old lover that inspires Marina to dream of better things than the war around them. It is this scene that guarantees the novel its privileged status as the last book to be burned. In paradoxical fashion, therefore, Nothomb, the writer, remains both marginal and central to her own highly satirical vision of canon formation.

Burning Books

Initially in *Les Combustibles,* the Professor and Marina represent two extreme positions with regard to literature and its relevance to the wider culture. On the one hand, reading books is depicted as an elitist activity, the sole preserve of academia with its professional gatekeepers, such as the Professor. On the other, books have no real value beyond their status as material objects, to be discarded as consumable and combustible items. This stance is exemplified by Marina who subverts the expectations and assumptions of her interlocutors by proposing the unthinkable, in this case burning books. Marina raises the uncomfortable question of a book's intellectual and cultural significance when compared with physical needs in times of war. During the siege, she debates whether any book is worth more than raising the room temperature two degrees by its burning. This leads to the following exchange over how to combat the cold:

LE PROFESSEUR: C'est parce que vous êtes trop frileuse. Normal: combien pesez-vous? Quatre-vingt livres?
MARINA: Je pèse deux mille livres: les livres que vous brûlerez pour me réchauffer, Professeur (*LC* 17).

The word play on *livres* as books or pounds of weight goes to the heart of Marina's dilemma as she struggles between feeding the body or the mind. Eventually, the pragmatist and survivor wins out; she who puts the need for warmth first. Yet, Marina's wish to burn the books in the library for self-preservation has disturbing parallels with scenes of book burning in Nazi Germany and elsewhere. For most readers, to destroy books is tantamount to an act of barbarism that threatens not only democratic freedoms but also the cultural heritage of a nation. As snipers pick off city dwellers in the main square, Marina's position would seem to represent the final victory of the enemy over the collective identity of a beleaguered people.

By the time that only ten books are left in the library, the Professor, Daniel and Marina have destroyed some of the great literary works of their culture. Daniel describes this as a sacrilegious act, akin to the fire that destroyed the library at Alexandria (*LC* 87). Yet, in a very real sense, burning the two thousand books in the library has staved off death. This is not only in physical terms. For while the books have indeed kept all three alive with the heat they generate, they have also, in a more fundamental way, given them the will to live. Literature has functioned as an inexhaustible subject of conversation, a means of blocking out the horrors of the war and remembering the past. It has also allowed the individual readers to reflect on their life histories and their values. In the final pages of the text, the choice of the last book to burn brings all three protagonists to argue for literature as the most elemental component of our identity as human beings.

Reading Strategies

In Daniel and Marina, the student lovers, Nothomb sets out contrasting reading strategies and approaches to literature. Daniel's vision of the literary project has much in common with Sartrean notions of *engagement,* while Marina represents the primacy of a purely aesthetic encounter between reader and text. As young readers not yet contaminated by the cynicism and reductive readings of the Professor, they offer alternative visions of literature's value to communities of readers.

The text's setting in an enclosed space, the library, with three warring protagonists brings to mind Sartre's *Huis Clos,* written and performed too at a time of war.[13] As in Sartre's play, *Les Combustibles* explores the *mauvaise foi* of three protagonists. It sets forth an image of human relations based on conflict where each character yearns for self-affirmation but is frustrated by others, unable and unwilling to fulfil their needs. The complex triangle of desire, attraction and rejection between Inès, Estelle and Garcin is reduced to the level of basic bodily needs in *Les Combustibles* as Marina betrays her student lover, Daniel, with their teacher, the Professor, for the extra heat generated by their love-making, otherwise seeing the encounter as 'abominable' (*LC* 82). For, despite its formal similarities with *Huis Clos, Les Combustibles* is more a parodic reworking of Sartre's philosophical paradigms than a homage to it. Here, the characters battle against outside forces as well as amongst themselves and the subjects of discussion are not past lives and the absence of conscience but the pressing need to survive when faced with the dual horrors of war and extreme cold. In a knowing twist of Sartrean prose, Marina asserts, 'l'enfer, c'est le froid' (*LC* 40).

Recasting *Huis Clos* for a different era does not mean, however, that the project of *littérature engagée* is sidelined in debates over fiction and its worth in *Les Combustibles*. In *Qu'est-ce que la littérature?,* Sartre presented the writer as someone embedded in the history of her/his age and the literary text as part of an ongoing struggle for freedom: 'la littérature vous jette dans la bataille; écrire, c'est une certaine façon de vouloir la liberté'.[14] Against a backdrop of war and conflict, *Les Combustibles* rehearses discussions over the role of literature at times of crisis in terms similar to Sartre who was writing over fifty years earlier. The doctoral student, Daniel, certainly celebrates the value of literature in terms of committed writing when he declares: 'on lit pour découvrir une vision du monde' (*LC* 74). Daniel presents writing as a social responsibility, a means by which the writer unveils the world to others in an act that modifies their perceptions. In his appreciation of the literature, Daniel understands that the role of the writer and the literary text is to generate new ideas and to speak to a generation struggling to overcome the vicissitudes of war: 'un livre, c'est un détonateur qui sert à faire réagir les gens'

(*LC* 83). Ultimately, for Daniel, literature has the potential to educate and enlighten readers, working as the 'conscience malheureuse' of a nation as it seeks to shape its future.

However, this vision of literature as a force for social good remains a fragile one in the fictional universe of *Les Combustibles*. In their battle of words, the Professor counters Daniel's views with a disparaging image of the average reader. In contrast to the literary didacticism of commitment writing stand the majority of readers who are 'égoistes, avides de plaisir et inéducables' (*LC* 75). For the Professor, to attempt to change such readers is futile and evidence of an outdated romanticism. As the war rages around him, Daniel's image of the humanizing potential of literature is seriously compromised. The siege of the city would seem to prove how little great minds and their noble creations have changed the world for the better.

Yet if readers are mistrustful of the Professor and his pronouncements, they are more prepared to accept Marina's rejection of committed writing. She too contests Daniel's vision of literature, claiming that the war has put paid to any notion of literature as 'ce langage d'espoir et d'honneur (*LC* 84). For Marina, a writer's role is rather to provide consolation and beauty in the face of horror. With the choice of Blatek's *Le Bal de l'observatoire* as the last book in the library, *Les Combustibles* would seem to endorse Marina's view of literature as a moment of intense and unparalleled pleasure at the imaginative potential of the written word.

In contrast to the sterile discussions of the Professor and Daniel, Marina's description of the seduction scene from Blatek's book conjures up the texture and beauty of fiction: 'ce langage de séduction qu'ils se renvoient l'un à l'autre comme une balle de soie. On croirait Eve parlant au serpent. C'est subtil, c'est à la fois divin et diabolique, c'est beau comme une lutte entre l'ange et la bête' (*LC* 82). This *roman de gare* embodies the contradictory impulses of the human condition—divine and diabolical, a struggle between good and evil, the angel and the beast. The beauty of the text, as Marina interprets it, constitutes her humanity, her feelings, thoughts and hopes, all those things that make her more than the sum total of animal needs for warmth, food and shelter. As this final book is thrown onto the fire amidst her protests, the Professor rightly points out its value as literature to her: 'Vous n'êtes pas encore tout à fait un animal. Il vous reste une seule chose humaine, et c'est ce livre. Et pour vous punir d'avoir menti, voici le sort que je réserve à votre dernière parcelle d'humanité. *(il le jette au feu)*' (*LC* 88).

Les Combustibles ends with the probable death of all three protagonists. Marina flees the library unable to watch *Le Bal de l'observatoire* burn. Daniel pursues her as he learns that she is headed for the main square and a suicidal walk within range of the snipers' guns. As the Professor enjoys the last flames consuming *Le Bal de l'observatoire,* he muses that he too will soon be joining their dead bodies on the main square: 'enfin, quand il n'y aura vraiment plus rien, plus aucun combustible *(il lève les yeux avec un sourire béat),* j'irai retrouver leurs deux cadavres sur la grand-place et je me promènerai, moi aussi, le temps qu'il faudra' (*LC* 89).

This ending is open to multiple interpretations. Readers may see in it a nihilistic image of the futility of all creative endeavour as the books have been burnt and all three protagonists are destined to die. Or they may interpret Marina's despair at the burning of her favourite book as the ultimate proof of literature's capacity to move the human spirit. Yet more than either of these possibilities, *Les Combustibles* ends by disrupting reader expectations of what constitutes literature and whose opinions count. In the place of the literary critic and the great author, Nothomb rehabilitates the primacy of the individual reader and their understanding of literature, whether this is as a means of acting on the world or as a thing of beauty to be savoured and loved. Either way, literature reveals something of the human condition that speaks of our hopes and desires, fears and anxieties.

Conclusion

Les Combustibles enacts less *l'assassinat de l'écriture,* with its scenes of book burning, than it reasserts the writer's role to ignite debate and to fire the imagination at times of crisis. In the play, burning books does not lead to the annihilation of culture but results instead in a renewed appreciation of literature and its transformative potential for the individual reader. By challenging any classical reverence for the written word, Nothomb forces a reassessment of how and why we invest so much of ourselves in these literary encounters. The universal appeal of the play is that it goes to the heart of such encounters encouraging both readers and spectators to muse on their own relationship with the written word and their perception of its value to the wider community.

This capacity to reach out and literally empower readers has also been one of the most unusual outcomes of the play. On its first performance in Quebec in 1996, *Les Combustibles* has had a striking impact on one local community. Since its production of the play, the Espace Go theatre company has operated an annual scheme 'Donne-moi un beau livre!'.[15] Each November, theatre-goers are asked to donate books that are then given to local projects to help children with their reading. Two books are distributed to each child and they keep one and pass the other on. So far, this initiative has led to the exchange of over 17,000 books. From book burning to book redistribution, this is perhaps the richest legacy *Les Combustibles* has bequeathed its readers so far.

Cardiff University

Notes

1. *Hygiène de l'assassin* (Paris: Albin Michel, Points, 1992), p. 127.
2. See Yolande Helm, 'Amélie Nothomb: "l'enfant terrible" des lettres belges de langue

française', *Études Francophones*, 11 (1996), 113–120 (p. 113) for details on the early reception of Nothomb's work.

3. The promotional material for *Stupeur et tremblements* (1999) is a good example with Nothomb depicted in geisha mode, wide eyed with red lipstick redefining her mouth in a sexually suggestive pout.

4. For example, *Cosmétique de l'ennemi* (2001), draws on Robert Louis Stevenson's sinister double personality, Dr Jekyll and Mr Hyde, for the characterization of Jérôme Angust and his alter ego, Textor Texel.

5. *Les Combustibles,* the opera, was adapted by Daniel Donies, with music by Daniel Schell. It was first performed in December 1997 in Paris. Schell clearly has a privileged relationship with Nothomb's work for he also wrote the music for *Hygiène de l'assassin* when it was performed as an opera in 1995.

6. See Helm, op. cit., p. 114.

7. *Les Combustibles* (Paris: Albin Michel, Livre de poche, 1994), p. 28. Subsequent references in the text will appear as *LC* followed by the page number.

8. Younger women challenging male authoritative voices have been a major feature of Nothomb's fictional universe to date. In *Hygiène de l'assassin,* Nina contests the pronouncements of Prétextat Tach, while in *Péplum,* the autobiographical figure of A.N. is transported to 2580 and engages the futuristic historian Celsius in combative dialogue.

9. I am grateful to David Gascoigne for this suggestive perspective on *Les Combustibles*.

10. Helm, op. cit., p. 120.

11. Nothomb makes passing reference to only two French writers, Marivaux (p. 19) and Bernanos (p. 40).

12. For a discussion of the influence of Plato's Socratic dialogues on Nothomb's work, see my 'Speaking Volumes: Amélie Nothomb's *Hygiène de l'assassin*' in *Women's Studies International Forum*, 23/6 (2000), 761–66.

13. *Huis Clos* was first performed in 1944 in occupied Paris.

14. Jean-Paul Sartre, *Qu'est-ce que la littérature?* (Paris: Seuil, 1947), p. 72.

15. For details of this scheme, see www.canoe.qc.ca/TempoLivres/novi_livres.can.html.

Susan Bainbrigge

'MONTER L'ESCALIER ANACHRONIQUE': INTERTEXTUALITY IN *MERCURE*

Published in 1998, *Mercure* is a novel rich in intertextual references.[1] One only has to glance at the back cover of the *Édition de poche* to read extracts from reviews which refer to Amélie Nothomb's 'goût, un peu effrayant, pour un romantisme morbide' (Bernard Le Saux, *Madame Figaro*) and to her 'érudition enlevée et jubilatoire' (Jennifer Kouassi, *Le Magazine littéraire*). The author's impressive erudition spans a variety of languages, genres and periods, and the predominance of intertextual references from 19th century works, mostly but not exclusively from the French canon, is striking. The attractions of the Romantic and the Gothic tale in particular act as a canvas on which the story is depicted. The 'escalier anachronique', the staircase constructed entirely of books which aids Françoise's escape from the Red room, is the pivot around which the story turns: here, books (literally) offer an escape from imprisonment, and the narrative itself becomes a self-reflexive exploration of this thesis, with the characters Françoise and Hazel's discussions about literature in the story foregrounding the theme of intertextuality itself. Is the selection of books in the ladder significant? The question is reminiscent of the ethical dilemma explored by the characters in *Les Combustibles,* and their discussions about what constitutes a great work of art and what, ultimately, is the purpose of literature.[2] In *Mercure,* the reader is confronted by obvious distortions of well-known tales, some the subject of detailed analysis by the central characters whilst in the background more subtle allusions to other writers can also be glimpsed. This article explores how the intertexts engage with a number of the author's key concerns regarding the role of literature and the reading act, and the dynamics of our relationships with others, especially in terms of oppression and freedom, in a text which escapes any neat generic categorization.

Mercure tells the story of the young Hazel Englert, who, since she was orphaned (in 1918), leads a secluded life on an island off the coast of Cherbourg with an old man, Omer Loncours. Led to believe that she has been badly disfigured by the bombardment which killed her parents, she is kept from seeing her reflection: there are no mirrors in the house, nor is there anything that would offer a reflection. Omer decides to employ a nurse to look after Hazel. Françoise Chavaigne arrives and is dumbfounded by the ways in which her employer and her charge lead their lives. She makes it her mission to enlighten Hazel about her situation (the fact that she is not hideously disfigured but of breathtaking beauty), but will find to her horror that when she finally gets the chance to expose the old man's deception, Hazel's response is perhaps not what she had bargained for. Even in the knowledge that the Captain, fifty-four years her elder, has tricked her, Hazel, who had protested to her nurse about her protector's lascivious advances and was dreading his forthcoming birthday 'surprise', clings to the fact that he loves her more than anyone else could, and maintains that he has protected her from a much worse fate in the outside world.

The two endings presented to the reader to conclude the story both culminate in the old man's death.[3] In the first version, Françoise manages to tell Hazel the whole story, and Hazel finally sees herself in the only mirror in the house. Yet Hazel's major objection seems to be that Loncours had loved someone else before her, a young woman called Adèle, and that she is the reincarnation of his first love who committed suicide. She puts a gun to her head and threatens to pull the trigger. Loncours insists that if anyone is to die it must be him. Once Françoise has retrieved the pistol, the discussion turns to the future. The two women will leave the mansion, set sail to New York, and live a peaceful life together, Hazel to be forever enchanted by the face she sees reflected in the mirror. The old man will leave his fortune to her, to be executed by Françoise, who will also be the only one to know about his suicide, since his letter has specified that Hazel must never find out. In the first ending the old man commits suicide and the two women live 'happily ever after'. In the second version, Françoise is caught by the guards on her way to Hazel's room and is escorted back to her room. However, the following day Hazel finally agrees to go for a walk, and thus presents Françoise with the opportunity to tell her the truth about her situation once out of the old man's earshot. When the old man sees them talking he presumes, erroneously, that Hazel knows everything. He rushes to them, asks for Hazel's forgiveness and throws himself into the sea, just as his first love, Adèle, had done. It is now Françoise who takes advantage of the situation by leaving Hazel in ignorance about her beauty, thus recreating the dependent relationship between Hazel and herself. It is only fifty years later that Françoise will tell Hazel the truth. Again, it is not anger but gratitude which Hazel shows her. Françoise's monstrosity in having perpetuated the old man's lies is confounded again by Hazel, who provocatively replies: 'Mais peut-il arriver mieux à une belle jeune fille que de tomber sur un monstre?' (ME 189).[4]

As is evident from this brief plot summary, the story would seem to lend itself to a pastiche of the 18th century Gothic romantic tale of mystery and terror, set, as it is, in a rambling mansion with creaking staircases, large, dark rooms, with few windows, and even clocks striking one at critical moments (ME 13, 15, 137). On this island, a hero-villain, a maiden, and the presence of secrets, criteria noted by Susan

Wolstenholme as prerequisites for the Gothic tale, are spiked by Nothomb's deflating humour.[5] In addition to these Gothic features, the references to 'malaises psychosomatiques', to the enclosed prison of Hazel's sickroom, and to the room in which Françoise will be imprisoned are all suggestive of the 'madwomen in the attics' of 19th century fiction.[6] In Fred Botting's study of the Gothic, he argues that such writing is characterized by excess and transgression, 'involved in constructing and contesting distinctions between civilization and barbarism, reason and desire, self and other'.[7] Particularly pertinent to *Mercure* are his references to stock devices such as 'doubles, alter egos, mirrors and animated representations of the disturbing parts of human identity', since the narrative is literally driven by mirrors, or the absence of them: Françoise makes it her mission to create a reflective surface from the mercury of many thermometers, and Hazel's discovery of her alter ego in Adèle produces the final twist in the tale.[8] Indeed, the author's predilection for mirrors and mirrorings can be found very early on in the old man's description of his first encounter with Hazel. Finding her amongst the carnage of a bombsite, he describes himself in the following terms: 'Je me trouvais dans un tableau de Jérôme Bosch: de toute part la laideur, la monstruosité, la souffrance, la déchéance—et là, soudain, un îlot de pureté intacte. La beauté au cœur de l'immonde' (*ME* 117). By inserting the character Loncours into a different picture, into a different frame of reference, the author offers a dual narrative perspective to the reader and plays with oppositions thematically too, contrasting beauty and ugliness, for example. Stock devices listed by Botting and mentioned above are used to good effect here. Botting also argues that 'signifying the alienation of the human subject from the culture and language in which s/he was located, these devices increasingly destabilized the boundaries between psyche and reality, opening up an indeterminate zone in which the differences between fantasy and actuality were no longer secure'.[9] Throughout *Mercure* the boundaries between art and life are shaken and reconfigured to the extent that life, as presented in the novel, is seen to mimic art, as the author ostentatiously waves canonical texts in front of the reader's eyes.

    Just as the planet Mercury circles within the orbit of Venus, Françoise becomes involved in the relationship between the old man and the young girl, becoming attached to Hazel in the process. She makes it her mission to communicate the truth to Hazel, and Loncours compares Françoise not only to Athena ('vous avez la beauté de l'intelligence' (*ME* 55)) but also to the mercurial messenger, by virtue of her profession, and her behaviour. This is spelt out to the reader in the dialogue between Loncours and Françoise: 'Avec une majuscule, le mercure devient le dieu messager, Mercure. Et quel est le symbole de Mercure? Le caducée!—Symbole de la médecine' (*ME* 132). Thus Françoise is associated with the caduceus, the winged staff of Mercury, and also with the serpent which is wound around it, spoiling the old man's self-professed Eden, since she is 'le serpent qui parle à mon Eve' (*ME* 179), the one responsible for giving knowledge to Hazel. Mercury was not only the Roman god of eloquence and skill, herald and messenger of the Gods and conductor of departed souls to the underworld, he was also God of trading and thieving.

In the second version of the story, Françoise would appear to live up to that name by appropriating Hazel for herself. Françoise is positioned, then, as the messenger but not in fact the principal storyteller, her identity fashioned from the mythological figure of Mercury.[10] 'C'est vous qui me racontez les belles histoires' (*ME* 83), she tells Hazel, providing a foil for her. Hazel, who is most intimately connected with the intertexts, assumes the role of storyteller from the beginning, since *Mercure* opens with her 'Journal de Hazel' before switching to a third-person account. Her main source of entertainment in the house has been reading books from the old man's extensive library. Hazel refers to one of the most famous storytellers, Shéhérazade of *Les Mille et une nuits,* in her conversations with Françoise.[11] As Charles Nunley notes in his study of Leïla Sebbar's use in her work of the narrator of the *Arabian Nights,* identification with Shéhérazade reinforces the female narrator's 'ties to literature as a source of identity and self-fashioning'.[12] Like Shéhérazade, Hazel maintains her privileged position by entertaining with her storytelling, and by playing on her self-avowed role in different ways. She calls herself both a 'sorcière' and a 'sourcière' (*ME* 60) conjuring stories rather than spells, and spins a web around Françoise by creating links with her and urging Françoise to share in the stories which she so admires. Hazel connects them to the same family tree, with her name, 'qui signifie noisetier', linked to Françoise's surname Chavaigne which sounds like 'châtaigne': 'Châtaigne, noisette, nous venons d'une famille identique' (*ME* 60). For Hazel, names are not arbitrary: 'Moi, je crois qu'ils sont l'expression du destin' (*ME* 61). Likewise, the reader senses that name-dropping in *Mercure* is not to be taken as arbitrary either, the image of the old man eavesdropping on conversations between Françoise and Hazel resembling the reader's role in gathering the clues dropped by the author into the narrative.

The intertexts chosen by our storyteller emphasize the liberating power of language and literature, in a narrative whose focus, ironically, is the image of the prison. The dilemma between freedom (into the unknown) and the safety of the familiar (if oppressive) status quo, is played out in the structuring of the story and in the dialogues between the two female protagonists.[13] Gothic and Romantic texts foregrounded by Hazel remind the reader of Nothomb's fascination with monsters and the monstrous, especially the demons lurking within the self.[14] These include *Le Comte de Monte-Cristo* (1844–46) by Alexandre Dumas, Stendhal's *La Chartreuse de Parme* (1839) and Sheridan Le Fanu's *Carmilla* (1874), not forgetting Lewis Carroll's fairytale, *Alice's Adventures in Wonderland* (1865) and its sequel *Through the Looking Glass* (1871).

Le Comte de Monte-Cristo, the famous Romantic work by Dumas, is the first text used to mirror the situation in which the two women find themselves. Hazel, upon meeting Françoise, compares their situation to that of Edmond Dantès and the Abbé Faria who find themselves imprisoned in the Chateau d'If:

Je suis dans la situation d'Edmond Dantès au chateau d'If. Après des années sans apercevoir un visage humain, je creuse une galerie jusqu'au cachot voisin. Vous vous êtes l'abbé Faria. Je pleure du bonheur de ne plus être seule (*ME* 24).

Hazel describes her gratitude towards Françoise in terms of freedom—specifically, the freedom to speak one's mind:

> Quand je suis avec vous, je sens que ma bouche est libérée—c'est le mot. Pour en revenir au *Comte de Monte-Cristo,* quand les deux détenus se rencontrent après des années de solitude, ils se mettent à parler, à parler. Ils sont toujours dans leur cachot, mais c'est comme s'ils étaient déjà à moitié libres, parce qu'ils ont trouvé un ami à qui parler. La parole émancipe (*ME* 40).

It is Françoise who reminds her that words as well as walls can be a means of imprisonment: 'Dans certains cas, c'est le contraire. Il y a des gens qui vous envahissent avec leur logorrhée: on a la pénible impression d'être prisonnière de leurs mots' (*ME* 40). She then remarks on the prophetic qualities of the tale when she finds herself imprisoned (*ME* 86), although at this point she is ignorant of the import of the books Loncours gives her to read. This mirroring can be found in one of the endings: the two female protagonists set sail to New York, where they will live happily ever after, just as the Count, in the final scene of the *Comte de Monte Cristo* had set sail with his mistress.

If the interplay with Dumas triggers the reader's curiosity, the presentation of Stendhal, and in particular, *La Chartreuse de Parme,* 'The Last Romance',[15] offers an even richer intertextual resource. A personal favourite of the author's,[16] his famous dictum, 'Le roman est un miroir que l'on promène le long du chemin' (*ME* 84), is cited in the narrative by Loncours, and reinforces the specular theme. No mirrors exist in Loncours's house except the ones offered by literature, and which are used to reflect the goings-on in the house. Ann Jefferson makes the point in her study of Stendhal that, 'Not only did he see that the mirror was positioned inside the world of which it purported to provide a reflection; but he also pointed out that the mirror is on the move within that world, strapped to the saddle-bag of a moving perspective. So that, on both counts, its objectivity and its impartiality are already under suspicion'.[17] This emphasis on distortion and fictionality is echoed in *Mercure;* the story is no more 'realistic' than the stories the protagonists exchange. At the same time, the fictional world is presented as a valid yard stick within the story for the protagonists to measure their actions. We are presented with layers of narrative which intersect, with mises-en-abyme, and ironic subversions of familiar tales.

What is the appeal of *La Chartreuse de Parme?* Henry James had summarized it as a work in which 'everyone is grossly immoral, and the heroine is a kind of monster'.[18] A text which Hazel professes to have read many, many times (sixty-four, to be exact)—'le même texte ou le même désir peuvent donner lieu à tant de variations' (*ME* 83)—it enables the themes of imprisonment and desire to be brought to the fore. Just as Françoise tells Hazel that she loves 'des histoires de prison' (*ME* 94), Hazel refers to Fabrice del Dongo of the *Chartreuse de Parme,* stating that, 'C'est qu'il y a dans l'incarcération un mystère formidable: quand un être humain ne dispose plus d'autres ressources que sa propre personne, comment va-t-il continuer à vivre?' (*ME* 94). Their discussion of Stendhal's text takes on an ironic significance for the reader only too aware of the mirroring between *La Chartreuse* and the story being recounted with, for example, Hazel's discussion of the paradoxes of freedom and imprisonment anticipating the ending of *Mercure*: 'Il peut arriver aussi que l'on prenne goût à sa geôle' (*ME* 94).

The conclusion of *La Chartreuse de Parme*, Clélia and her child's death, and Fabrice's voluntary imprisonment in the charterhouse reinforces the paradox explored in *Mercure* that happiness may be found ultimately not in freedom but in chains. Victor Brombert has argued that, 'The most important function of the Stendhalian prison is that it restores his heroes to their own selves—or rather, that it allows them to discover the self, and even to create it. The prison thus assumes a protective and dynamic role. It liberates one from the captivity of social existence'.[19] In Françoise's prison, she is liberated to a certain extent by reading, and books, quite literally, also help her to escape. Françoise accuses the old man of imprisoning Hazel 'à l'intérieur d'elle-même' (*ME* 119). The psychological hold he enjoys over her reinforces again the theme of voluntary imprisonment of the self which has recurred in the intertexts, and which the old man justifies as a situation not necessarily worse than the one in which she might find herself in society. Here, echoing Brombert's argument, he comments that she leads 'une vie de princesse romantique' as opposed to a life in society as 'une reproductrice bourgeoise' (*ME* 128). The reader is confronted with a dual narrative in which the books being cited offer an additional commentary on the story being recounted.

In a similar vein, Hazel's next recommendation to Françoise is Sheridan Le Fanu's *Carmilla* (*ME* 106). The entry of the female vampire into the narrative, especially one who preys on a young girl, reinforces the image of the double and provides a humorous metatextual commentary on the story being recounted; the relationship which develops between Laura and Carmilla mirrors their friendship, and serves perhaps as a sly warning shot about Françoise's vampiric behaviour at the end. It anticipates, Loncours hopes, the relationship between Hazel and Françoise, as he excitedly urges them to discuss the book, feeding them literature in the hope that he will then be able to enjoy eavesdropping on their discussions,[20] and complaining when their conversations revolve around less provocative subjects, more akin to a 'salon des précieuses' (*ME* 131).[21]

These stories within stories are numerous, and culminate in the presentation of the 'escalier anachronique' itself. Taking the theme of imprisonment and freedom one step further, Françoise envisages her escape by taking Hazel's pronouncements about the liberating and salvatory aspects of literature literally: 'Nous allons voir à quel point la littérature a un pouvoir subtil, libérateur et salvateur, ricana-t-elle' (*ME* 133). By piling up the books in her room she creates a ladder high enough to reach the window. Books are judged according to different criteria now, those relating to their size and shape, the irreverent narrative reminiscent of the decisions to be made in *Les Combustibles*:

Elle commença par les plus larges et épais pour obtenir une assise stable sur la chaise: les œuvres complètes de Victor Hugo furent un matériau de premier choix. Elle continua par des compilations de poésies baroques, rendant grâce à Agrippa d'Aubigné. Après *Clélie* de la Scudéry vint Maupassant, sans que la maçonne se rendît compte de l'énormité d'un tel rapprochement. L'escalier anachronique comporta ensuite saint François de Sales, Taine, Villon, Madame de Staël et Madame de La Fayette (elle pensait avec plaisir au bonheur de ces deux dames à particule à se voir ainsi réunies, les *Lettres de la religieuse portugaise,* Honoré d'Urfé, Flaubert, Cervantès, le *Genji monogatari,* Nerval, les contes élisabéthains de lady Amelia Northumb, les *Provinciales* de Pascal, Swift et Baudelaire—tout ce qu'une jeune fille du début de ce siècle, cultivée, sensible et impressionable, se devait d'entrouvrir.

Il lui manquait juste un ou deux volumes pour parvenir à la fenêtre. Elle se rappela avoir laissé *La Chartreuse de Parme* et *Carmilla* dans le tiroir de la commode. La tour livresque atteignit alors la hauteur requise.

« Et maintenant, si la pile s'écroule, c'est qu'il n'y a rien à espérer de la littérature » , se dit-elle.

L'escalade fut périlleuse: sans ses longues jambes et sa stabilité naturelle, elle n'aurait eu aucune chance—pour affronter le monde des livres, rien de tel que d'avoir le pied sûr (*ME* 134–35).

Bearing in mind that Françoise is the mercurial messenger, both volatile and unstable, the reference to her 'stabilité naturelle' offers an ironic touch in this passage which juxtaposes literal and metaphorical meanings.[22] Here, fact and fiction combine, in terms of real and invented authors. Amélie Nothomb resituates herself in a fictional English setting, as lady Amelia Northumb, author of 'contes élisabéthains' (*ME* 134), and the texts could be viewed as the possible stepping stones to a cultivated mind, a notion Nothomb gently pokes fun at by inserting fictional references and by framing the passage with deflating humour as Françoise's heroic climb is depicted in terms bordering on the burlesque and the absurd (*ME* 135).

These numerous intertexts are pointed out explicitly to the reader and their significance discussed, prompting us to reflect on the recurring themes which are built upon these 18th and 19th century literary foundations, and to delight in the collisions of genre, style and language which ensue. However, a less obvious intertext offers another lens through which to read the work: Charlotte Brontë's *Jane Eyre*.[23] The room in which Françoise is imprisoned by Loncours is called the 'chambre cramoisie', a scarlet room reminiscent of the infamous red room in which Jane is imprisoned.[24] In *Jane Eyre* it is a symbolic space: in the early part of the novel it is the room where Jane is imprisoned by her aunt and in which she experiences a moment of crisis, the eruption of her emotions signalling her refusal to conform to a certain type of behaviour expected of her. Eventually ill health brought on by this crisis results in her being freed from the room which has become her prison. After Jane refuses to become Rochester's mistress, despite her longing for him, she dreams of the Red Room, and of a voice telling her to flee temptation. Jeannette King has argued that this dream 'is a reminder of the loss of consciousness, of identity, which follows abandonment to intense feelings and visions born of the imagination. [. . .] He [Rochester] is asking her to surrender her view of herself and the world for his'.[25] In *Mercure,* the first mention of the red room is preceded by Loncours's reference to Stendhal's image of the mirror. The 'chambre cramoisie' offers a reflection of the red room in *Jane Eyre:* this is where Françoise is imprisoned and where she undergoes a personal transformation, her idea of the world enlarged by the books which the old man gives her to read. These are books which offer not only an escape through literature into the world of the imagination but literally the means to escape from the room itself, via the 'escalier anachronique'. In *Jane Eyre* and *Mercure* the red rooms imprison their heroines, both physically and emotionally, and coincide with moments of crisis for the protagonists in which they explore the nature of love, and in particular, fulfilment of the self through love, and possibly, subjugation.[26]

Secondly, the references to the character Adèle Langlais, Hazel's alter ego, find another double in *Jane Eyre.* Adèle Langlais is an enigmatic figure whose presence haunts the narrative in a manner befitting a tale of magic and mystery. We learn that Hazel has a precursor, Adèle, another beautiful young girl, who, orphaned, was taken under the wing of Loncours twenty years earlier but who committed suicide. Supporting the Romantic framework of the story, we discover that she throws herself into the sea clad in a long white night gown (*ME* 58–59). Adèle and Hazel's names (Langlais and Englert respectively) and situation are shown to mirror each other and Loncours refers to Hazel as Adèle's reincarnation: 'Adèle est revenue sous les traits de Hazel' (*ME* 126). If the reader's attention is drawn to the similarity between their names (*ME* 68, 127), the English resonance in both Englert and Langlais and the name Adèle itself are not highlighted specifically. In the context of *Jane Eyre,* Adèle Langlais has a counterpart: the young French orphan, Adèle, who is taken under the wing of Rochester, and becomes Jane's pupil at Thornfield Hall.[27] Viewed in this light, our storyteller Hazel, and her double Adèle, offer a further rescussitation of one of Brontë's less memorable characters, Adèle. This time it is the turn of the less than heroic, frivolous but charming young French girl from her novel to be given a voice. Just as Rochester's first wife, Bertha, the madwoman in the attic of Thornfield Hall has her say in Jean Rhys's *Wide Sargasso Sea,* an evocation of the early life of the first Mrs Rochester, here *Mercure* opens up an intertextual space for this lesser-known orphan.[28] Brontë's Adèle has elicited little critical interest to date. Does she get a new lease of life in this melodramatic, gothic tale? Different intertextual configurations are possible: the two orphans called Adèle, and Hazel, all embark on a voyage of discovery, guided by their respective mentors. Françoise, like Jane, experiences a moment of crisis in her red room, but her role is transformed from governess of a young orphan to her life-long companion, thus her positioning mirrors both the Jane/Adèle relationship and the romantic Jane/Rochester one.

What is to be made of the relationship between the characters and the texts with which they interact? Françoise struggles to come to terms with Hazel's apparent mirroring of Fabrice del Dongo in her willing acceptance of imprisonment: 'Les prisonniers ne veulent pas de la liberté. Vous me faites le coup de Fabrice del Dongo: vous aimez votre cachot' (*ME* 142). Hazel, by not resisting her subjugation to another, despite her protestations about her treatment at the hands of the other, seems to be articulating the author's view that all relationships can be viewed in terms of a continual playing out and reconfiguration of the balance of power between two people.[29] This gives rise to the paradoxical situations in which our protagonists find themselves. Even Françoise is not immune, and the reader's possible identification with her is confounded when she changes tack: 'Ce fut un coup d'Etat en gants de velours'; 'Françoise quitta la chambre cramoisie pour celle du Capitaine. Il n'est pas rare que le trajet le plus court pour prendre le pouvoir passe par la prison' (*ME* 185). Books may offer an escape from imprisonment, but nothing can legislate for the unpredictable desires of the self, Nothomb's characters seem to tell us. This fascination with the dynamics of the duo adds weight to Nothomb's self-perception as a 'dialoguiste'. As readers, the far-fetched and often incongruous events described in *Mercure* distance us from the characters and from any attempts to analyse their actions in terms of their psychology. In this respect an exchange between Françoise and Hazel seems to sum up nicely Nothomb's writing practice. 'J'adore votre façon de raconter de jolies histoires pour ensuite en poignarder la poésie', Françoise tells Hazel (*ME* 98).

Nothomb self-consciously combines different forms and genres, including myth, fairytale, legend, the Gothic and the Romantic. Given the attention paid to the mirror and the theme of the double in the text, and the metatextual commentary on the nature of the relationship between life and art, *Mercure* plays out to good effect Nothomb's 'specular' writing practice. Thus the grand mirror in the mansion, the 'psyché', just happens to lie hidden behind Stendhal's *Le Rouge et le noir* in the old man's room. Through Stendhal, the author urges us, we can examine our own situation albeit through a distorted lens. The myriad references created by the textual hall of mirrors present the reader with familiar textual landscapes but playfully subvert and deform them, often using a language of excess. As a result, we are forced to reconsider the ways in which we read, and the extent to which our reactions to texts are governed by prevailing norms and expectations. Jolted out of our complacency, Nothomb takes us on a voyage of rediscovery. She brings old classics into new contexts, her intertextual practices highlighting her desire to share her love of literature with her readers. Is this also her way of playing with themes of freedom and confinement? She weaves associations with other writers and works into her texts, perhaps unable (or unwilling?) to escape the clutches of her literary predecessors. Reworking familiar tales is not stifling to her creativity but unleashes it. In this respect Nothomb makes explicit the intricate relationship between the act of writing and literary influence.

These wide-ranging intertextual encounters would not appear to create any obvious links to the author's Belgian origins.[30] Yet, the combination of real and unreal worlds, of dream and reality, of dark humour spiking serious questions, and of language viewed as a playful medium suggest affinities with surrealism, and open up a space for a final tentative connection which I would like to make. In the

Magritte's *Le Miroir magique*

Dean Gallery of Modern Art in Edinburgh hangs a painting by Magritte entitled *Le Miroir magique* (1929). An outline of a mirror, on which is written in black lettering 'corps humain' is the focus. The flesh colour and shape of the mirror resemble a disembodied head, its face a blank canvas. Yet the stark surround, reminiscent of a bathroom, draws attention to other ways of viewing the mirror; it could be interpreted as an aerial view of a toilet bowl, suggesting perhaps the materiality of existence through a somewhat clinical image. What we might expect to see in a mirror, our own or someone else's features, is replaced by text, which has the effect of depersonalizing the individual. We look in the mirror in search of confirmation of our own self but here this is confounded by the reminder that the individual is just one of many 'corps humains'. In *Mercure,* Hazel is prevented from seeing her face in a mirror; and she only gets a sense of herself through reading and through the insights offered by the other characters. The image seems to offer an additional commentary on Amélie Nothomb's narrative practice and her relationship to the absurd. In *Mercure* and *Le Miroir magique* a depersonalized and deromanticized vision of existence is offered; glimpses of beauty are overridden by attempts to 'poignarder la poésie', to cut through illusions and surfaces to reach a brute, material reality.

Mercure escapes precise generic definition in its reflections and deflections of literary giants. It confirms Nothomb's place as a compelling storyteller, the ultimate mercurial messenger, who makes us reflect upon the role of literature in our lives, upon the ways in which we interact with others, the limits to which we can be driven in our intersubjective experiences, and finally, how we mask and unmask ourselves and the worlds we inhabit. In *Mercure* we are reminded of the ways in which literature can be viewed as recreational and as re-creation, both for the author and for the reader willing to take up the challenge.

University of Edinburgh

Notes

1. *Mercure* (Paris: Albin Michel, 1998, Livre de poche, 2001). Subsequent references in the text will appear as *ME* followed by the page number.
2. The article on *Les Combustibles* by Claire Gorrara in this volume explores such questions in detail.
3. Ruggero Campagnoli analyses the escape scene and the two endings in terms of their relationship to literary norms and genres such as modernism and postmodernism, and the function of melodrama, in '«Mercure» d'Amélie Nothomb au sommet de la tour livresque', *Les Lettres belges au présent,* Actes du Congrès des Romanistes allemands (Université d'Osnabrück, du 27 au 30 septembre, 1999) (Frankfurt: Peter Lang, 2001), pp. 309–18.
4. Françoise's incredulity is revealed in her ironic recapitulation of events: 'J'arrive dans une maison inconnue, je rencontre une jeune fille séquestrée, elle se plaint à moi des sévices que lui inflige son vieillard de geôlier, elle est sans défense, elle me regarde avec de

grands yeux suppliants en me disant que je suis sa seule amie, et moi, naïve provinciale, je suis bouleversée, je mets mon existence en jeu pour venir en aide à cette pauvre victime, j'achète tant de thermomètres que je passe pour une empoisonneuse, je suis emprisonnée à mon tour, je m'évade au péril de ma vie, au lieu de m'enfuir à la nage je viens me remettre dans la gueule du loup pour la sauver, je lui dévoile enfin l'odieux mensonge dans lequel son tuteur la fait vivre—et le résultat de mes efforts, c'est que la jeune dinde dit au vieux salaud, de sa voix la plus douce : « J'éprouve plus que de la tendresse pour vous! » Vous vous fichez de moi?' (*ME* 155).

5. Susan Wolstenholme, 'Charlotte Brontë's Post-Gothic Gothic', in *Gothic (Re)Visions* (New York: SUNY, 1993), p. 57. In the opening lines Hazel announces: 'Pour habiter cette île, il faut avoir quelque chose à cacher. Je suis sûre que le vieux a un secret' (*ME* 7). Later she mentions to Françoise that she is convinced that Loncours is hiding something from her (*ME* 93).

6. This is the title of Sandra M. Gilbert and Susan Gubar's groundbreaking work, *The Madwoman in the Attic: The Woman Writer and the Nineteenth-century Literary Imagination* (New Haven: Yale University Press, 1979).

7. Fred Botting, *Gothic* (London: Routledge, 1996), p. 19.

8. Ibid., p. 11.

9. Ibid., pp. 11–12.

10. Terry Castle points out in her book *The Female Thermometer: Eighteenth-Century Culture and the Invention of the Uncanny* (Oxford: Oxford University Press, 1995), that a 'mercurial personality' was one characterized by fickleness, emotional variability and a susceptibility to hysteria, often attached to women (p. 25). In this respect Françoise's actions at the end of *Mercure* would appear to corroborate those characteristics.

11. This is a work that, according to Charles Nunley, originally shaped France's romanesque view of the Orient. See 'From Schéhérazade to Shérazade: Self-fashioning in the Works of Leïla Sebbar', *Thirty Voices in the Feminine,* ed. by Michael Bishop (Amsterdam: Rodopi, 1996), p. 239. Lucie Armitt, in *Contemporary Women's Fiction and the Fantastic* (New York: Palgrave, 2000), defines her as follows: 'Scheherazade is *the* archetypal female storyteller, the frame narrator of *The Thousand and One Nights* [. . .]. King Shariyar, disenchanted with all women since the proven infidelity of his own wife, selects a new virgin with whom to sleep every night, only to command her execution in the morning. Soon Scheherazade is the only virgin left in the land, but [. . .] she determines to outwit him by ravelling him up in the spell of her tale, spinning an elaborate tapestry of interconnecting narratives, each one embedding itself in the next as the last is closed off so that at least some of the threads of the tapestry always remain hanging and the Sultan remains gripped by the (narrative) possibilities of the next night' (p. 9).

12. Nunley, op. cit., p. 246.

13. The paradox to be teased out from them is encapsulated in a short exchange between the old man and Françoise, on the relationship between love and freedom: 'Vous ne savez pas ce que c'est, vous, le bonheur d'être aimée', to which Françoise replies, 'Je connais, moi, le bonheur d'être libre' (*ME* 78).

14. Nothomb's most recent publication, *Cosmétique de l'ennemi* (Paris: Albin Michel, 2001), is a detailed exploration of the enemy within.

15. This is the term used by Michael Wood in his study entitled *Stendhal* (London: Elek, 1971). Roger Pearson notes the novel's 'affiliation to ancient traditions of epic and romance, of fairy tale and oral narrative', in *Stendhal: The Red and the Black and The Charterhouse of Parma* (London: Longmann, 1994), p. 17.

16. The author comments in the interview in this volume that Stendhal played an important role in her adolescence, and that her first trip to Europe as a teenager had been a huge disappointment because of the extent to which she had idealized it from her readings of *La Chartreuse de Parme* (See also *Le Logographe,* 3 avril 1998).
17. *Reading Realism in Stendhal* (Cambridge: Cambridge University Press, 1988), p. 231.
18. In 'Henri Beyle', *The Nation* (17 Sept. 1874), cited by Pearson, op. cit., p. 13.
19. In Pearson, op. cit., p. 109.
20. Michael H. Begnal's study, *Joseph Sheridan LeFanu* (Lewisburg: Bucknell University Press, 1971), highlights LeFanu's purpose in creating Carmilla to 'comment on the self-destruction of a total submission to sexuality' (p. 44).
21. He objects to their discussions of Honoré d'Urfé, Madame de Staël, and Saint François de Salès, for example (*ME* 131–32).
22. When asked about her upbringing in Japan, the author replied that literature offered a certain stability in her life: 'La seule stabilité [. . .] était la langue que je parlais, le français, et la bibliothèque parentale qui suivait', in Stéphane Lambert's *Les Rencontres du mercredi* (Paris: Ancre rouge, 1999), p. 31.
23. First published in 1847.
24. I am grateful to Dr France Sharratt for first drawing my attention to the link between 'la chambre cramoisie' and the Red room in *Jane Eyre.*
25. In *Jane Eyre* (Milton Keynes: Open University Press, 1986), p. 48.
26. Red rooms have appeared in numerous works of fiction, often depicted as spaces of claustration, suffocation, death or intimacy. See, for example, H. G. Wells (*The Red Room and Other Stories,* 1997), Françoise Mallet-Joris (*La Chambre rouge,* 1955), Cocteau (*La Machine infernale,* 1934), Angela Carter (*The Bloody Chamber,* 1979).
27. *Jane Eyre* (Hertfordshire: Wordsworth Classics, 1999), p. 94.
28. Critics have explored the extent to which Bertha is Jane's alter ego or repressed self. See for example, *The Madwoman in the Attic: the Woman Writer and the Nineteenth-century Literary Imagination,* op. cit. Other incidental connections include references to Guadeloupe as the birthplace of Brontë's Bertha and Nothomb's Adèle; the fires which kill the parents of the two Adèles; and the brief entry of a character named Bertha in *Mercure.*
29. In Paul Ames's review 'Diplomat's daughter rocks French literary scene with dark novels', 16 August 1996, Nothomb mentions that in her view all relationships are driven by sado-masochism, available online at *http://www.canoe.ca/JamBooksFeatures/ nothomb_amelie.html.* Margaret-Anne Hutton explores in detail the sadomasochistic relationship as it is played out in Nothomb's texts in ' "Personne n'est indispensable, sauf l'ennemi": l'œuvre conflictuelle d'Amélie Nothomb', in *Nouvelles Écrivaines: nouvelles voix?,* ed. by Nathalie Morello and Catherine Rodgers (Amsterdam: Rodopi, 2002), pp. 111–27.
30. Nothomb distances herself from the term 'belgitude' but does recognize affinities with surrealism in the interview in this volume.

David Gascoigne

AMÉLIE NOTHOMB AND THE POETICS
OF EXCESS

In the fire-and-ice universe of Amélie Nothomb, the fissile nuclear material is, first and foremost, language. Nowhere in her writings are we left in
any doubt of its elemental power. In her quasi-autobiographical texts, she
highlights the Pandora-like discovery of this power by her child-persona. In *Métaphysique des tubes,* out of the impassive, god-like, self-sufficient, speechless *infans*[1]
of the opening, there emerges, belatedly, a screaming and furious two-year-old. In
this preternaturally docile child, vocal self-expression has at last been generated by
anger, occasioned apparently, we are told, by some intrusive and disruptive mental
image or perception: 'Quelque chose était apparu dans son cerveau qui lui avait
semblé insoutenable' (*MT* 28). This idea of the origins of voice already casts a rich
reflection on Nothomb's other works—how often the lava-flow of rhetoric has at
its source an irritant, an intruder, an unwelcome arrival in an ordered world: Bernardin, the tiresome neighbour, for Émile in *Les Catilinaires;* A.N., the uncoopera-
tive hostage for Celsius in *Péplum;* Nina, the irrepressible interviewer for Prétextat
Tach in *Hygiène de l'assassin;* the narrator in *Stupeur et tremblements,* with her im-
portunate aspirations; Xavier, the unwelcome rival for Epiphane Otos in *Attentat;*
the garrulous Textor Textel, for Jérôme Angust in *Cosmétique de l'ennemi.* Each of
these irritant presences generates first discomfort, then fully voiced outrage in their
interlocutor, the developed equivalent of the child's screaming. The scream is an
expression of excess, of an extreme emotion which cannot be contained, and
which overflows into utterance pushed to the limits of its intensity. When, a little
later in *Métaphysique des tubes,* the child first shows the capacity for speech, the trigger this time is intense pleasure—the first taste of white chocolate, Belgian chocolate of course, and the explosion of euphoria it unleashes (*MT* 36). Thus, in this
mock-Genesis of a text, Nothomb places the voice, and language, firmly under
the aegis of passion, be it pleasure or anger, viewing language as the channelled
response to an overflow of feeling.[2] The recognition of such excessive feeling is,

Nothomb avers, the very source of the sense of self, and of the self's linguistic sign: 'Le plaisir profita de l'occasion pour nommer son instrument: il l'appela moi—et c'est un nom que j'ai conservé' (*MT* 39).

'Nommer son instrument' brings us to the process of naming. The primal linguistic act is arguably that of naming. Naming objects is a way of controlling a dangerous world: as the narrator A.N. says in *Péplum*, 'nommer les choses, c'est leur enlever leur danger'.[3] The two-year-old of *Métaphysique des tubes* 'avait observé que les parents et leurs satellites produisaient avec leur bouche des sons articulés bien précis: ce procédé semblait leur permettre de contrôler les choses, de se les annexer' (*MT* 29). Naming people is even more an act of power, a way of controlling and annexing people, as the same child comes to realize. When she first names her sister, Juliette, the act unleashes an ecstatic and definitive reaction:

> Le langage a des pouvoirs immenses: à peine avais-je prononcé à haute voix ce nom que nous nous prîmes l'une pour l'autre d'une folle passion. [. . .] Tel le philtre d'amour de Tristan et Iseut, le mot nous avait unies pour toujours (*MT* 49).

By a logical corollary, her odious brother is denied the privilege of being named: 'je décidai de ne pas nommer Hugo, pour le châtier' (*MT* 76). In a similar fit of pique, the seven-year-old of *Le Sabotage amoureux* tries to rename Trê, the Chinese woman who cares for her, by foisting on her the name of an earlier, more gratifyingly obsequious Japanese nanny[4]—names are here seen as a magic spell to exert power and to reconfigure the world. Some names carry what Nothomb calls 'le privilège onomastique d'un [. . .] mythe',[5] an associative electric charge which captivates its hearers—names like China (*LS* 8),[6] or Quasimodo (*A* 57). When our Quasimodo, Epiphane Otos in real life, is turned down for a job on tacitly discriminatory grounds of ugliness, he has no resource for revenge save a veiled threat based on the coincidence of his name, Otos, with that of a lift manufacturing company—a feeble weapon, but the only one he has (*A* 46).

In the dialogues, naming one's interlocutor is a powerful weapon. In *Hygiène de l'assassin* Nina is discomfited when Tach calls her by name, and with reason—it is the start of a declaration of love:

> — [. . .] Ignorez-vous ce que signifie le besoin de nommer certaines personnes? [. . .] Si on éprouve au fond de soi le besoin d'invoquer le nom d'un individu, c'est qu'on l'aime.
> — . . .?
> — Oui, Nina. Je vous aime, Nina.[7]

The impact of the spoken name is likewise seen in *Le Sabotage amoureux,* at a moment when the narrator is trying to maintain a façade of indifference to the object of her infatuation, the beautiful Elena.[8] With the deadly instinct of the *femme fatale,* however, the precocious Elena knows and uses the power of naming:

J'essayais de réfléchir quand Elena prononça mon nom.
C'était la première fois.
Je ressentis un malaise extraordinaire. Je ne savais même pas si c'était agréable ou
non. Mon corps se figea des pieds à la tête, statue sur un socle de boue (*LS* 116–17).

Naming is a key part of Elena's strategy to reassert her dominance, and through
the utterance of a name Iseut's potion works its irresistible magic again. Thus, in
Amélie Nothomb's world, words make love and war, and sometimes both at
once—'Gloire aux mots', exclaims Epiphane Otos exultantly, 'gloire à mes mots
qui baisaient mieux que le sexe de mon rival!' (*A* 97). As Epiphane's idol Ethel
comes to understand, just before her death at his hands, 'rien n'est plus physique
que les mots' (*A* 151).

More generally, a ritual or incantatory use of language is part of the armoury of
Nothomb's characters. This is most obvious in the epic formal tirades which characterize the pecking-order in *Stupeur et tremblements*. Omochi's devastating public
castigation of Fubuki transcends the verbal to resemble physical assault, or rape,[9]
demonstrating that indeed 'rien n'est plus physique que les mots'. This ritualistic
deployment of language is also apparent in *Le Sabotage amoureux*, when the gang
of children gleefully rehearse suggestions for possible tortures for their hapless
prisoner-of-war (*LS* 26–29), or in *Hygiène de l'assassin*, when Nina repeatedly lists
the titles of Tach's books, a tactic which serves effectively to breach his defences
(*HA* 96–102). A virtuoso of linguistic warfare like Tach can make an interviewer
physically ill simply by reciting the details of his own daily diet (*HA* 37–38). Thus
excess in language generates physical excess. Indeed, the two are frequently associated: it is striking how often the metaphor of vomiting is used by Nothomb as a
linguistic marker of disgust and rejection.[10] In *Les Catilinaires*, Bernardin's provocation is the opposite, and yet to similar effect: in a society where small talk is
viewed as the indispensable lubricant of social relationships, his persistent silence
appears as aggressive as polemic—what Nothomb calls elsewhere the implacable
power of the force of inertia, 'l'effroyable emprise de l'immobile' (*MT* 15). The re-
sentment which Émile feels in the face of this implacable inertia finds expression in
an ironically erudite logorrhea, a kind of verbal vomiting, the excess of exasperation and rage finding temporary satisfaction in baroque excesses of rhetoric. The
sought-after prize in such dialogic encounters is itself often linguistic. The loqua-
cious Émile struggles throughout to make Bernardin speak, to say anything which
can offer him some kind of bridgehead in this man's being. He seeks a modus vivendi, or more precisely a *modus dicendi,* some way of generating a discourse capable of encapsulating and thus disarming the disturbingly enigmatic phenomenon of the neighbouring couple. In other confrontations, the aim may be to make
the adversary utter particular words, such as, in *Hygiène de l'assassin*, the dictated
apology which Nina extracts from Tach (*HA* 86), or, in *Cosmétique de l'ennemi,*
Texel's struggle to get his victim Isabelle to pronounce her own name (*CE* 74, 80).[11]

Such evidence thus reveals how, throughout Nothomb's writings, the origins
and ongoing generative well-springs of language are the most basic and intense

human emotions: euphoric pleasure, anger, repulsion, cruelty, love, jealousy, the delectation of power—all that is emotive and instinctual, one might say, rather than rational or intellectual. Yet, of course, it is also only language which makes possible rational thought, and Nothomb's 'monstres sacrés'—Tach, Celsius, Omer Loncours—seek to crush their opponents by the apparent inner logic and consistency of their position and to justify their project, however bizarre it may be. Characteristically, they are masters of a closed system. Celsius is a lynchpin in a society of rigidly defined castes, and boasts of how he managed to obtain the consent of his co-equals for his pet project of the destruction-preservation of Pompeii by his skilful use of rhetoric and tendentious argument: 'Je dus déployer des trésors de sophistique et de diplomatie pour que le dossier soit recevable' (*PE* 121).

The similarly rigid hierarchy of the Yumimoto company in *Stupeur et tremblements* is likewise maintained by a constant conventional rhetoric of superiority and inferiority, of flattery and humiliation, where any individual initiative, to be accepted, requires astute presentation within the norms of the prevailing company discourse. These are examples of collective, totalitarian orders. Omer Loncours and Prétextat Tach maintain their domination in smaller, individualistic empires, but once again linguistic mastery is essential to their hegemony—Tach in his ability to crush others with his verbal charisma, Loncours in his capacity to use language (among other means) to conceal the truth from Hazel and to keep control of the inquisitive Françoise. The systems which these authoritarian language strategies are thus used to maintain and defend are however fraudulent, in this sense: while they lay claim to a logic and an order which is so important that all else must be subordinated to it, they finally manifest at their roots the very forces of unreason which their logic implicitly claims to exclude.

The apparent logic of Tach, of Loncours, of Émile and of Celsius implodes into a kind of Dionysian madness; it is used to justify acts of deception, imprisonment, murder and mass devastation, while the narrative, as it lays bare the roots of these manifestations of excess, invariably reveals that the common factor in each case is an irrational passion. As Jérôme, in *Cosmétique de l'ennemi,* puts it: 'Le pire, avec vous, c'est que vous trouvez des prétextes intellectuels à vos actions lamentables et sadiques' (*CE* 92). It is Tach's desire, against all reason, to halt the ageing process and to continue a timeless idyllic relationship with his cousin which leads him to murder, and it is Celsius's desire to turn back time and to rescue his loved one (in this case a city) from oblivion which leads him likewise to the paradoxical decision to lay waste the object of his infatuation, to preserve it through death. Émile's murder of Bernardin, so eloquently rationalized, can be seen as designed to protect the moral innocence of the love he shares with Juliette, even as it destroys his own integrity. Texel's discourse presents rape and murder as spontaneously generated by all-consuming love and beauty. In all of these cases, love and violence, even love and murder, are inextricably mingled, and prevail both over rationality and over conventional humanist ethics.

'Je n'avais d'ambitions que guerrières et amoureuses', we are told of the seven-year-old of *Le Sabotage amoureux* (*LS* 77). It is the figuration of such 'ambitions guerrières et amoureuses' which underlies the would-be logic of the worlds, childish and adult, individual and collective, present and future, which we find in Nothomb represented and constructed by language. How that reflects back on language, how that in fact works itself out through language, can be seen for instance in the implicit debate about metaphor in *Hygiène de l'assassin*. When his first interviewer uses the word 'metaphor', Tach seizes on it to deconstruct it and denounces metaphor as a figure of 'mauvaise foi' (*HA* 21), a mind-set which enables readers to avoid facing up directly to the salutary horrors and brutalities which he offers in his writings. 'Je peux me permettre d'écrire les vérités les plus risquées, on n'y verra jamais que des métaphores' (*HA* 126). This does not prevent him, of course, from indulging in an outrageous extended metaphor, worthy of Jean Genet, to characterize the attributes he admires in a writer—'des couilles' represent a writer's capacity to resist the prevailing bad faith, 'la bitte' a capacity for literary creation, and so forth (*HA* 65ff). However, when his interviewer tries to add 'le cœur' to the list, Tach wrongfoots him by insisting on a referential understanding of the word, 'un bête cœur plein de cholestérol' (*HA* 73). This contradiction, between Tach's luxuriant deployment of metaphor and his diatribe against it, is not resolved until the moment, late in the book, when, on reaching the climax of his narrative of Léopoldine's death, he speaks of his fingers gripping her neck, 'ce tissu spongieux qui deviendra le texte' (*HA* 154). Here we have, in Nothomb's first published fiction, a master-metaphor, a metaphor of language-as-figuration, text figured as flesh ('rien n'est plus physique que les mots', we recall), and the birth of literary creativity figured as self-realization through ecstatic love and murder. Challenged by Nina as being 'en flagrant délit de métaphore' (*HA* 154), Tach claims, against all appearances, that his words are beyond metaphor, and that metaphor, the glue by which we piece together mere fragments of meaning, is transcended by his privileged vision of the totality of things. Earlier, in his no-holds-barred demolition of a journalist, Tach had perversely collapsed the metaphor of 'heart' in the direction of referentiality, denying it any possible figurative value. Here, by contrast, speaking of the defining experience of his life, the murder of Léopoldine, he this time pushes metaphor in the direction of the wholly figurative. His life-project is not, he claims, subject to normal morality or judicial logic: it can only be understood and validated by a *poetic* reading of the facts, an acceptance of a private, figurative truth which outweighs and transcends outward appearances.[12]

A similar battle over metaphor takes place in *Stupeur et tremblements*. There the narrator Amélie finds an analogy for her confrontation with her immediate superior Fubuki in the relationship between the two protagonists (likewise European and Japanese respectively) in the film *Merry Christmas, Mister Lawrence*.[13] In that story about a Japanese PoW camp, she finds a multiple reflection—of her own sense of imprisonment and victimization, of the physical beauty of her authoritarian opposite number and of the ambiguous relationship between the two of them. When she attempts to explain this similarity to her superior, however, Fubuki simply collapses the metaphor in the direction of literal referentiality: 'Je trouve que vous ne ressemblez pas à David Bowie' (*ST* 143). By contrast, in their final meeting, when Amélie provides Fubuki with an almost orgasmic thrill by her ritual self-abasement, the narrator secretly marks up a victory in metaphor by an extraordinary inner monologue of masochistic passion which plays on the poetics of Fubuki's name, which signifies 'snow storm' in Japanese:

> Chère tempête de neige, si je peux, à si peu de frais, être l'instrument de ta jouissance, ne te gêne surtout pas, assaille-moi de tes flocons âpres et durs, de tes grêlons taillés comme des silex, [. . .] (*ST* 158).

It is a triumph of poetic excess, inspired by violent love, over the constraints of convention and the rituals of hierarchy.

The most compelling metaphors in Nothomb's writing have this quality of being grounded in a private, figurative truth which defies referentiality. When the narrator of *Le Sabotage amoureux* writes enthusiastically of her horse, it is some while before the figurative horse is resolved into a real bicycle, and by that time the figurative transformation has infiltrated the reader's imagination and thus retains much of its power. When, later, she lies in bed, the love the narrator feels for her idol Elena summons up fantasies in her mind, 'des histoires, que d'aucuns qualifie-raient de métaphores' (*LS* 59). These 'récits expérimentaux' have no referentiality beyond the well-springs of desire which sustain them, just as the 'horse' metaphor is the sign connoting that overflow of euphoria which she feels as she rides off on her bicycle. At the heart of these fictions of pure figuration is a state of Dionysian intoxication, whether through love or pleasure.[14] Moreover, as the same narrator suggests later, extraordinary works of literature—the *Divine Comedy, Alice in Won-derland, Lolita*—have been born of a man's all-consuming passion for a very young girl (*LS* 71). Love as an absolute imperative, creating its own transcendent order of beauty and faith as in the myth of Tristan and Iseut, is constantly proclaimed in Nothomb's writing. 'Ne comprenez-vous pas que l'on peut aimer un être en de-hors de toute référence connue?' exclaims Prétextat Tach, adding: 'L'amour ne sert à rien d'autre qu'à aimer' (*HA* 172–73). '[. . .] En dehors de l'amour, rien n'est inté-ressant', echoes Nina (*HA* 118). In *Attentat,* Epiphane Otos writes to his adored Ethel that others, such as Xavier, 'ne croient pas en toi, ô unique religion révélée. Moi, j'ai foi en toi et je puise en ton culte une force inconnue des mortels' (*A* 140). Epiphane's response to the epiphany of beauty he has been vouchsafed is an ex-tended ecstatic hymn of devotion in which the personal beauty of Ethel tends to disappear behind the mystical intoxication of the emotion she inspires. It is for this reason, perhaps, that she, like Léopoldine in *Hygiène de l'assassin,* Isabelle in *Cosmétique de l'ennemi* and the city of Pompeii in *Péplum,* can be sacrificed, because their 'culte', and the 'force inconnue' it bestows on the male worshipper, has out-grown its object. Love has its own autonomous rights, and ordinary notions of justice, truth and morality must cede before the commanding presence of love and beauty. 'Est vrai ce qui est beau', proclaims Celsius in *Péplum* (*PE* 130). He quotes the case of the courtesan Phryne, on trial for profaning the Eleusinian mysteries, whose testimony had to be believed simply because she was so beautiful.[15] Beauty trumps reason and judgement. Marina, the most enthusiastic book-burner in *Les Combustibles,* discovers in the end that saving a book that one loves for its beauty is of the utmost importance in an ugly, intolerable world.[16]

Nothomb never conceals the destructive face of Dionysos: her *Liebestode* are love-murders rather than ethereal love-deaths. Nevertheless, it is those who found their lives on passion who, in the end, emerge as justified, not through morality or reason, but through the self-justifying poetic vision which inspires them and gives meaning to their life. The lives of Nothomb's characters, whether fictional or quasi-autobiographical, bear witness to this poetics of excess, this need in a life truly lived for the passion which overflows reasonable and decent limits. More particularly, this poetics is also central to Nothomb's theory and practice of language. Language for Nothomb is born of pleasure and anger, and it is first of all a gratuitous poetry of excess before it ever becomes the servant of reason and morality. It is in constructing the lives and charting the obsessions of characters who invest their passions in the most extreme situations, combining beauty and violence, nobility and degradation, that she puts her own writing practice in touch with its roots, and with that primal well-spring of raw emotions on which, as her fictions insistently suggest, our very being is founded.

University of St Andrews

Notes

1. Nothomb refers to the etymological root of 'enfant', deriving from *infans,* 'unable to speak'. See *Métaphysique des tubes* (Paris: Albin Michel, 2000), p. 77. Subsequent references to the text will appear as *MT* followed by the page number.
2. Otto Jespersen refers, somewhat dismissively, to a speculative theory of the origins of speech known as the interjectional theory (or, by nickname, the *pooh-pooh* theory), whereby 'language is derived from instinctive ejaculations called forth by pain or other intense sensations or feelings'. See O. Jespersen, *Language: its nature, development and origin* (London: Allen & Unwin, 1922), p. 414. Nothomb's narrative can in this respect be read as a hyperbolic development of that notion.
3. *Péplum* (1996) (Paris: Albin Michel, Livre de poche, 2000), p. 109.
4. See *Le Sabotage amoureux* (1993) (Paris: Albin Michel, Livre de poche, 2000), p. 7. Subsequent references to the text will appear as *LS* followed by the page number.
5. See *Attentat* (1997) (Paris: Albin Michel, Livre de poche, 2000), p. 57. Subsequent references to the text will appear as *A* followed by the page number.
6. The narrator admits that she deliberately makes reference to her life in China 'quand je trouve que quelqu'un ne m'admire pas assez' (*LS* 8).
7. See *Hygiène de l'assassin* (1992) (Paris: Albin Michel, Points, 1995), p. 171–72. Subsequent references to the text will appear as *HA* followed by the page number.
8. This passage recalls Julien Sorel's similar efforts to act coldly towards Mathilde de la

Mole, with whom he is infatuated. See Stendhal's *Le Rouge et le noir,* Livre II, ch. 25 ff. . Nothomb refers quite frequently to Stendhal in her work: in *Mercure, Le Rouge et le noir* is the volume which reveals the mirror that launches the dénouement of the story. See *Mercure* (1998) (Paris: Albin Michel, Livre de poche, 2000), p. 145.

9. *Stupeur et tremblements* (1999) (Paris: Albin Michel, Livre de poche, 2001), p. 117–24.

10. See, for example, *HA* 174, *PE* 114 and also *Cosmétique de l'ennemi* (Paris: Albin Michel, 2001), p. 63.

11. A conjectured, but crucial, episode of the same kind turns on the vow which the adolescent Tach allegedly extracted from his cousin Léopoldine, sealing the pact which underpins his perverse project (*HA* 109).

12. In his cynical inconsistency, Tach is exploiting the ambivalence which Ricœur analyses in his theory of *tension* (or *controversion*) in the referential relationship of the metaphorical statement to reality, and in particular in 'the tension between two interpretations: between a literal interpretation that perishes at the hands of semantic impertinence and a metaphorical interpretation whose sense emerges through non-sense'. See Paul Ricœur, *The Rule of Metaphor* (Toronto: University of Toronto Press, 1977), p. 247.

13. See *ST* 155–6. *Senjo no Merii Kurisumasu (Merry Christmas, Mr Lawrence)* (dir. Nagisa Oshima, 1983) deals both in extreme passion and violence and in repressed homosexual desire. Oshima's earlier controversial film *Ai No Korrida (In the Realm of the Senses)*(1976), dealing with sexual obsession, murder and mutilation, is referred to by Prétextat Tach when he describes how he strangled Léopoldine (*HA* 149).

14. On this Dionysian aspect, see the following article in this volume by Laureline Amanieux.

15. At the climax of his speech her advocate, Hypereides, had her uncover her breasts, and the jury was so moved by her beauty that she was acquitted. See for example the article 'Hypereides' in *The Oxford Companion to Classical Literature,* ed. by M.C. Howatson, 2nd edn. (Oxford: Oxford UP, 1989), p. 291–92.

16. See *Les Combustibles* (1994) (Paris: Albin Michel, Livre de poche, 2000), p. 86.

Laureline Amanieux

THE MYTH OF DIONYSUS IN AMÉLIE NOTHOMB'S WORK

Everything in Amélie Nothomb's work reveals the mark of Dionysus, not only because her heroes experience absolute desires, but also because the author herself feels invested during the creative process by an overwhelming force.[1] As God of duality, Dionysus embodies a tragic and fascinating power. This essay explores the inscription of Dionysus's presence within Amélie Nothomb's work, and considers the importance of a 'Dionysian' force in the author's writing process. I shall present and compare several examples of Dionysian characters in Nothomb's works in order to demonstrate the ambivalence and necessity of their sublime feelings and their monstrosity. I shall further argue that the author combines these dual feelings in the creative momentum of writing.

The Legend of Dionysus

The first duality of Dionysus can be traced from his peculiar birth: he is the son of Zeus and of a mortal, Semele, who was struck when she asked her lover to appear in all his glory.[2] Zeus took the baby from his mother's womb and hid it in his thigh until the expected date of his birth. This explains why Dionysus is called the 'twice born God' (this theme of the double birth is central in Nothomb's writing, for example in the novel *Métaphysique des tubes*).[3] According to the legend, he was born horned with his head crowned with snakes. This repugnant image of the god is counterbalanced when he reaches adulthood. He then appears in Greece at the court of King Icarios, disguised as a handsome adolescent. Thus Dionysus embodies the duality beauty/ugliness, a binary opposition characteristic of Nothombian novels.

To return to the legend itself, hunted down by Hera's jealousy, he was torn into pieces by the Titans and thrown into a cauldron. His grandmother Rhea put the pieces back together again and re-animated him: thus, life and death intermingle within him. In order to flee the goddess's anger, Dionysus had to use strategies to conceal his identity: these blurred the oppositions between the masculine and the feminine sex, or between human beings and animals; thus he disguised himself as a young girl or a lamb. As an adult, he travelled around the world followed by Selene, by satires and the Maenads, who taught him the art of growing grapes and making wine. As God of wine, his excesses essentially involve women, who, in a state of drunkenness and religious trance, experience climax but also abandon themselves to violent crimes, and go mad. However, Dionysus is also the king of absolute love, the love he bears to Ariadne, abandoned by Theseus and whom he will marry. Eventually, he finds himself in Mount Olympus, at Zeus's right-hand side, along with his mother who also becomes immortal. Inspired by this God's dual characteristics, Amélie Nothomb's protagonists, men as well as women, are always both monstrous and sublime, and driven in pursuit of purity and absolute love.

Dionysian Characters in Nothomb's Works

Among these characters, Prétextat, in *Hygiène de l'assassin,* is the perfect embodiment of Dionysus as he is possessed by destructive love and an appetite for monstrous purity.[4] Omer, in *Mercure,* as well as Epiphane in *Attentat,* by their profound yet perverse love, are progressively invaded by the God's madness which transforms feelings into incandescent love.[5] Love is not the only means of possession: the Professor in *Les Combustibles* turns out to be Dionysian in his relationships by wielding unhealthy authority over two of his former students, which ends when they commit suicide.[6] Omer, Epiphane and the Professor distinguish themselves by their witty eloquence, by their desire to justify themselves, and by their tendency to succumb to sudden fits of anger, provoking a deafening hullabaloo characteristic of Dionysus's mad outbursts. Yet, the characters invaded by Dionysus remain sometimes fixed in a gloomy and paralyzing silence. Palamède, in *Les Catilinaires,*[7] embodies a terrifying yet silent Dionysus: this Dionysus is no longer delirious and thus emptied of his substance. The human being is invaded by nothingness. By essence, Dionysus is double: presence and absence, boisterous delirium and deathly silence.[8]

Starting with their physical appearance, Amélie Nothomb's characters reveal their duality, Prétextat appearing for example as a handsome young ephebe before Léopoldine's death in *Hygiène de l'assassin.* Nonetheless, his smooth face which reflects naivety and purity shelters a tormented soul which, in its delirium, is ready for murder and horror. Françoise, in *Mercure,* looks gorgeous in Hazel's eyes, but this beauty turns to coldness in the second ending of the novel, when Françoise drives Omer to commit suicide. Beauty, then, is the beauty of horror, of a vice indissociable from virtue.

Dionysus enjoys being surrounded by gorgeous women, the Maenads, who, thanks to him, display spellbinding and cruel charms. Their fatal beauty provides perfect pleasures, absolute submissions, but they don't hesitate to destroy whoever yields to them. In the same way, Amélie Nothomb's characters confront each other with this Dionysian violence which drives them to tear each other to pieces. Like panthers, Amélie Nothomb's heroines are seldom tender or gentle; they are always bursting with vitality and energy and at the same time try to outdo each other in elegance. Like the Maenads, they are driven by their Dionysian madness and do not hesitate to swoop down on their victims in order to torture or kill them. Women play with their half-dead victims in a sadistic and sophisticated way: 'Et l'avatar contempla ses mains avec admiration' (*HA* 180). Likewise, Nina and Françoise do not hesitate to kill with an obvious pleasure; Françoise makes no mystery of her jubilation to Hazel, 'ravie d'avoir tué son ennemi grâce à un malentendu bien orchestré' (*ME* 183). Their savagery is all the more fascinating as it is an explosive expression of an appalling desire to swoop down on the victim. Dionysus enjoys bloodshed: murder is thus experienced as an infinite delight for Prétextat when he strangles Léopoldine during 'cent quatre-vingts secondes édéniques': 'on se sent revitalisé, quand on a étranglé une personne aimée' (*HA* 149). Thanks to the power he procures, Dionysus makes crime easy and efficient: 'Avec un cou délicat comme le sien, l'étreinte fut d'une aisance!' (*HA* 150). In the same way, Émile, who murders his exasperating neighbour in *Les Catilinaires,* asserts: 'Personne ne peut imaginer combien c'est facile' (*CA* 149).

In order to defeat his enemies, Dionysus resorts to metamorphosis into a savage beast.[9] He then revives the ancestral duality between man and animal. The diversity of transformations he undergoes is a testimony to his propensity for madness and ecstatic love which ends in death. For instance, in Euripide's *Bacchantes,* he appears in the form of a bull.[10] He appears to the Maenads as a raging bull, symbol of sexual power and animal force, but his vitality is overtaken by fearsome fury. This is exactly how Epiphane fantasizes himself in a dream scene in *Attentat* taken from *Quo Vadis,* where he is embodied in the raging aurochs which rapes the beautiful and pure Lygia. This is a dream of carnal possession, where the other's body is nothing but a toy moulded according to one's fantasy to discover its most delicious aspects. In this sadistic dream of sexual superiority, 'J'enfonce mes cornes dans ton ventre lisse: c'est une sensation fabuleuse' (*A* 39). This is also an orgiastic scene, since it takes place under the cheering of an intoxicated crowd. Here the bull is both destructor and genitor as he produces a pleasure in which ecstasy and agony intermingle: 'Ton visage blafard a une expression exaltée, proche du sourire: je savais que tu aimerais ça' (*A* 41). The supreme joy lies in the facial expression of the victim, the bull's eye devouring and even absorbing the beauty of Lygia's features: 'je laisse ton visage intact afin que ces expressions restent lisibles' (*A* 41). Possession of the loved one can only take place in the most cruel violence and in an osmosis in the sensual pleasure of death: 'au même instant, toi et moi, nous mourons de plaisir' (*A* 42). Dionysian delirium imposes on the character a carnivorous appetite, a desire to tear raw flesh (Lydia's 'ventre lacéré' for Epiphane), or the need to trample underfoot her body which 'ressemble désormais à un fruit éclaté' (*A* 40–41). This extract is the most violently sensual and carnal in Amélie Nothomb's novels. In this passage, the fight between the torturer and the victim acquires its most powerful sadomasochistic dimension, where physical climax stems from destruction. The bull symbolizes the savagery of pleasure which can only lead to death. When the dream comes true, Epiphane kills Ethel with the sharp edges of a diadem, symbolizing the horns of the bull, while whispering sweet nothings. As a God of sexual frenzy, Dionysus unleashes passions in which pleasures of love and pleasures of death merge.

The Monstrous and the Sublime

Dionysus's limitless vitality drives him to be both monstrous in his destructions and sublime in his liberating fervour. This ambivalence also characterizes Amélie Nothomb's heroes, which makes it difficult for the reader to distinguish between good and evil, because their actions and sayings seem both fine and cruel. Everything in Dionysus is marked with excessiveness and immoderation. The sublime and the monstrous are born out of a lack of limits. They fuse contradictory feelings such as astonishment, fear, attraction and repulsion. In turn, the reader experiences the same feelings towards the characters: Omer is sublime in his love but he is also vile because of his deception; Prétextat is a genius in his evil ingenuity. Nothing is sublime *per se* but the experience of disproportionately strong or overwhelming emotions brings us closer to what Kant called the feeling of the sublime.[11]

The sublime opposes triviality, mediocrity, and cowardice. In this respect, even the most sordid murderers can be said to be sublime. The real monster is arguably the one who does not transcend his or her mediocrity, who refuses to experience the excesses of emotions and acts according to the destructive desire to exclude oneself from the basic pleasures of life, from the only important and necessary thing: love. Nina is a monster because she ignores ecstasy; she is unable to give meaning to life. At first, her sole desire is to pry into Prétextat's past without any concern for his dignity or right to privacy. Françoise's life could be charged with mediocrity, given her ignorance of love, of its sublime shivering, of its power and imperatives, before meeting Hazel and being convinced by Omer that 'L'amour n'est pas une expérience très courante chez les humains' (*ME* 77). Also, in *Le Sabotage amoureux,* the young Amélie, before meeting Elena, is unaware of the humanity given by love, so preoccupied is she by the cruel games the children play.

Dionysus's mark is to be recognized in the insatiability and intemperance the characters display in their search for uncommon absolutes: Prétextat and Epiphane only want to live intense moments provided by an exceptional hence monstrous love. 'Monstrum',[12] a term of religious vocabulary referring to a marvel, a divine intervention, has been applied to mythological creatures, and in the 16th century in France the word still designates a miracle. Thus, the ambiguity between the monstrous and the sublime is first of all linguistic. The monstrous is primarily the bizarre before becoming synonymous with the morally repulsive. The actions, thoughts and feelings of Amélie Nothomb's characters echo so well the threshold of absolute and excess, that what first appeared sublime in their determination becomes monstrous. In *Les Catilinaires,* the story is seen only through Émile's eyes, which makes his murder all the more ambivalent as well as his justifications, which oscillate according to the nocturnal or diurnal side of the hero. In the absence of any omniscient narrator, suspicions surround both depictions of the sublime and the monstrous.

The hero's ideals are born out of evil, but they drive him into the sphere of a deceitful sublime. For instance, Ethel declares to Epiphane: 'Ton amour a ses racines dans le fumier: c'est peut-être pour ça que ses fleurs sont si belles' (*A* 203). According to these hero-murderers, to kill the loved one in spite of oneself is to save oneself from mediocrity and degradation, to accord oneself an almost divine status; however, every ideal is dubious and disturbing with Amélie Nothomb, and instead of edifying, it leads towards gloomy, chaotic depths:

> La pureté est toujours monstrueuse. J'ai un grand idéal de pureté tout en étant consciente que cette pureté est elle-même monstrueuse, et donc l'inverse est vrai: la monstruosité recèle une véritable pureté. Quelque part, la monstruosité, c'est un excès de courage. Je pense que nous avons tous en nous la possibilité d'être monstrueux et que rares sont ceux qui la développent. Alors la question qui se pose, c'est ceux qui la développent le font-ils parce qu'ils ne peuvent pas faire autrement ou au contraire par courage? Eux, au moins, osent le montrer. Ce qui est certain, c'est que beaucoup de mes personnages assument leur propre monstruosité.[13]

Amélie Nothomb: a Dionysian Creation

According to the autobiographical elements provided in *Métaphysique des tubes,* the author herself resembles Dionysus. Indeed, she experiences a double birth, like the twice born God: during the first two years, she compares herself to a pot plant, in a vegetative state; then she is born a second time, suddenly taken out from this state by an uncontrollable anger which ends only with the discovery of pleasure.

Also, as far as the creative process itself is concerned, Amélie Nothomb experiences a Dionysian drunkenness, in the sense that she describes herself as being taken over by a trance-like state which is beyond explanation or mastery. The author plunges into her most obscure and mystical depths to find inspiration to write:

> C'est ça qui est fou, quand j'arrive dans ce versant de moi, j'appelle ça aussi descendre dans mon sous-marin, quand j'ai vraiment réussi à descendre au fond de mon sous-marin, à ce moment-là, c'est un moment miraculeux: il n'y a plus de différences entre le mot et la chose, il n'y a plus de différences entre le verbe et l'acte. Si j'écris et que je tue, je tue vraiment mais dans une jouissance parfaite et une impression de grandiose parfaite.[14]

Writing is the very release, the catharsis of Dionysian pulsions which enables her to avoid madness. Writing transcends everything that in humanity is dual, horrible, or sublime; writing offers this 'accès direct et surnaturel à la vie des autres' (*HA* 134) in the uncontrolled surging forth of words:

> Il y a des moments, ce n'est pas tout le temps, mais il y a des moments où j'écris, où vraiment, je vois que le dionysiaque l'emporte. C'est le meilleur moment; ça veut dire: là, j'ai forcément raison.[15]

The author experiences a Dionysian jubilation through a writing of destruction:

> La personne qui se trouve devant vous serait incapable de commettre un crime, mais quand je suis dans ces moments dionysiaques, je suis capable de tout! Heureusement que je me contente d'écrire (. . .) C'est terrible, la scène du taureau, je l'ai totalement vécue, bon, bien sûr, jamais dans la réalité. Je n'ai jamais été un taureau dans la réalité. Mais quand je l'ai écrit, c'était tellement dionysiaque que je l'étais à fond. J'étais aussi bien la jeune vierge que le taureau: j'étais tout à la fois, c'était prodigieux et tout ça dans une jouissance totale. Et tout ce que ce taureau a fait, je l'ai fait; et tout ce que cette jeune fille a subi, je l'ai subi.[16]

The author's own use of the term 'Dionysian' reinforces its significance as a motif, as a powerful source of inspiration in her writing. As a motif imbued with apparently contradictory impulses, Dionysus, as a God of beatitude as well as of savagery, monstrous in his deeds and in the eruption of his murderous madness, bears within himself a tragic ambivalence. The force of his drunkenness and the extremes of his love for Ariadne stem from this very ambivalence. Amélie Nothomb's characters represent oppositions that he incorporates: beauty and ugliness, beast and human, human and god. She creates a monstrous sublime by shedding light on the motivations of such excessive heroes whose quest for ideals and perfect love has turned them into sordid and sadistic criminals.

The author herself seems driven by a Dionysian force, her creativity shaped by both the executioner's and the victim's *modus vivendi*. She brings together these two schismatic parts of human beings in her writing, with the effect that seemingly intractable binaries, love and hate, beauty and ugliness, murderer and victim, are merged in an ecstatic and sometimes ambiguous fusion of opposites.

Université de Nanterre, Paris X
Translated by Rémi Bourdot

Notes

1. I am grateful to the editors of the journal *Religiologiques* for permission to print this article, an amended version of which appeared in French in the Spring 2002 issue.

2. Nadia Julien, *Le dictionnaire des mythes* (Paris: collection Marabout, 1992) pp. 203–7.

3. *Métaphysique des tubes* (Paris: Albin Michel, 2000).

4. *Hygiène de l'assassin* (Paris: Albin Michel, Livre de poche, 1992). Subsequent references in the text will appear as *HA* followed by the page number.

5. *Mercure* (Paris: Albin Michel, Livre de poche, 1995); *Attentat* (Paris: Albin Michel, 1997). Subsequent references in the text will appear as *ME* and *A* followed by the page number.

6. *Les Combustibles* (Paris: Albin Michel, Livre de poche, 1994).

7. *Les Catilinaires* (Paris: Albin Michel, Livre de poche, 1995). Subsequent references in the text will appear as *CA* followed by the page number.

8. F. Otto Walter, *Dionysos, le mythe et le culte* (Paris: Mercure de France, 1969) p. 101.

9. Ibid., p. 120.

10. 'Apparaît sous la forme d'un taureau', ibid., p. 117.

11. E. Kant, *Observations sur le sentiment du beau et du sublime,* trans. by M. David-Ménard (Paris: Garnier-Flammarion, 1990). Original title: *Beobachtungen über das Gefühl des Schönen und Erhabenen,* 1790.

12. *Le dictionnaire historique de la langue française, sous la direction d'Alain Rey* (Paris: Le Robert, 1993).

13. Interview with Laureline Amanieux, available online at *http://multimania.com/fenrir/ nothomb.htm,* 27/04/2001.

14. Ibid.

15. Ibid.

16. Ibid.

Mark D. Lee

AMÉLIE NOTHOMB: WRITING CHILDHOOD'S END

'Les avocats invoquent une enfance malheureuse comme circonstance atténuante.
En sondant votre passé, je me suis rendu compte qu'une enfance trop heureuse
pouvait elle aussi servir de circonstance atténuante'.[1]

The evocation of childhood and its loss has long been a source of creative inspiration for writers and a subject of literary analysis for critics. For Amélie Nothomb, it is perhaps the very *moteur* of her creative writing project. In a review article and interview with journalist, Martine de Rabaudy, Nothomb makes the following connection between writing and childhood: 'L'écriture, c'est la continuation de l'enfance par d'autres moyens'.[2] Taking this affirmation as my starting point, I will argue that although childhood does—in reality—end, for Nothomb this ending is an oddly productive beginning. By adopting *other* means, childhood and its end are incessantly re-imagined, displaced and condensed into strange, often unrecognizable forms. They are given, through writing, a sort of *survie*—both an afterlife and a survival—that continues potentially indefinitely.

Nothomb's affirmation raises a number of questions for critics. What kind of temporality is implied in the recurrence of a moment that has, on some level, already achieved closure? How does one read a writing that—according to Nothomb's own description—enters into a supplementary relationship with childhood itself? Finally, what do the various forms taken by the scene of childhood's end tell us about the role of narration? While these questions may be explored by looking at the whole of Nothomb's literary production, I will focus my analysis in great part on two major works where the problem of childhood's end is most strikingly performed: *Hygiène de l'assassin,* the author's first published novel, and *Métaphysique des tubes*,[3] her most recent autobiographical fiction. We shall see that in continuing childhood *par d'autres moyens* Nothomb not only throws into question the veracity of any 'true' narrative of childhood, but she especially binds herself as author to re-enact—by different means—a narrative of closure that, although it refuses mastery, ultimately defines and drives her literary imagination.

Prolonging Childhood: Ugliness and Sex

If '[l]'écriture, c'est la continuation de l'enfance par d'autres moyens', then the most visible consequence of this statement in Nothomb's writing is the odd array of childlike figures who populate her novels. I am not speaking here of child characters themselves, found principally in her autobiographical works *Le Sabotage amoureux*[4] and *Métaphysique des tubes,* but rather of adults who by different means display or are forced to maintain traits usually associated with children, well after childhood should have ended.[5] In this first section I will mention but a few of these characters and the means by which they prolong their childhood.

Epiphane Otos, the narrator of Nothomb's 1997 novel, *Attentat,* is one of these ostensibly adult, yet childlike characters.[6] Naïve to the point of painful, comic embarrassment and although in his late twenties, Otos has a level of maturity and experience—especially sexual and emotional—that does not correspond to his years. He explains the cause and means of his perhaps involuntarily extended childhood by describing himself in the following manner: 'Ma copie était vierge. Au fond, la laideur m'avait conservé en une fraîcheur extrême: je devais tout inventer. Je n'avais plus vingt-neuf ans, j'en avais onze' (*A* 26). Sheer physical *laideur*—at least in this novel—is apparently enough to preserve not only one's virginity but also one's youth. Otos' unfortunate recipe finds a similar yet different elaboration in the character of Hazel, in *Mercure*.[7] In contrast to Otos, Hazel only *believes* herself to be hideously deformed when she is in reality strikingly beautiful. Yet, this belief is enough to keep her in a complicit state of childlike dependency. Imprisoned while still very young on an island where no mirrors exist, she literally cannot see her true, beautiful, adult self. And therefore, somewhat like Otos, ugliness incarcerates her both psychologically and physically in a different sort of prolonged childhood.

Contrary to what one might expect, sexual precociousness also seems to be related to the extension of childlike characteristics into adulthood. Or, put another way, it is associated with the repression of adult-like characteristics during one's more mature years. This is true of Epiphane Otos, who remarks that, 'Je me rendis compte que c'était mon enfance qui avait joué le rôle de mon adolescence: à l'âge de treize ans, j'avais mis mon sexe au placard' (*A* 33). And, it is also the case for Émile and Juliette, the newly retired couple in *Les Catilinaires*[8] who believe they have found at the end of their working lives the idyllic, isolated home 'auquel nous aspirions depuis notre enfance' (*CA* 14). This couple started having sexual relations at six years of age (*CA* 57). Perhaps indelibly marked by this first encounter at a moment when they were too immature, Émile, the narrator of *Les Catilinaires,* claims he regards his sixty-six-year-old spouse as if she were still a child: 'je n'avais d'yeux que pour la fille de six ans' (*CA* 18). Indeed, according to a confused genealogy, he sees his wife as a strange combination of child and adult, claiming she is her own child as well as his: 'Les anges n'ont pas d'enfant, Juliette non plus. Elle est son propre enfant– et le mien' (*CA* 83). Indeed, Émile and Juliette are—in one significant, emblematic way—still very much pre-pubescent, infertile beings well into their sixties. Like virtually all adult characters in Nothomb's fiction, they are childless. The suggestion here is that they either do not, or cannot procreate because, like many adult figures in Nothomb's writing, they are still children themselves in many respects. [9]

Preventing Childhood's End: Food, Sex and Death

By far the most dramatic recipes for maintaining and extending childhood, however, are to be found in *Hygiène de l'assassin,* a work that does nothing to dispel the commonplace of literary criticism that an author's first novel announces the many preoccupations that will nourish her future works. Prétextat Tach, *Hygiène's* principal character and Nobel-winning writer, is somewhat of an amalgam of later Nothomb characters, yet with certain traits exaggerated so that they bring to the foreground issues often implicit in subsequent incarnations. Like the figures previously discussed, Tach was sexually active before puberty –even going so far as to assert that he is technically still a virgin as an adult (*HA* 76), since he has not had sex since he was a child. Much is made by him and other characters in the novel of his *laideur,* and of his strangely smooth, hairless skin, despite his eighty-three years and grotesquely incapacitating obesity. To top off this portrait, he also possesses a markedly puerile, sadistic disposition in his adult years.

Yet, while Tach does qualify as a childlike adult, unlike the other characters previously discussed he is the sole figure to offer explicit recipes for *preventing* the onset of adolescence, for staving off childhood's end as long as possible. While in their early teens, he and his pre-pubescent, cousin-lover, Léopoldine, develop a concerted project to stay forever young, whereas characters in other books are rather unaware and passive in prolonging their childhoods. Nothomb constructs her first published novel around the following situation: with only a few weeks to live Tach, a Nobel prize-winning author, accepts to be interviewed by several journalists. He trounces them all until he finds himself face to face with one named Nina. Drawing upon details from Tach's sole, unfinished novel, also entitled—by a modernist twist—*Hygiène de l'assassin,* Nina confronts Tach with the detailed 'hygiène d'éternelle enfance' (*HA* 110) devised by himself and Léopoldine as adolescents, in order to prolong their childhood indefinitely:

> Persuadé que la puberté fait son œuvre pendant le sommeil, vous décrétez qu'il ne faut plus dormir, ou du moins pas plus de deux heures par jour. Une vie essentiellement aquatique vous paraît idéale pour retenir l'enfance: désormais, Léopoldine et

vous passerez des journées et des nuits entières à nager dans les lacs du domaine, parfois même en hiver. Vous mangez le strict minimum. Certains aliments sont interdits et d'autres conseillés, en vertu de principes qui me semblent relever de la plus haute fantaisie: vous interdisez les mets jugés trop 'adultes', tels que le canard à l'orange, la bisque de homard et les nourritures de couleur noire. En revanche, vous recommandez les champignons non pas vénéneux mais réputés impropres à la consommation tels que les vesses-de-loup, dont vous vous gavez en saison. Pour vous empêcher de dormir, vous vous procurez des boîtes d'un thé kenyan excessivement fort (*HA* 110–11).

I will return to elements of this description later, but it would be negligent not to at least remark on the obvious parallels between the *hygiène* outlined here and Nothomb's own notorious predilection for strong tea, near rotten food and little sleep.[10] What are the physical consequences—in this novel—of following such a regime? Nina claims to have recovered a photograph of Prétextat and Léopoldine, taken when they were seventeen and fifteen respectively, at the peak of their extended childhood:

Enfants, oui, même vous qui ne présentez aucun signe d'adolescence. C'est très curieux: vous êtes tous les deux immenses, maigres, blafards, mais vos visages et vos longs corps sont parfaitement enfantins. Vous n'avez pas l'air normal, d'ailleurs: on dirait deux géants de 12 ans. [. . .] A croire que vos délirants préceptes d'hygiène étaient efficaces (*HA* 121).

Of course, on one obvious level childhood does end both for Tach and for Léopoldine. As Nothomb's narrative goes, he and Léopoldine made a pact to kill the other at the first physical sign of either one entering adulthood. And so, moments after having sex with Prétextat on her birthday, Léopoldine starts menstruating while floating in a pond on the property of their noble ancestors. Tach strangles her to death, claiming that not only Léopoldine but he too died in the experience: 'je suis mort à dix-sept ans' (*HA* 125). His subsequent life has been but a sort of 'non-vie' (*HA* 134) where, although he becomes a successful writer, nothing essential really happens after childhood's end. For Tach, like all other childhood survivors in Nothomb's fiction, the only recourse to having survived this passage is to spend the present and future in a sort of exile, looking back on childhood. This sentiment is articulated particularly clearly by the autobiographical narrator of *Le Sabotage amoureux,* who states: 'J'ai toujours su que l'âge adulte ne comptait pas: dès la puberté, l'existence n'est plus qu'un épilogue' (*LS* 25). And the narrator later reiterates this sentiment with the statement that, 'Nous n'abordions pas non plus l'inepte question de notre avenir. Peut-être parce qu'instinctivement nous avions tous trouvé la seule vraie réponse: "Quand je serai grand, je penserai à quand j'étais petit"' (*LS* 55). The closing statement in *Métaphysique des tubes,* Nothomb's autobiographical recounting of her early childhood and its end, fully corroborates and amplifies this sentiment. Having brought the reader to the ripe old age of three, the narrator concludes, 'Ensuite, il ne s'est plus rien passé' (*MT* 171).

The Double Bind: Nothing New, *Again and Again*

It would appear from these statements and previous ones that Nothomb's writing is governed by a purely retrospective temporality, by a looking back at a lost and finished moment in childhood. Nothing, however, could be more mistaken. For although the above statements suggest nothing new, nothing of essence happens in adulthood, childhood—at least on the level of the imaginary, of aesthetic reality—is by no means finished. Nor is its writing simply retrospective. Instead, childhood *happens again and again,* perhaps unbeknownst to the characters and the writer herself. A closer reading of *Hygiène de l'assassin* alerts us that Tach's childhood and its dramatic end recur at least a second time during the novel, enabled by an uncanny temporality of repetition and return. Thanks to a contradictory, condensed gesture, the act of narration enables a space whereby the past—childhood—may be briefly resurrected while simultaneously put to death. Having been forced both to hear his story told by Nina and to recount it again himself, Tach suddenly exclaims, to his morbid pleasure, 'Ne voyez-vous pas qu'à l'instant même où je vous parle, je suis en train d'étrangler Léopoldine?' (*HA* 154). We should recall that *Hygiène de l'assassin* is also the title of Tach's only, unfinished novel. By means of a joint narration, Tach hopes to finish it, and the murder of childhood it recounts, once and for all. He suspects that, through a performative narration, he will be able to alter the laws of time and give closure to that which refused completion previously. Building on a metaphor of cartilage tissue, he announces the temporality that enables the re-writing of childhood's end not only here, but across Nothomb's fiction: 'Comprenez-moi: les cartilages sont mon chaînon manquant, articulations ambivalentes qui permettent d'aller de l'arrière vers l'avant mais aussi de l'avant vers l'arrière, d'avoir accès à la totalité du temps, à l'éternité' (*HA* 153).

Narration—like writing—sets up a double bind in Nothomb's fiction. It initially allows childhood's end to be re-enacted, yet this time the writer has the ability to perhaps change the outcome by being active—as an adult—where in the past she was passive—as a child. Similar to a *travail de deuil,* the act of narration also opens up the possibility that the past may be put to rest, finished off once and for all. Thus, Tach first seeks to re-enact his crime in a rather literal fashion, by offering to strangle Nina. But the name *Nina,* it must be remarked, re-inscribes in a cunning condensation the figure of the female child returning to confront her assassin. And so, by a significant reversal, Tach convinces Nina to give him this closure by having *her* kill *him.* Nina, no longer the passive child, but an uncannily active adult-yet-child agrees to kill Tach by the same means he killed Léopoldine many years ago.

One may therefore be tempted to conclude that childhood is indeed put to death here, that the knot of ending but not ending is at last untied. In fact no. Many features essential to Nothomb's subsequent works counter this conclusion, revealing that childhood persistently recurs in her œuvre with differing levels of visibility. As already discussed, it may be recognized in the displaced form of child-

like adult figures populating her novels. It also manifests itself in the literary project of writing three autobiographical fictions, of which two deal directly with
childhood and its end, and the third of which, *Stupeur et tremblements,* recounts a
young adult's readiness to submit to any and all forms of punishment in order to
reintegrate the nation of her childhood: 'Ce premier exil m'avait tant marquée que
je me sentais capable de tout accepter afin d'être réincorporée à ce pays dont je m'é-
tais si longtemps crue originaire'.[11] More recently if less visibly, Nothomb's 2001
novel, *Cosmétique de l'ennemi,* indirectly takes up once again the question.[12] Like
Hygiène, it tells the story of a man brought to confront the murder of a woman he
cherished and who now finds himself excluded from his previous world of innocence—a *chute* reinforced by several explicit references to Adam and Eve and the
Garden of Eden in the text (*CE* 78, 130–31). Indeed even *Péplum*—Nothomb's
pseudo science-fiction novel about the remarkable preservation of Pompeii—is
predicated on exactly the same dilemma that defines her relationship to an unfinished childhood's end.[13] Its recounting of how a future civilization becomes obsessed with a past moment and attempts to bring it perfectly preserved into the
present through murder reproduces not only Tach's contradictory desire to resurrect yet destroy the moment he strangled Léopoldine, but also Nothomb's task as
writer of childhood and its end.

From *Hygiène* to *Métaphysique:* Returning to the Scene of the Crime

Given this weight of evidence, and especially Nothomb's statement about the
function of writing and its relationship to childhood, I would assert that *Hygiène
de l'assassin*—by an obvious *mise-en-abyme*—is also Nothomb's unfinished novel,
par excellence. The mere fact that Nothomb is a professed *graphomane,*[14] that she is
unable to stop writing, suggests that something constantly brings her back to the
scene of a crime at childhood's end, that something profoundly unresolved in this
experience escapes her mastery. Indeed, the name, Prétextat Tach, tells us as much
in its own, roundabout way. It announces that this character, his dilemma and his
unfinished novel stand as the proto-type or pre-text to the task or *tâche* that is the
writing of Nothomb's subsequent fiction. The task of writing, or *tâche d'écriture,* if
you will, is predicated on another sort of *tache* marking childhood's end: a 'tache'
in the sense of an indelible stain or mark that cannot be erased or washed out, but
only re-inscribed, re-enacted. In Nothomb's first novel this 'tache' is the crime of
killing childhood, and its literalization, the sudden appearance of menstrual blood
trickling from Léopoldine as she floats in the water. This blood signals the end of
childhood, the start of adolescent fecundity and, consequently, the risk of becoming a mother and no longer a child.

The most obvious recurrence of this writerly task may be found, of course, in
Métaphysique des tubes—a work that lends itself to being read as a sort of palimpsest
of *Hygiène de l'assassin*. When Nothomb writes about her idyllic childhood and its
end in Japan, many common elements reappear—mixed up and re-composed into

uncannily similar yet different configurations—to the point where it becomes diffi-cult if not impossible to decide which work is the repetition or 'continuation' of the other. Given the fluid, overlapping temporality of re-enactment afforded by 'les cartilages', it is not surprising that Nina, in *Hygiène,* should signal a future, intertextual relationship. Speaking of Tach's unfinished novel, *Hygiène de l'assassin,* and by implication of Nothomb's novel too, Nina declares 'j'ai de bonnes raisons de penser que ce roman est strictement autobiographique' (*HA* 119). While Nina reports January fourteenth as the day she learned of Tach's imminent death, having just returned from vacation (*HA* 137), Nothomb reports in *Stupeur et tremblements* that she started writing *Hygiène de l'assassin* on a January fourteenth (*ST* 186)—having just exiled herself for the second time from Japan, where she had quit her professional, adult career, and broken off her engagement to a Japanese fiancé.[15] The culminating scenes in both *Métaphysique* and *Hygiène* happen at the same time of year: Léopoldine dies in a lake 'le 13 août, 1925' (*HA* 141), and Amélie—the nar-rated child—nearly drowns 'fin août 1970' (*MT* 171). Prétextat calls Léopoldine 'l'hiérinfante' (*HA* 141), while Amélie's first years of life in Japan are qualified as 'un état divin' (*MT* 153) where she is especially cherished by her Japanese governess, Nishio-san. Whereas Tach kills Léopoldine on her birthday—by no coincidence, also Nothomb's birthday, August thirteenth—having followed their regime for three years, Amélie falls hypnotized into the water while feeding the three fish she had just received for her third birthday.[16] Amélie, like Léopoldine and Prétextat, leads, 'une vie essentiellement aquatique' (*HA* 111), as if she too were following the 'hygiène d'éternelle enfance' (*HA* 110) set out by this odd couple. She spends a sig-nificant amount of her Japanese childhood in the water, either floating in the nearby 'Petit Lac Vert' (*MT* 114), lying out in the rain, walking flooded streets with her father, swimming at the seaside or finally almost drowning in the garden fish pond.

As if obeying the implicit law of repetition that characterizes the problematic of childhood in her œuvre, Amélie drowns not once, not even twice, but at least three times in the novel, where the first, at the seaside, and the last, in the garden pond, actually happen in water. In between the two, however, a metaphorical drowning marks the definitive end of her childhood perfection. When Amélie learns that Nishio-san has resigned, that there is a term to her Edenic sojourn in Japan, No-thomb renders Amélie's disorientation in this manner: 'J'étais dans la mer, j'avais perdu pied, l'eau m'avalait, je me débattais, je cherchais un appui, il n'y avait plus de sol nulle part, le monde ne voulait plus de moi' (*MT* 135). Thus, when we do ar-rive at the final drowning scene, it is almost a supplement to the preceding verbal and metaphorical version, or at least a 'continuation' of all previous versions.

Repression and Return: Bloodstains and Scars

Yet, not only shared, similar elements encourage us to read these scenes together. If we look at the differences between them, we find other, tacit connexions. Of course the most obvious difference between *Hygiène* and *Métaphysique* resides in the fact that the first protagonist, Léopoldine, is a pre-pubescent, sexually active fifteen-year-old who is strangled to death, whereas Amélie is a young, sexually in-experienced child who nearly drowns. But on these points the two texts enter into a silent conversation with each other that the critic may only perceive by reading them as rewritings of each other. Asked why he did not simply drown Léopoldine since she was already floating in a lake, Tach states he was deterred by the idea of making an obvious literary reference to the death of Victor Hugo's daughter, of the same name (*HA* 150). However, Tach's reasoning also holds true for Nothomb herself: she apparently wishes to avoid a literary reference to *her own* near drowning in *Métaphysique des tubes*. Even though it was as yet not writ-ten—or at least, not published—its literary, aesthetic and imaginary status is real enough to provoke this curious difference and its repression. Indeed, this variant raises a question *Métaphysique des tubes* does not ask explicitly of its culminating scene, but which is clearly articulated in the intertext. The whole issue for Nina in her confrontation with Tach is to find out the following: 'Monsieur Tach, j'ai besoin que vous me disiez la vérité: Léopoldine fut-elle réellement et consciem-ment consentante?' (*HA* 137–38). Was she murdered or did she let Tach kill her, by what we might call a strange form of assisted suicide? By displacement, we are brought to ask the same questions of Amélie: does she consciously consent to terminate her life in this drowning scene, knowing that her Edenic, Japanese childhood was coming to an end anyway, or is her near-death on some level an at-tempted murder, committed by an external force? And, listening to that question again, 'fut-elle réellement et consciemment consentante?', one cannot help but also hear Nina asking whether Léopoldine willingly consented to sexual relations with Tach.[17]

The presence of blood at both scenes encourages us to pursue these lines of interpretation. Although Amélie strikes her head as she falls into the garden carp pool, no mention of blood or her injury is made until after she is pulled from the water. The bloody wound is elided until she is in the car with her mother racing to the hospital where Amélie is warned that she has a bleeding 'trou', a 'fente' that she must not touch, and that must be sewn up (*MT* 169–70). Read intertextually with the scene of Léopoldine's murder, Amélie's bleeding and near death at three years of age suggest at the very least the sudden appearance of a symbolic menstrual blood, marking her irrevocable passage from childhood to adolescence. And the mother's remarks suggest, by displacement, a bid to stop this symbolic, menstrual bleeding, to repress the transition from innocence to knowledge.

However, given Nina's question from *Hygiène*, 'fut-elle réellement et consciem-ment consentante?', we are led to wonder if the scene of childhood's end in both works –Léopoldine's murder and Amélie's too sudden knowledge of her impend-ing exile—is not also characterized as a rape of innocence. For Amélie, blood ap-pears as a *result* of her injury whereas for Léopoldine, blood is the *cause* of her death, since it incites Prétextat to kill her. We should perhaps consider that by com-parison with Amélie the blood Léopoldine sheds is also the *consequence* of an act, an injury to which she was not fully 'consentante': adult sexual intercourse with a male who, as we remarked earlier, nevertheless claims he is 'technically' still a virgin since he has never had sex as an adult (*HA* 76). Of course the counterpart to this intertextual reading is the suggestion that the bloody end of Amélie's three-year childhood is also characterized as a rape. This interpretation is silently encouraged by the presence of the three carp in the pool where Amélie incurs her injury, as the novel earlier tells us that carp are explicitly marked as symbols of the male sex in Japan (*MT* 93–94). Even the names Amélie gives these fish—Marie, Jésus, Joseph—betray both her desire to announce and to hide their sexual connotations, since we have combined in these three the mystery of a virgin fecundation and birth.

The adult narrator of *Métaphysique des tubes* intervenes at the end of this scene, which is also the end of the novel, to cast a modicum of doubt on the veracity of this event's narration: 'Parfois, je me demande si je n'ai pas rêvé, si cette aventure fondatrice n'est pas un fantasme' (*MT* 171). However, to dispel any lingering doubts about the phantasmatic nature of her memory, she claims she need only look in a mirror to see the scar, a sort of *tache,* left on her head by the episode in the garden carp pond. This scar suggests by an interesting condensation that Léopoldine or Amélie's assailant-assassin and his crime have left an indelible mark on her body and mind forever.[18]

Rising to the Surface: Nishio-san and the Power of Narration

One final scene of childhood's end seems to have particularly marked Nothomb's writing. Given that it dates from a period when, according to *Métaphysique des tubes,* Amélie was just entering the symbolic register of language, it is difficult if not impossible to decide whether the scene is her own *fantasme,* someone else's, or some conjugation of both. Significantly, the most striking example of this painfully pleasurable narrative drive is to be found not in Amélie's mouth but displaced and condensed in the mouth of Nishio-san. Ironically, the Japanese domestic whose imminent departure first metaphorically drowned Amélie is also the person who not only physically pulls her from her watery grave in the fish pond, effectively giving Amélie back her voice and the possibility of narration, but also the person who imparts a model of narration uncannily similar to Nothomb's own. In fact, Amélie's own story of childhood's end—and potentially all other versions of this dilemma in her writing—seems mediated in an important fashion by Nishio-san. As Amélie's substitute mother figure, Nishio-san provides not just the story of another sort of drowning, but perhaps the very master-narrative of childhood's end that, because it precedes Nothomb's own repeated recountings, appears to found and inform all others.[19] Having learned of the existence of death—her grandmother just died in Belgium—Amélie turns not to her parents but to her Japanese governess for guidance. This important step in Amélie's loss of innocence is punctuated, at the child's behest, by Nishio-san reciting the tale of how, during the war, her own childhood ended under a rain of bombs—'les bombes avaient commencé à pleuvoir' (*MT* 58)—when she was seven years old.[20] She transfixes Amélie with her own story of near death, destruction and symbolic resurrection, of being buried alive under the rubble of her childhood home, of repeatedly trying to climb to the surface, gasping for air, only to slip back down again and again under the blast of another explosion (*MT* 59–61). Nishio-san's drowning in rubble, her multiple efforts to reach the surface, her doubts about whether it would be better to give up and stay below the surface—'C'est encore ici que je suis le plus en sécurité' (*MT* 60)—or to return to the world above, which has become a nightmarish scene of fire and dismembered bodies, all these elements pre-articulate the dilemma of Amélie's own, future drownings in *Métaphysique des tubes,* and by extension in all Nothomb's novels. Indeed, Nishio-san's repeated recounting of this scene and of the death of her sister, crushed two years earlier by a train (*MT* 51), appear to teach Amélie the immense power of narration to resurrect and to kill the past through language—'À chaque occurrence de ce récit, sans faillir, les mots de ma gouvernante tuaient la petite fille. Parler pouvait donc servir aussi à assassiner' (*MT* 51).[21] In this manner, Nishio-san's narratives stand as a master metaphor for the recurrent writing of childhood's end across Nothomb's works. Striking with the force of a bomb, this scene initially disorients but subsequently, relentlessly 'climbs back to the surface' of this author's writing.

In the end, it is of course impossible to decide which of the many versions of childhood's end is the most 'true'. As if to announce this impossibility, Amélie informs us in *Métaphysique des tubes* that telling the truth or fabricating stories elicits a similar accusation from her listener: 'tu mens tout le temps' (*MT* 127). What counts, finally, for Nothomb is the drive to repeat, to re-enact and to continue *par d'autres moyens* the fascinatingly endless story of childhood's end.

Mount Allison University

Notes

1. *Hygiène de l'assassin* (Paris: Albin Michel, Édition Points, 1992), p. 107. Subsequent references in the text will appear as *HA* followed by the page number.
2. 'Occupons-nous d'Amélie: Portrait', *L'Express,* 2521, 28 octobre 1999, 140–41 (p. 141).
3. (Paris: Albin Michel, 2000). Subsequent references in the text will appear as *MT* followed by the page number.
4. (Paris: Albin Michel, Livre de poche, 1993). Subsequent references in the text will appear as *LS* followed by the page number.
5. In counterpoint, the child narrators of these autobiographical works have strikingly adult-like characteristics (discernment, memory, language skills) only partially attributable to the overlapping voices of an adult narrator writing about a child narratee.
6. (Paris: Albin Michel, Livre de poche, 1997). Subsequent references in the text will appear as *A* followed by the page number.

7. (Paris: Albin Michel, Livre de poche, 1998).
8. (Paris: Albin Michel, Livre de poche, 1995). Subsequent references in the text will appear as *CA* followed by the page number.
9. This lack of interest in procreation suggests not only that Émile and Juliette are fixed at a childlike stage where their bodies are not mature enough to reproduce, but also that they are not interested in having children since—on an imaginary level—they are of the same sex, as an autobiographical reading would suggest. Émile and Juliette are rather transparent substitutions for Amélie, the author, and Juliette, her sister. Together they dreamed of forever staying together, of never being separated in adulthood (Rabaudy, op. cit., p. 140). A similar refusal to reproduce is also demonstrated by the sole female character in *Les Combustibles* (Paris: Albin Michel, Livre de poche, 1994) who would rather die than enter into a married, maternal, bourgeois existence. See pp. 52–53.
10. Jean-Baptiste Hareng, in a review article of *Cosmétique de l'ennemi,* resumes Nothomb's well-documented eating and sleeping habits. See 'L'Échappée belge', *Libération,* section Livres, 30 août 2001, IV-V (p. V).
11. (Paris: Albin Michel, Livre de poche, 1999), p. 27. Subsequent references in the text will appear as *ST* followed by the page number.
12. (Paris: Albin Michel, 2001). Subsequent references in the text will appear as *CE* followed by the page number.
13. (Paris: Albin Michel, Livre de poche, 1996). Subsequent references in the text will appear as *PE* followed by the page number.
14. See Hareng, op. cit., p. V, or Rabaudy, op. cit., p. 140.
15. This detail is provided in Hareng's review article, op. cit., p.V.
16. In an at present unpublished interview with Nothomb, conducted in February 2002, I asked the author about the significance of dates in her works. She stated that dates in several novels, particularly in *Hygiène de l'assassin* and *Stupeur et tremblements* are important for her, describing a veritable obsession deriving from her decision to remember the events of every day of her life from the moment she and her sister decided to become anorexic, January 5th 1981. This superposition of dates creates, in Nothomb's words, potentially never-ending, cumulative, even erotic effects: 'chaque jour était tellement lesté d'événements. Il y a même un de mes "dits" premiers romans—un de ceux que je n'ai jamais montrés—qui s'appelle *Le Stupre des anniversaires,* parce que je constatais que chaque fois qu'une date revenait, et il y en avait beaucoup qui revenaient, j'en éprouvais une émotion! Mais presque de l'ordre de l'érotisme. Alors que la date commémorée n'était pas forcément érotique'.
17. In fact the question of consenting or being forced to have sexual relations runs through many of Nothomb's works, and will be the object of a future study.
18. It should be noted that Nothomb's novel, *Péplum,* also ends with the revelation of a scar as proof of an encounter (*PE* 153).
19. Nishio-san and Kashima-san, the two Japanese domestics who work in the family home, are in effect substitute parents for Amélie. They distribute into two separate bodies the 'good' and 'bad' traits that characterize parents in a child's *imaginaire.* Nishio-san is the loving, forgiving parent of humble origins while Kashima-san is noble, stern, critical and punishing. Moreover, many elements of their description lend weight to the idea that they not only form part of Amélie's personal, particularly Japanese *roman familial,* but also act as a model for the divided self later illustrated in Nothomb's *Cosmétique de l'ennemi.*
20. This scene of being orphaned in a bombing recurs in Nothomb's novel, *Mercure.*

21. The dramatic, tragic separation of Nishio-san from her sister may be seen as a projection and transformation of Nothomb's own fear of being separated from her elder sister, Juliette, and their pact to remain inseparable throughout life. Moreover, Nishio-san's twin children—whom Amélie, the narrator, has linguistic difficulty distinguishing one from the other—are likely another transformation of this fear and desire.

Marinella Termite

'CLOSURE' IN AMÉLIE NOTHOMB'S NOVELS

Why choose to give a novel two endings? This is the umpteenth challenge thrown down by Amélie Nothomb with her 1998 novel, *Mercure*.[1] Coming as it does under the aegis of Stendhal, with echoes of Julien Sorel's duality and Fabrice Del Dongo's imprisonments, any attempt to unravel the action in this novel is rendered problematic as are any strategies for tackling the textual periphery within the scope of its oblique writing. I shall take up the challenge by reading this writer's works backwards, a paradoxical step perfectly in keeping with Nothomb's own style. Firstly, I shall isolate the characteristics of this writing by using examples from a large number of her novels. In these examples, the ironic infrastructure is based on an interplay of different levels within the text which feed its economy right up to the elaboration of their closing sequence. From this, concentrating principally on *Mercure,* I shall deduce a typology of endings which are highly characteristic of Nothomb's writing.

The amused tone of this 'graphomaniac's' paradoxical tales is regulated by an irony tinged with cynicism, an often perverse sense of provocation and a continual sabotage of the conventional status quo. This encompasses the titles she chooses for her texts, as well as her tragi-comic characters and a panoply of rather bizarre themes which the writer always manipulates by means of an overall destabilizing effect. Indeed, the unexpected seems to result in a displacing of meanings, both on an etymological and a cultural level. The questioning attitude of the characters also guarantees a dual approach, in which there is room to swing from one point of view to another. Even the perception of a human seen through the prism of his or her deformity underlines this tendency to show the reverse side of the coin. Hazel's distorted vision in *Mercure* or Epiphane Otos's exemplary ugliness in *Attentat* describe an anthropophagic space in which cruelty is tempered with the most fluid lightness of touch.[2] Confronted with over-exploited images, such as that of a terribly damaged face which is held dear by female tradition from Duras to Nobécourt,[3] or the physical monstrosity of dwarves,[4] the tone here does not fall back onto easy formulae but strives to deploy the duality so that its closely coupled presence produces disarmingly surprising effects.

Amélie Nothomb's writing exploits certain mechanisms which facilitate this sort of parodic mix of literary genres, metatextual interventions and experimentation with endings. It is within dualistic frameworks, complete with two different standpoints, that Amélie Nothomb experiments with several hypothetical 'closures' and narrative dénouements. This is a far cry from the interactive forms so dear to writers helped or constrained in their creation by the use of computers. The parodic quality and the singular presence of the author's voice guarantee the minute construction of her works. But, rather than breaking up the closing sections, the network of connections creates a resonance that can prolong its own effects to the very last word. Hence the instigation of a specular system of tones between suspense and completion. In an analysis of this young Belgian writer's work, two types of 'closure' reveal these choices. The first one, the convergent type, shall be discussed in the first part of this article; the less used type is the divergent one, which I shall consider in the second part which focuses on *Mercure*. If the convergent type is inspired by the desire to bring the narrative to a close, the divergent closure is characterized by the absence of a choice of a specific ending, which means that several endings exist simultaneously.

The Convergent Closure

This form of closure plays on two circular plots which draw together to complete the narrative, and is used for example in *Les Catilinaires, Péplum, Stupeur et tremblements, Hygiène de l'assassin, Métaphysique des tubes* and *Attentat*.[5] Despite variables specific to each novel, the argumentation is shot through with a dual standpoint and a metascriptural presence in such a way that, in the end, the plots reshape themselves around generalizing positions which contradict the writer's own position and her precision in demonstrating it, producing anti-conformist solutions. Hence we find syllogisms, maxims and self-contained metascriptural loops.

The 'closure by syllogism' model is used in *Les Catilinaires*. The final paragraph introduces the questions of time and of the identity of a 'je' who, having illuminated and established his individual space, discovers the unknowability of the self. By comparing the first sentence of *Les Catilinaires* with the last, the change of subject becomes apparent:

> On ne sait rien de soi (*CA* 9).
> Je ne sais plus rien de moi (*CA* 151).

In this example initially we have the major premise, the starting point for any precise, deductive reasoning which has no need for external corroboration. Hence the off-hand attitude to the question of time. Perceiving the conventional nature of time does not preclude resorting to a hypothetical unity of time (a year) at a point, in fact, when the plot seems to be concentrated within one location with one distinguishable action: the disturbing appearance of the neighbour's unsettling face at the same time every day. The three unities—or Nothomb's versions of them— are only there to be undermined, helped along the way by a pronominal generalization, the 'nous' which has a soothing influence on a climate of madness. The weirdness of the situation is presented in preparation for the dual approach to the plot achieved by the discrepancy between the subject and his or her actions. The use of 'on' introduces this kind of generalization, but it is the imperative form which plucks the 'je' from the abyss: 'Sachez qui vous êtes et vous vous prendrez en grippe'(*CA* 9). The provocative heterodoxy of this statement is clear from the opposition between the ancient dictum 'Know thyself—being conventionally a path to wisdom—and the formula 'vous vous prendrez en grippe', which already suggests a dissonant doubleness of the self.[6] The transition from 'on' to 'je', via the use of 'nous', moves from the general to the particular only to double back and to confirm the loss of any lasting identity.

Taking the first and final sentences as a starting point, a syllogism can be constructed, one that demonstrates—by means of a strict sequence of logic—the disarming power of questions; the paradox emerges in the 'je' which, deprived of any concretization, ends up wafting helplessly in a vacuum, despite the assured argumentation. The parallel stances stand their ground even as they converge towards the initial conceits, forming the same maieutic system of enquiry used by Socrates. The reader has a guarantee of a moral; this mimics the pattern of endings in fairy tales. But here the author had already reversed the place—from the end to the beginning—and then the meaning, making a paradox of this concluding effect.

The endings of *Péplum* and *Stupeur et tremblements* are characterized by the setting up of two narrative planes which create a metascriptural short-circuit around the author's identity. This is not merely a question of editorial commentary offered at the end to highlight the text, but it is a narratorial self-representation which reveals the author's use of mechanisms directly contradictory to the novel form. Amélie Nothomb implicates herself in the action and not only parodies the role of the writer—and this is clearly endorsed throughout her work in pseudo-paratextual passages—but also sends herself up. She features with indicators such as 'Amélie-san'[7] or Lady Amelia Northumb (*ME* 161) that make her easy to identify. To the homophonous elements of the name she adds a false title and attributes works which do not exist (what is more, they are *contes* not novels) in an era when their particular genre was not used. By comparing these two types of authorial presence in her work, important indicators of the endings can be seen. For example, if the Amélie-san offered at the end of *Stupeur et tremblements* concludes the narrative by disclosing the writer's Japanese identity, then Lady Amelia Northumb's more novelistic trajectory opens up a virtual dimension. Situated on the 'anachronistic staircase', this name—and the amused, ironic tone—guarantee a subversion of fixed codes of time and space. Within the structure of *Mercure* and its dual dénouements, the presence of this virtual axis is a clue to the specular nature of the stories and the dramatic effects created by the play of reflections, as constructed around the author's name, and which also features in the Adèle-Hazel couple.

In *Péplum,* however, the opening section and the final section are more clearly traced than in other works, thanks to clear thematic shifts. Rather than an authorial intervention, it is the transition from one time to another which determines the dislocation. An incident that is as banal as it is fertile in Nothomb's economic presentation of paradoxical situations provides the means for the dénouement of the argumentation. The beginning outlines the novel's thesis: '– Cherchez à qui le crime profite. L'ensevelissement de Pompéi sous les cendres du Vésuve, en 79 après Jésus-Christ, a été le plus beau cadeau qui a été offert aux archéologues. A votre avis, qui a fait le coup?' (*PE* 5). The middle section pursues this demonstration in a tense dialogue with the scientist Celsius.

Once the dialogue is over, the ending brings together the evidence. The two oscillating timeframes finally anchor themselves in a 'contemporary' reality. Hence the extraordinary importance of the *péplum,* the only thing that links the different temporal axes involved (the Pompeii era, the time in which the author is writing, and Celsius's age). The ending also deals with the way in which the plot is written and with the author's 'need' to write a novel: 'Quand j'ai eu fini de rédiger ce manuscrit, je l'ai apporté à mon éditeur. J'ai précisé qu'il s'agissait d'une histoire vraie. Personne n'a daigné me croire'(*PE* 154). Just as in the *note* in *Mercure,* confronted with this inevitable requirement to disclose her *modus operandi,* the author subverts her own role, thanks to her supposed ingenuousness. The meticulous details about her writing poke fun at any kind of paratext and, apparently shyly and inoffensively, Nothomb also plays on the pseudo-scientific environment she has created.

The two planes of the narrative, centred on the element of time and on the interplay between the different standpoints in the dialogues, are resolved in the concluding passages when the metascriptural elements toy with reality. As well as the problem of the Cassandra-writer, there is the Italian editor who intervenes to invite Amélie to Naples just as she is finishing *Péplum,* and who becomes a key to the overlapping of different spaces in the novel. There is a detective-story connivance between the editor's office and Pompeii, the subject of the plot, a connivance which eventually interconnects with the disorientating effects and the conspiracy theory to which the author falls victim. From the virtual to the real, this metascriptural closure brings together the two points of view deployed throughout the work.

This metascriptural strategy also governs the closure of *Stupeur et tremblements,* at the point where it completely overturns the 'anonymous' nature of the Japanese character. The text is pervaded by a sense of confused identity thanks to the constant use of a 'je' who has no sense of belonging. Her alienation, presented also in passages in the second person, is constructed as her involvement in the Japanese system evolves. The tone of the introductory passages is clear, with sequences of similar sentences pushing the foreigner into another dimension. The two levels of the narrative are structured around her point of view and the action until the gaping void is shown up by the vocative 'tu', a technique also used in *Le Sabotage amoureux*.

The ending of *Stupeur et tremblements,* which is broken up and reduced to a few tightly crafted paragraphs, offers a maxim and a series of metadiscursive elements which, as in *Péplum,* reconstruct the characters' standpoints around another authorial identity. The apparent break is marked by the end of the disorientated feeling of not belonging and the resumption of the author's 'je'. The phrases used to indicate this step forward play repeatedly on the images at the end of the book: 'La fenêtre était la frontière entre la lumière horrible et l'admirable obscurité [. . .] Une ultime fois, je me jetais dans le vide. Je regardai mon corps tomber. Quand j'eus contenté ma soif de défenestration, je quittai l'immeuble Yumimoto. On ne m'y revit jamais' (*ST* 173–74). The window is a physical barrier which has become an obvious escape route to deliver the character from the rigorous Japanese work ethic. Everything seems to evolve towards death, which is never mentioned but given as a possible final deliverance on both narrative levels, in keeping with the Samurai practice of hara-kiri: 'Aussi longtemps qu'il existerait des fenêtres, le moindre humain de la terre aurait sa part de liberté' (*ST* 174). The window-freedom opposition is ironically undermined by the haughty tone and the intermediary use of 'moindre' which breaks up the multiplicity of 'fenêtres' with the unicity of that desire for freedom. This passage is followed by short paragraphs, clearly separated by blank space, in which the narrator mentions her return to Europe and the fact that, several years later, she receives a note from Mori Fubuki written in Japanese. Through the language, a connection is established between the narrator and her former host country, revealing a recognition of a sense of belonging. The circular nature of the narrative is, therefore, established in both these concluding hypotheses, the one seen through the window and the other offered by the *note,* converging towards the acquisition of a Japanese identity. Using this technique, Amélie Nothomb trammels her narrative along two routes before closing them off.

Métaphysique des tubes provides another example in this vein, as its last lines constitute a link to the core of the text. The beginning both imitates and subverts the opening of the Book of Genesis, and there is a corresponding plural closure, identified by a grouping of three paragraphs. In the first the state of suspense is based on a comparison: '[. . .] la boutonnière de ma tempe, comme un couturier retouchant un modèle à même la cliente' (*MT* 170). After a gap, a series of negations and interrogations re-open the text: 'Ainsi s'acheva ce qui fut ma première—et, à ce jour, ma seule—tentative de suicide' (*MT* 170). At the same time, by resorting to maxims, the author endorses the stilted rhythm of the ending, by contributing to the closely knit structure of the sentences and also with the help of the backtracking offered by the imagery of the dream: 'De toute façon, le salut n'est qu'un faux-fuyant' (*ME* 171). When a timorous future catches sight of itself in the mirror, the very last sentence—isolated by the blank space around it—closes any kind of opening, and the action stops completely: 'Ensuite, il ne s'est plus rien passé' (*ME* 171).

Attentat, a novel published one year before *Mercure,* provides thematic analogies very close to *Mercure*'s major themes (the beauty and the beast couple, the references to mirrors, the metatextual presence of Stendhal on the subject of imprisonment, and the double *dénouement*). In *Attentat* these analogies are used to advocate the development of closure-strategies as the 'I-Amélie-writer' hides increasingly in the wings leaving only a mocking voice to perform on stage. At the same time, the desire to play with reflections and their myriad connotations as well as the possibility of contesting the end of a known story (*Quo vadis?*) by rewriting it along the lines of a cynical bullfighting mentality, which can cast aside man and his noble feelings in order to favour the animal, feature here. These desires underline the creation of two levels of subversion: the presence of literary references which are more obvious and more pronounced here than in the other novels and which become blatant citations, and the disconcerting interplay concerning who is actually being addressed (also found in the ending of *Mercure*). Yet these succeed, with the help of a mocking tone, in reaching a conclusive convergence.

It is in this context that the last sentence has all the weight of a maxim: 'Il n'y a pas d'amour impossible' (*A* 153). Its brevity is arresting and it brings to a close the debate which sparks the novel. The sentence-maxim, produced at the end of the argumentation, overturns the questions of beauty and ugliness, but it is also disturbing in so far as the litotes is undermined by the negation of the impossible. In this world of the possible, opposites can co-exist but they have to be revealed.

The Divergent Closure

In contrast to these variations of convergent endings, divergence emerges as a *modus operandi* within the infrastructure of *Mercure,* both on a narratological and an aesthetic level. This novel has two possible conclusions with an important *note* about this particular strategy. By moving away from pseudo-biographical detours, here relegated to the *note,* and by playing on a fictional presence with comic tendencies, Amélie Nothomb pursues the Stendhalian dictum: 'Le roman est un miroir que l'on promène le long du chemin' (*ME* 103). The author deploys a veritable treatise on reflections which—given their effects of convergence and divergence— underline the decisions to sabotage the end of *Mercure.* This ambiguous oscillation between the novel—as it is described on the cover—and the *conte*—the structural fabric of the text—takes a stand somewhere between novel and autobiography. The veiled references to fairy tales, as well as characters such as the fairy Carabosse, the magic elements such as the mirror, or the rules that are there to be broken, suggest other kinds of parallels.[8] Personal diaries, dialogue and epistolary material end up parodying a mixture of genres. Indeed, having identified those aspects that are at once the most characteristic and the most debated, the author has fun turning them inside out. With its use of ultimately laughable hyperbole, black humour contributes to this capsizing of the moral equilibrium.

The first part of *Mercure* is characterized by the setting up of a prism in which the mythological, structural and literary references multiply the different levels of perception. Right from the beginning duality opens up a path for itself in the face of the prescriptive attitude of the first sentence: 'Pour habiter cette île; il faut avoir quelque chose à cacher' (*ME* 9). The definition of a limited universe—that of the island—created by the metaphorical 'Mortes-Frontières' and port de Nœuds, clarify the idea of moving towards death and the subsequent dissolution of all links with the point of departure. Nothomb bases around these two poles the divergence offered by the first route to a closure, but, in the meantime, this one-way ticket incorporates the interplay of internal and external voices which nuance the balance of relationships between the three central characters.

The interplay of opposites becomes all the clearer in the themes introduced by the characters of the nurse, the young girl and the Captain. Beauty and ugliness, happiness and sadness, honesty and dishonesty, the body and the soul, love and hate, freedom and imprisonment, and the role of literature are constantly examined, giving a very marked branching effect which acknowledges the reflections within the text.

The personal stories of the protagonists are touched with several forms of duality. The most obvious duality, which is integral to the plot, is the correlation between the two accounts (with their very different tones and forms) of the Captain's 'women'. His ambiguous attitude to the young girl, which is flagged up by the nurse, eventually breaks apart in the two endings, thereby facilitating the possibility of further subdivision through the two letters written by Loncours to the two women.

Thanks to the intervention of sleep—a method of suspension very familiar to the author—the action stops before the final *dénouement,* just as the writer explicitly proposes two different *dénouements.* The first is characterized by an extension of the interplay of reflections and by the lyrical aspect of the destructive trajectory. The irony, sometimes loaded with the nurse's anger, is counterbalanced by Hazel's poetic disposition towards the Captain. In the first, Françoise gradually breaks down the young girl's arguments by using a series of paradoxes which eventually form lacerating maxims: '[. . .] l'amour n'est pas la spécialité des humains' (*ME* 189). She resorts to hyperbole in order to turn her meaning upside down. Other revealing features of the narrative include: her choice of adjectives in 'funeste miroir' (*ME* 168); 'heureux bienfaiteur, stratagème habile, votre gentil Capitaine, saint homme' (*ME* 169); the superlative used in elaborately polite forms of address, for example in '– Heureux bienfaiteur qui, par un stratagème habile, a eu pour maîtresses les deux plus belles filles du mondes! Et dites-moi donc quel serait mon intérêt de prendre tant de risques pour venir vous noircir la réputation de ce saint homme?'(*ME* 169); the way in which the characters' qualities are established with 'méchanceté, fourberie, malhonnêteté' (*ME* 169) and their magic gifts, like 'beauté, fortune et liberté' (*ME* 195). These and the moralizing turns of phrase are all examples of how fairy tales are subverted. This is a climate of twisted argumentation in which, for example, two sentences appear side by side, constructed in the same way but with their reference points reversed: 'Les deux amies montèrent sur le rafiot. La cadette, livide, contemplait l'île qui s'éloignant. L'aînée, radieuse, re-gardait la côte qui s'approchait' (*ME* 121).

The nouns, adjectives and verbs used demonstrate the way in which the action-sentences evolve. Their point of convergence is guaranteed by the pairing of 'contemplait / regardait' and 'île / côte', as this indicates two elements of anchorage. Both verbs refer to the same action of looking but, with the younger girl, there is a connotation of mysticism and dreaminess, as if she were losing herself in the image to the point of being absorbed by it. In the case of the older girl, her pragmatic nature dominates, confirming her maieutic role. Their separation from the island is experienced as an idyllic retreat. Alongside these two synonyms, Amélie Nothomb enjoys herself with a game of opposites which carries on as follows: 'Françoise partit aussitôt à Tanches rencontrer le notaire du Capitaine. La pupille s'assit face à la mer et ouvrit l'enveloppe de son tuteur' (*ME* 201).

The letters sent to the two girls by the Captain become as much an arena for metalepsis about death as a long-distance dialogue between the three characters. In fact when the Captain writes to his ward he does not mention the death he has chosen for himself; he uses syllogisms to support his justification for his very singular love and to give this sentiment a universality. The coincidence of opposites—'love / death'—is provided by the letter, with its driving force by balancing the commemorative act with reincarnation as bipolar reflections of a former time. As for the other letter, addressed to Françoise, it discloses the exact nature of the relationship between the Captain and the nurse. Here Omer talks of his death and asks for collaboration from the elder girl to hide the truth from Hazel. The tone is pragmatic and abrupt. The first letter is dominated by the element of eternity whereas, in the second, time and place fix the event and anchor the action. The letters establish a long-distance dialogue, quite unlike the swordsman's sparring which pervades the entire book in the turn-taking games (two characters speaking, so to speak, on stage while a third is concealed from view or battles it out with monologues), given that here there are no direct responses to the Captain's words.

The last sequence resumes the techniques used in the conclusions of fairy tales. Wonderful things described in superlatives ('[. . .] partageaient la palme de la plus belle passagère. Elles partageaient aussi la plus belle cabine [. . .]' (*ME* 203)), and a sense of magnificence, a shifting towards myth, a Narcissus-style metamorphosis ('Je suis en train de devenir une fleur') are combined with the impersonal nature of the sentences ('Il faisait bon vivre quand on avait de l'argent. [. . .] Il leur arriva bien des choses à chacune, mais elles ne se quittèrent jamais' (*ME* 204)). With the help of the past historic ('achetèrent' and 'arriva'), the story could actually come to an end, since the two protagonists have found their equilibrium with the happiness granted to them by beauty and wealth. 'Elles ne se quittèrent jamais' (*ME* 204) sanctions the heroine's victory after all the events with the forbidden mirror. But after this eloquent grandeur which accompanies the 'happy ending', the metalepsis imposes convolutions of hidden stories. The adversative 'mais', associated with the reflections and with the end compensates for the divergence of the individual stories by recreating the magical attraction between the two women. This word with all its undertones of sabotage rekindles the sparring of the dialogued argumentation, built out of objections and comments. In this way, the technique of rekindling and connecting the dual closures becomes a clear sign of a 'false ending'.

The second *dénouement* is introduced by the *note*, in which the author explains the origins of her choice, using words such as 'fin', 'dénouement' and 'issue'. The word 'dénouement' is linked to Nœuds, the privileged port-connection to the outside world, and 'issue' has connotations of escape routes for the protagonists. By defining the first solution to the plot as 'happy', the writer advocates the more violent nature of the second. She does not, however, use the variant 'clôture' which would continue to play on the ambiguity of the word 'fin' by adding the perception of something closing, a very important aspect for a text — like *Mercure* — based on an enclosed space from which characters attempt to escape. The parody of the author's interventions on the subject of her experiences as a writer, such as the prefaces or postscripts, lies in the fact that the *note* is placed between the two endings, altering the traditional position of paratexts, and of apologies to the audience. Nothomb justifies her mischievousness with a style dominated by the negatives of the deliberations and argumentations, demonstrating the way in which the pen steers the author's will. In the next paragraph Amélie Nothomb legitimizes her voice in the handling of the narrative space presented to the reader; this is a writer who circumvents their objections by maintaining a defensive stance, before attacking and consolidating her own ideas. Here again there is a meta-scriptural clash of swords which catches the reader out by 'demanding' that he or she re-read the novel itself.

The second ending distinguishes itself from the first thanks to a rapid sequence of events which instils a more taut and less lyrical sense of cruelty than the former. The Captain's suicide as an act of love is counterbalanced by the nurse's own ambiguous plans for the future. Here too we find a fairytale style of writing, but, instead of the closing off which brought together the connections in the first *dénouement,* in this case an opening up of the text occurs. Is the nurse a saint or a murderer? With this paradoxical game she ends up revealing her secret to Hazel, who, on the other hand, defends herself with her questioning; the latter does not bring the plot to a close as in the first *dénouement,* but demonstrates the capacity that the young girl has acquired for imitating her tutor in her adroit use of language as a weapon:

— Nierez-vous que je suis un monstre?
— Certainement pas. Mais peut-il arriver mieux à une belle jeune fille que de tomber sur un monstre? (*ME* 226).

The rhetorical question offers two aspects of beauty, in the guise of moral and physical monstrosity, by establishing its traditional point of reference in a moral plane.

Together, therefore, the two *dénouements* succeed in prolonging the poetics of reflection by revealing a mechanism of dual standpoints which, in the convergent closures of the other novels, shatters the final moments but also connects them by syllogisms or maxims. The way in which the writer reveals herself is linked to this desire to bring the narrative to a close. Yet, Amélie Nothomb's writing can only ever have false endings, since her continual sabotage points towards a conclusion and at the same time offers several *dénouements*. In so doing she goes beyond the clear distinction between closing and opening in her handling of reality. But with these labyrinthine choices she exploits the interplay of ambiguities in her oblique writing by means of one final blow of the sword which is, at heart, to parody the concept of closure itself by avoiding any closure at all.

Università di Bari
Translated by Adriana Hunter

Notes

1. Amélie Nothomb, *Mercure* (Paris: Albin Michel, 1998). Subsequent references in the text will appear as *ME* followed by the page number.
2. Amélie Nothomb, *Attentat* (Paris: Le livre de poche, 2001). Subsequent references in the text will appear as *A* followed by the page number.
3. See, for example, Marguerite Duras, *L'Amant* (Paris: Minuit, 1984) and Lorette Nobécourt, *La Démangeaison* (Paris: J'ai lu, 1998).
4. Portrayed for example by Michel Del Castello, *La guitare* (Paris: Seuil, 1984) and Bertrand Visage, *Au pays du nain* (Paris: Seuil, 1977).
5. Amélie Nothomb, *Les Catilinaires* (Paris: Le livre de poche, 2000); *Péplum* (Paris: Le livre de poche, 2000); *Stupeur et tremblements* (Paris: Albin Michel, 1999); *Hygiène de l'assassin* (Paris: Seuil, coll. Points, 1995); *Métaphysique des tubes* (Paris: Albin Michel, 2000). Subsequent references in the text will appear as *CA, PE, ST, HA* and *MT* followed by the page number.
6. I am grateful to Dr David Gascoigne for his comments on this aspect of the text.
7. This pseudonym is frequently used in *Stupeur et tremblements*.
8. *Beauty and the Beast* in the case of *Attentat*, *Snow White* in *Mercure* and *Cinderella* in *Stupeur et tremblements*.

TRANSLATING AMÉLIE NOTHOMB

Andrew Wilson

'SABOTAGE, EH?' TRANSLATING
LE SABOTAGE AMOUREUX FROM THE
FRENCH INTO THE CANADIAN
AND THE AMERICAN

'La petite peste de la littérature française'—that was what first caught my eye. The place was Vancouver, Canada, the year was 1993, and the words were a headline in the French-Canadian news magazine *Actualité*. Amélie Nothomb had just published *Le Sabotage amoureux,* and the magazine had run a two-page spread about her and the new novel.

I remember idly wondering how best to translate the headline, and settled on 'the brat of French literature'. It certainly fit the mischievous, twenty-two-year-old face in the accompanying photograph. (Neither the face nor the image has changed much in the intervening years.)

If the title and photo caught my attention, the article sold me on the book. Who could resist the premise: a multi-national gang of children re-fighting World War Two in Beijing's diplomatic compound during the era of the Gang of Four. I ordered the book, enjoyed it hugely, and started telling my friends about it . . . Which was thoroughly unsatisfying, since you can't really have a discussion about a book other people can't read. Vancouverites are far more likely to speak Cantonese or Punjabi than French, and few of my friends there read French comfortably, or at all.

I knew that literary translations usually lag behind the original by several years, which seemed a pity. *Le Sabotage amoureux* was only one hundred and ten pages long, and the vocabulary seemed pretty basic. So I decided to translate it. At two hours a day, *Petit Larousse* at my side, it took two months. I duly showed it to my friends, most of whom liked it as much as I did. And that was that. I liked what I'd done, but always assumed that someone, someday would translate it properly.

Fast Forward to 1998 . . .

As it happened, *Sabotage* never did get translated into English by anyone else. In fact, five years passed before anything by Amélie could be read in English. I didn't much care for the spiky, unsympathetic *Les Catilinaires* (published in English as *The Strangers Next Door*): it seemed an unfortunate choice to introduce her to English-speaking audiences. After a few inquiries, I got in touch with the agency that represents French publishers in North America, the French Publishers Bureau, in New York. The English-language rights were still available—a sad commentary on the North American market for literary translations, but a pleasant surprise for me.

From there it was relatively easy to find a small Canadian publisher willing to take it on: Vancouver's Hurricane Press (owned, conveniently, by my younger brother). That had a happy knock-on effect a few months later, when the Bureau placed it with New Directions, the American literary publishers, who had wanted to publish Nothomb for years.

Less happy was my realization that I had to get serious about this translation. It was good enough to give friends an idea of the jewel Amélie had written, but I was pretty sure it wasn't yet ready for the literary marketplace. The fact is, I'm not a professional translator, nor even a serious student of literature. For the past decade I've been a freelance technical writer and editor, specializing in topics like public health, social services, and AIDS. My French gets regular exercise as I work frequently in Geneva for the United Nations AIDS programme, and about one in twenty of the books I read for pleasure is in French. But that just meant I had enough French to know how limited my command of it was.

Word Wrangling

Luckily, one of my best friends is a professional translator who now lives in Nijmegen, Holland. (Among other accomplishments, Kevin Cook is the author of the droll, wonderfully readable *Dubbel Dutch,* a guide to idiomatic Dutch). I diffidently sent him the translation, asking him to 'give it a look'. He responded with no less than a dozen pages of suggestions, and a coda explaining that 'the whole exercise of working out and describing why certain translations work better or worse than others fascinates me so I tend to go to town on it'. I immediately incorporated most of his suggestions into the text, for they were corrections of errors, pure and simple, the result of gaps in my knowledge of French language and Belgian and French culture. But others I wanted to argue.

For example, I'd never heard of parataxis—the placing of clauses or phrases one after another without coordinating or subordinating connectives—until Kevin questioned my translating Amélie's use of it word for word. For example, when the kids find themselves battling with the Chinese authorities and provoking them into locking up a fire escape, the narrator chortles parataxically (as I've translated her), 'The height of glory. And even more, the wonderful news: our enemy was an idiot' (*LS* 54). Kevin wasn't convinced. Because parataxis is much more common in French than in English, he felt I shouldn't use it so frequently in the translation. But I liked it. It wasn't exactly standard English, but it wasn't incorrect, and I felt it gave the text a bit of an 'accent' that reflected Amélie's unique voice.

And there were a few passages I simply wasn't sure about. One is the scene where Elena, knowing exactly what she is up to, makes the narrator run until she has an asthma attack. The word 'sabotage' is a key element in the scene, and I had translated it literally. Kevin's comment was,

I hate to say it, but I feel the whole sabotage word-play fails in English. In English, 'sabotage' is perceived as an entirely fortuitous word, unconnected to any other item of vocabulary and so devoid of the very resonance/connotations the narrator refers to . . . . *'You want me to sabotage myself for you?'* As far as I'm concerned this just isn't acceptable English—you can only sabotage things, not people. 'Sabotage' in French has a far broader meaning: to botch, to mess up, to ruin. . .

As I happened to be in Geneva at the time, we agreed it might be a good idea for me to come for a visit and give the manuscript a final polish. We spent a weekend dividing our labours between Kevin's kitchen and several of Nijmegen's very pleasant bars and restaurants. Wherever we parked ourselves, the modus operandi was the same: I read the English translation out loud while Kevin scanned the French.

He set up his first roadblock a mere eight words into the book's first sentence. The French is, 'Au grand galop de mon cheval, je paradais parmi les ventilateurs', which I had translated as 'With a great thundering of hooves, I galloped among the electric fans'. Kevin didn't mind that the translation was far from literal, but challenged my use of the word 'galloped' for 'paradais'. I stood my ground: the obvious, and otherwise quite acceptable translation—'paraded'—sounded too slow and clunky, given that the opening paragraphs are all about speed. ('Clunky' was a word I used a lot that weekend: above all, I wanted the translation to reflect the elegance of Amélie's voice.)

We batted it back and forth and discussed other possibilities for a few minutes. Then, satisfied that I had a fairly solid reason for what I'd done, he accepted 'galloped'. We moved on, but a few words later he stopped me again, this time catching a real error (which I'm too embarrassed to describe here). And so it continued all weekend. It was exhausting, and sometimes chastening, but invaluable to have just about every word, every turn of phrase challenged.

Our session confirmed for me that it is acceptable, and sometimes necessary, in literary translation to sacrifice literal accuracy for the sake of euphony. For example, I used the word 'pathfinder' to translate 'éclaireur', the narrator's rank in the Allied army, which she describes with relish as a word she could ride like a mustang or hang from like a trapeze ('Je pouvais attraper ce mot-là d'un bout à l'autre, dans tous les sens, l'enfourcher comme un mustang, m'y suspendre comme à un trapèze. . .'). 'Scout' would be more accurate in purely military terms, but isn't such a proud mouthful of syllables as 'pathfinder', hasn't its resonance with James

Fennimore Cooper's classic adventure tale, and is contaminated by its association with the vaguely insulting 'boy scout'.

Less successful, and something that still bothers me when I see it on the printed page, is the scene in which the Allies capture a German kid, pull his pants down, and subject him to verbal torture. Amélie does a nifty little wordplay on the words 'gonades' and 'grenades', ending with 'On lui dégoupillera les gonades' (literally, 'we'll pull the pin out of his gonads') It just didn't work in English—'gonad' and 'grenade' sound too different. So I ended up using a very different wordplay on 'nuts', the slang I remember using when I was a schoolboy. It's okay, but not as good as the original.

From Canadian to American

The manuscript finally in publishable shape, I sent it to my Canadian publisher. Copy-editing generated few surprises, and the process of graphic design—which authors usually have little to do with—was fun. When it got to the American publisher, however, I re-discovered some of the subtle differences that operate above and below the 49th parallel. Standard Canadian English sounds very much like standard American; but it still retains vestiges of its more recent connection with Britain. New Directions' editor David Savage did his work with a discreet, sensitive touch, but we had differences on some very subtle issues of syntax and tone.

You can see it on the first page of the book, where the narrator rides her horse on The Square of the Great Fan, 'appelé plus vulgairement place Tienanmen'. I had translated the phrase as 'known more commonly as Tienanmen Square'; David felt it should be 'more commonly known as Tienanmen Square'. In a note to him about this and other questions, I wrote, 'I'd prefer "known more commonly as" because her construction feels a bit more high-falutin' than simply "more commonly known as"'. The latter sounded to me like a cop describing someone's use of an alias ('AKA John Doe'), rather than the way an erudite European would describe one of the world's great squares. I got my way on this passage in the Canadian edition, but not in the American one. It's no big deal, but it still bothers me a little, and I still think it matters. As Amélie herself says later on in the book, 'Rien n'est moins innocent que la syntaxe' (Comparing notes with Adriana Hunter, the highly accomplished translator of *Stupeurs et tremblements,* I found I got off lightly—her American publisher didn't even do her the courtesy of discussing the changes they eventually made).

And Finally, Amélie Herself

It was 6 in the morning when the phone rang.

'Allo', she said, in her lightly accented English. Then, hearing my sleep-muddled reply, 'Oh, I'm sorry—it is not the same time as New York?'

Nope. Actually, Vancouver is three time zones behind New York, the result of distances that many Europeans can't quite imagine. But I was thrilled to finally hear Amélie's voice and get her opinion on the final draft that we'd sent for her approval.

'La petite peste de la litterature française' was charming and very complimentary of the translation, but she had a few things on her mind. The biggest issue for her was the title. Neither the Canadian nor the American publisher liked the literal translation, 'Loving Sabotage'. They both thought that 'In the City of Electric Fans' would work better, advertising both the exotic and the quirky virtues of the text. I was ambivalent, but had the feeling that there was something clunky about 'loving sabotage' as a phrase. It doesn't sound quite . . . right, though at the same time it isn't wrong.

Amélie, however, was adamant. *Sabotage* had by that time been published in ten languages, and she'd noticed that the versions with literal translations of the title did well (bestsellers in Germany and Italy, for instance), while other solutions didn't (Holland, which went for the fans — *Vuurwerk en Ventilatoren*). I quote from a fax she sent her publicist:

> Ce n'est pas du narcissisme d'auteur . . . Qu'on ne vienne pas me dire qu'en anglais ça sonne bizarre (grand argument passe-partout des traducteurs): en français aussi, cela sonne bizarre, et c'est précisément pour cette raison que cela marche!

So 'Loving Sabotage' it was, and is.

Parataxical afterthought: I think it marches like crazy.

Adriana Hunter

NARRATIVE VOICE IN AMÉLIE NOTHOMB'S *STUPEUR ET TREMBLEMENTS:* A TRANSLATOR'S IMPRESSION

Stupeur et tremblements was one of those books that I stumbled across by happy chance. As a literary translator, I am most frequently commissioned by editors to translate work; occasionally I will hear of a promising book and follow it up, but far more pleasing are the works that I chance across, fall in love with and then champion (asking the French publisher whether the English Language rights are available, translating a sample chapter and then touting it around those editors who are most likely to be susceptible to its particular style and content). *Stupeur et tremblements* fell into this last category, and I was delighted when St Martin's Press in New York picked up the rights for the book and had the courage to succumb to my hustling and use a non-American and—to them—untried translator.

Cynics might think that I was ambitiously trying to chalk up an award-winning novel from a hot young writer on my *curriculum vitae,* but I am ashamed to say I had not previously heard of Nothomb and had actually started 'promoting' the book before it won the *Grand Prix du roman de l'Académie française* (in fact, I was almost distressed by this accolade because I felt sure this book I had 'discovered' would now be snatched up by an editor who already had a translator in mind). No, what attracted me was the way the book carries the reader along with its fluid, engaging style, irrepressible humour and distinctive narrative voice.

It is that voice which most struck me: in *Stupeur et tremblements* the content, intelligence, virtuosity, humour and irony all add up to Amélie Nothomb's very particular voice as an author and Amélie's voice as the first-person narrator of this specific book. Re-creating the voice is one of the key factors in translating fiction.

Being a translator is something like being an actor: where the actor loses his or her identity in the character, the translator loses his or her voice in the writing. An actor representing a real person, such as Winston Churchill, will never be Churchill but he will strive to be as good a Churchill as can be had in the absence of the real thing. The translator can never write exactly the same book as the original because of the limitations and possibilities represented by a change of language, but they too can offer the next best thing to the reader who does not have access to the 'real thing'.

The actor and the translator can love, marvel at or even disagree with their material—empathy is, oddly enough, not a prerequisite for getting the most out of the material (there is a scene in one of his films where the actor Ian McKellen—a committed vegetarian—skins and guts a rabbit on camera; similarly, I have recently worked on an autobiographical pornographic book in which the sexual behaviour was in places very distasteful to me and such light years from my own experience as to seem to belong to another species). But with Nothomb's book I felt instantly at home, and translating it—or writing it in English—felt extremely natural. Obviously there were difficult passages and phrases, but in general it flowed so easily that it sometimes felt like copy-typing, reading the words in French and letting them scroll up onto the screen in English.

It felt, in fact, as if I were writing in my own voice. I began to wonder at this and to draw parallels between Amélie Nothomb's life and my own: a diplomat's daughter, well travelled, introduced to languages at a young age, writing . . . I even began to think that, if I had anything remotely interesting to say, I would make a passable novelist myself. It was not long, however, before I realized that, instead of all this self-congratulation, I should look more closely at the original material. My translation and the facility of the work were only a response to the clarity of Amélie Nothomb's writing.

My delusions of grandeur were further deflated when I read Andrew Wilson's excellent translation of *Le Sabotage amoureux* in which he achieved perfection in a sentence again and again. All credit to Andrew Wilson, because one cannot pluck just anyone off the street and expect them to produce an exquisite translation, but I feel sure that in his case, as in my own, there is no escaping the fact that the original material demands and dictates this perfection. A truly hopeless tennis player (the athletic equivalent of the man on the street who could not translate a No Smoking sign) will crumble and give up in the face of a very good player, but a competent one will find his or her game surprisingly improved. Similarly, Andrew and I both seem to have got a great deal out of the 'matches we played' with Amélie Nothomb's writing.

Nothomb's powerful voice steers—corners, even—the translator into using words such as 'behoves' and 'vexatious' (Andrew Wilson put these words—absolutely correctly—into the mouth of the seven-year-old narrator of *Loving Sabotage*),[1] phrases such as 'sublimely fallow' and 'voluptuous mindlessness',[2] and expressions such as 'not unhappy' with all its subtle implications instead of 'happy'. The narrative voice tells the translator how to translate an apparently innocuous sentence, for example, 'C'était une idée à laquelle je pensais depuis quelque temps' (this specific sentence constitutes an illustration and is not an extract) could be, 'It was an idea on which I had been dwelling for some considerable time', or, 'It was something I'd been thinking about for ages'.

This produces a paradoxical situation in which the translator may struggle not to use a particular word or turn of phrase because it sounds too bland, blunt or obvious in the context of the prose, in which he or she fights to match the elegance of Nothomb's clarity. Even clarity, however, can be interpreted differently by two different people. One of the frustrations of this particular commission was that my work was quite heavily edited and Americanized and I was offered no power of veto (which would normally be the case). Here is an example from the closing sentences of the book where my original interpretation of the text has been altered by the sub-editor:

> En 1993, je reçus une lettre de Tokyo. Le texte en était ainsi libellé:
> "Amélie-san,
> Félicitations.
> Mori Fubuki"
> Ce mot avait de quoi me faire plaisir. Mais il comportait un détail qui me ravit au plus haut point: il était écrit en japonais (*ST* 175).

This passage was originally translated by me as:

> In 1993 I received a letter from Tokyo. It read as follows:
> "Amélie-san,
> Congratulations.
> Mori Fubuki."
> This note certainly made me happy. But there was one detail about it which completely delighted me: it was written in Japanese.

But it appeared in the published version as:

> In 1993, I received a letter from Tokyo. Written in elegant Japanese characters, it read in its entirety as follows:
> "Amélie-san,
> Congratulations.
> Mori Fubuki."
> The letter brought me great happiness.[3]

I feel that much of the impact, nuance and strategic timing of Nothomb's writing has been lost by unnecessary editing. In this example, not only has Fubuki capitulated by recognizing Amélie's success as a writer, she has acknowledged the fact that Amélie speaks Japanese. By putting this at the very end of the very last sentence, Nothomb endorses the importance of the point, which has been lost in the published version. Perhaps, though, it was merely a different and equally valid interpretation of the original. Such are the endless possibilities of translation.

Despite such potential discrepancies, Amélie Nothomb's writing lends itself to elegant translation into English because of her simple sentence structure (a simplicity, incidentally, offset by the sophistication of her vocabulary). In general French prose is susceptible to and often riddled with sub-clauses—families of them, whole armies of them within one sentence. This reduces the translator either to using endless ramifications of the various forms of parenthesis (commas, dashes, brackets, square brackets and any combination of the above) to render the sentence intact in English, or to snipping the original sentence up into smaller less fertile ones. Such punctuational gymnastics and grammatical sabotage are rarely necessary with Nothomb, whose sentences succeed in being both incisive and picturesque: incisive in form and picturesque in content.

Amélie Nothomb's voice carries the translator into new territory and even lets him or her say some shocking things. She made me feel quite at home with the hallucinatory and surreal passages in *Stupeur et tremblements* (I have never wanted to throw myself, even figuratively, out of a window or wanted to degrade myself systematically as Amélie does); and she made Andrew Wilson speak brilliantly with the voice of an obsessive and politically incorrect little girl (and however obsessive or politically incorrect he may or may not have been, he presumably has never been a little girl!).

Even though the character/narrator Amélie in *Stupeur et tremblements* took me beyond myself in this way, I felt I identified with this ambivalently well-meaning and humorously irreverent European in the face of Japanese inscrutability and their rigorous hierarchy. Given that I was working for an American publisher, I secretly felt it was right that my *English* English voice should speak for Amélie in the Japanese setting that I loosely identified with the puritanical work ethic of the United States. My American editor, however, felt that the Japanese could be identified with the British, their class structure and their reserve, and that Amélie represented a freer, pioneering American spirit.

I hope the fact that Amélie Nothomb herself told me she was 'extremely happy' that an English translator was working on the book for the American market vindicates my point of view, but, as with most aspects of translation, even that remains open to conjecture.

Notes

1. Translation published by Hurricane Press, 2000.
2. My translation from *Fear and Trembling* (NY: St Martin's Press, 2001).
3. Op. cit., final page.

INTERVIEW WITH AMÉLIE NOTHOMB
(25/01/02)

Susan Bainbrigge/Jeanette den Toonder: D'abord nous tenons à vous remercier de nous avoir accordé cet entretien. Nous sommes heureuses de vous rencontrer et nous aimerions entamer cette rencontre par parler de votre position vis-à-vis du milieu littéraire en France. Comment vous situez-vous par rapport à l'établissement littéraire en France ou ailleurs?

Amélie Nothomb: Ce n'est pas pour l'institution littéraire que j'écris: qu'elle soit honorifique ou universitaire, ce n'est pas pour elle que j'écris. Cela ne signifie pas le moins du monde que je la méprise ou que je la dédaigne; mais a priori, moi j'écris pour tout le monde et j'ai plus d'émotion à être reconnue par Monsieur Tout le monde qu'à être reconnue par une institution. Ceci ne signifie pas que je n'aie pas d'émotion à être reconnue aussi par une institution; être reconnue par l'université c'est . . . c'est tellement impressionnant que c'en est comique. On se dit 'ils vont se rendre compte que c'est une erreur, que c'est une plaisanterie, que je ne suis pas du tout un écrivain. . .'. Mais il semblerait qu'il y ait des universitaires qui s'intéressent à moi? Cet intérêt me fait beaucoup d'effet. Je me souviens encore tellement bien du temps où c'était moi qui travaillais sur les auteurs, et qui ne dormais pas la nuit en pensant à telle ou telle chose. De penser qu'il y ait des étudiants maintenant, voire même des professeurs . . . alors cela me paraît de la science-fiction. Sinon, l'institution honorifique, non, elle ne me préoccupe absolument pas. Je ne la méprise pas et quand j'ai gagné le *Prix du roman de l'Académie française,* j'étais contente. Mais c'est vraiment la dernière de mes préoccupations.

JdT/SB: Est-ce que, dans *Les Combustibles* par exemple, vous parodiez d'une certaine manière le snobisme institutionnel?

AN: Il s'agit de remettre l'institution universitaire en cause par le jeu de la citation. J'ai une pratique assez perverse, mais innocemment perverse, de la citation, puisque beaucoup des citations que je fais sont absolument inventées. Bon, la plupart sont vraies, mais une fois de temps en temps j'invente. Je sais que cela met en colère certains de mes lecteurs qui, eux, ne savent pas que j'invente, et qui se disent: 'Oh, qu'est-ce qu'elle est pédante! Il faut dire qu'elle nous cite des auteurs grecs dont on n'a jamais entendu parler. . .'. Mais l'auteur grec, par exemple, que je cite dans *Les Catilinaires,* Tachandre de Lydie, et dont je cite plusieurs passages soi-disant traduits du grec ancien, c'est moi qui l'ai inventé: il n'y a jamais eu de Tachandre de Lydie! C'est déjà une remise en cause, là aussi, de l'institution littéraire.

JdT: Pourtant il y a aussi des renvois explicites aux auteurs réels.

AN: Cela me pose beaucoup de problèmes avec certains lecteurs, parce que certains lecteurs disent: 'Écoutez, cessez d'étaler votre culture! On sait . . . Franchement, c'est énervant!' Mais il ne s'agit pas le moins du monde d'étaler ma culture: je crois qu'il y a vraiment un malentendu au sujet de la citation, en tout cas au sujet

Susan Bainbrigge/Jeanette den Toonder: Firstly, we'd like to thank you for granting us this interview. We're very pleased to meet you and would like to begin by discussing your position vis-à-vis French literary circles. How do you situate yourself with respect to the literary establishment in France or elsewhere?

Amélie Nothomb: I don't write for the literary establishment, be it honorary or academic, that's not why I write. That doesn't mean in the least that I look down on it or that I scorn it, but, in principle, I write for everybody and I get more pleasure from being recognized by the man in the street than by being recognized by an establishment. This doesn't mean that I don't get any pleasure from also being recognized by an institution. Being recognized by universities is . . . it's so astonishing that it's funny. You say to yourself 'they're going to realize that it's a mistake, that it's a joke, that I'm not a writer at all. . .'. But it would seem that there are academics who are interested in me? This interest affects me a lot. I still remember so well the time when it was me who was working on authors, not sleeping at night for thinking about one thing or another. To think that there are students now, teachers even . . . well, that seems like science-fiction to me. Otherwise, honorary institutions, no, they don't worry me at all. I don't look down on them and when I won the *Prix du roman de l'Académie française* I was pleased. But, really, it's the last thing on my mind.

JdT/SB: Do you parody establishment snobbery to a certain extent, for example, in *Les Combustibles*?

AN: It's a matter of calling into question the academic establishment by playing a quotation game. I have quite a perverse, though innocently perverse, practice of quotation because a lot of the quotations that I use are entirely made up. Well, the majority are real, but once in a while I invent them. I know that this angers some of my readers who don't know that I'm making them up and who say to themselves: 'Oh, she's such a pedant! To think that she quotes Greek authors whom we've never heard of. . .'. But the Greek author that I cite in *Les Catilinaires,* for example, Tachandre de Lydie, and from whom I quote several passages allegedly translated from ancient Greek, I invented him. There has never been a Tachandre de Lydie! That's already a way of calling into question the literary establishment.

JdT: All the same, there are also explicit references to real authors.

AN: This causes me lots of problems with some readers because some readers say: 'Listen, stop flaunting your erudition! We know . . . Frankly, it's irritating!' But it's not in the least a matter of flaunting my erudition. I think that there's a real misunderstanding on the subject of quotation, or in any case on the subject of my

des miennes. La citation, pour moi, et c'est ici la Japonaise qui parle, c'est de l'humilité: au Japon on m'a assez appris la reconnaissance envers les maîtres, je sais ce que je dois à mes maîtres, et simplement, plutôt que d'inventer que c'est moi qui ai inventé ça, ce qui est tout à fait faux, je dis d'où ça vient. Si cela peut jeter mes lecteurs dans le grand jeu de piste de la littérature, tant mieux. La littérature est un tel bonheur!

SB: Ce désir de partage fait-il partie de votre éthique de la littérature?

AN: J'ai bien remarqué que tout ce qui était bon dans la vie devenait meilleur quand on le partageait. Donc, plutôt que de le garder bêtement pour moi, ce qui limiterait mon plaisir, autant agrandir, même égoïstement, autant agrandir mon propre plaisir en le partageant . . . Et quand je vois que c'est partagé, alors là c'est le sommet du plaisir! On pourrait dire que c'est l'éthique du plaisir. Je pense que le plaisir est une très grande éthique.

JdT: Vous avez tout à l'heure mentionné le Japon: en ce qui concerne la réception de vos œuvres au Japon, êtes-vous au courant de ce que les lecteurs en pensent?

AN: Je n'ai eu que le courrier de Japonais francophones. La maison d'édition japonaise ne m'a pas transmis les courriers . . . En quoi elle a raison: parce que moi je ne lis pas le japonais. Par contre, j'ai reçu pas mal de lettres de Japonais francophones, très contrastées. J'ai reçu par exemple une lettre furieuse d'une Japonaise qui m'écrivait: 'Et si vous avez été si mal traitée dans votre entreprise, c'est parce que vous l'avez bien mérité'. Comme il me semble quand même que je prends la défense des femmes japonaises, cette réaction est une réaction d'orgueil.

Sinon il y a eu aussi des réactions très émues, de Japonais, bien sûr de petits employés, mais pas forcément: il y a eu aussi des gens plus hauts dans l'échelle sociale, comme par exemple des diplomates japonais francophones, qui m'ont dit qu'ils étaient vraiment bouleversés, et par *Stupeur et tremblements,* et par *Métaphysique des tubes.* Bon, évidemment *Métaphysique des tubes* les a un petit peu réconciliés avec moi, parce que *Métaphysique des tubes* ne peut pas les fâcher; *Stupeur et tremblements* peut les fâcher. Je sais qu'il y a des chefs d'entreprise comme le PDG de Sony, qui, paraît-il, était furieux et a dit que c'était de la calomnie, que c'était de l'invention pure. Je suis persuadée que le PDG de Sony ne sait pas comment sont traités les employés de sa propre entreprise, donc il a peut-être été de bonne foi en disant que c'était de la calomnie.

JdT: Mais on a lu le livre.

AN: Oui, on l'a lu, c'est déjà remarquable. Soyez sûres que si j'avais écrit un tel livre sur la Chine actuelle, la Chine ne l'aurait jamais traduit. La Chine actuelle a traduit *Le Sabotage amoureux,* mais *Le Sabotage amoureux* traite d'une période antérieure.

quotations. Quotation, for me—and here it's the Japanese woman in me who's speaking—is a form of humility. In Japan I was taught well enough to show gratitude towards my teachers, I know what I owe to my teachers and, quite simply, rather than saying that it's me who thought it up, which would be completely wrong, I say where it comes from. If this plunges my readers into the great literary treasure hunt, so much the better. Literature is such a source of happiness!

SB: Is this desire to share part of your literary ethic?

AN: I noticed that everything that was good in life became better when it was shared. So, rather than foolishly keeping it for myself, which would limit my own pleasure, it would be just as good to increase my own pleasure, even egotistically; it would be just as good to increase my own pleasure by sharing it . . . And when I see that my pleasure is shared, well that's the height of pleasure! You could say that it's the ethics of pleasure. I think that pleasure is a very strong ethic.

JdT: You mentioned Japan earlier: as far as the reception of your work in Japan is concerned, do you know what Japanese readers think of it?

AN: I've only had letters from Japanese francophones. The Japanese publishing house hasn't passed on any letters . . . With good reason because I don't read Japanese. On the other hand, I've received quite a few letters, very varied letters, from Japanese francophones. For example, I received a furious letter from a Japanese woman who wrote to me: 'And if you were so badly treated in your firm it's because you deserved it'. As it seems to me that, for all that, I take the defence of Japanese women; this reaction is one of pride.

   Otherwise, there have also been some emotional reactions from Japanese people, from minor employees, of course, but not necessarily. There have also been people higher up the social ladder, like, for example, francophone Japanese diplomats who have told me that they were really bowled over both by *Stupeur et tremblements* and by *Métaphysique des tubes*. OK, obviously *Métaphysique des tubes* reconciled them with me a little bit because *Métaphysique des tubes* can't anger them; *Stupeur et tremblements* can make them angry. I know that there are company directors like the president of Sony who, apparently, was furious and said that it was slanderous, that it was pure fabrication. I'm convinced that the president of Sony doesn't know how employees in his own firm are treated, so he was perhaps being sincere in saying that it was slanderous.

JdT: But the book was read.

AN: Yes, the book was read, which is already remarkable. Be certain that if I had written such a book on present-day China, it would never have been translated in China. *Le Sabotage amoureux* has been translated in China, but *Le Sabotage amoureux*

D'ailleurs, les Chinois ne se préoccupent pas beaucoup de ce qu'on pense d'eux à l'étranger, tandis que les Japonais se préoccupent beaucoup du jugement de l'étranger: donc ils ont traduit le livre, ce qui est déjà remarquable. Alors il y a eu des articles fielleux, et j'ai eu des interviews épouvantables de Japonais qui n'étaient même plus des interviews, qui étaient des enquêtes policières. Dans le livre, somme toute je suis très gentille, je ne dis même pas le nom de l'entreprise; je cache tous les noms. Même si le Japon reste le pays au monde que j'aime le plus, j'ai appris à me méfier des interviews des Japonais. D'autre part, on peut les comprendre, puisque tous les peuples sont les mêmes en ceci que les peuples acceptent la critique quand elle vient de l'intérieur, mais la critique qui vient de l'extérieur, c'est beaucoup plus dur!

SB: En parlant de la réception de votre œuvre dans des pays autre que la France, nous aimerions insister également sur la Belgique. En ce qui concerne le peuple belge, on entend de plus en plus parler de 'belgitude'. Que pensez-vous de ce terme?

AN: Ce que je n'aime pas dans le mot de belgitude, c'est la notion de souffrance: tout mot qui se termine par –tude a l'air d'impliquer quelque chose de douloureux. Or moi, franchement, je suis très contente d'être belge. Cela devient bien, de dire qu'on est belge. Il y eut un temps où, en France, on se cachait, parce qu'on avait droit à toutes les plaisanteries. Aujourd'hui on a toujours droit à toutes les plaisanteries, mais on a aussi droit à beaucoup d'estime: c'est devenu bien, dans l'intelligentsia française, d'être belge. On est vu comme des originaux, ce qui est vrai, d'ailleurs: franchement, moi si je compare la littérature d'expression française, aujourd'hui, en France et en Belgique, je trouve que nous avons plus d'originalité en Belgique, tout simplement parce que la vie littéraire en Belgique est moins organisée, je crois. En France la vie littéraire est tellement institutionnalisée que le risque est grand qu'il y ait une contagion entre tous les auteurs, et c'est un peu ce qu'on voit.

SB: Également par rapport à la Belgique, vous vous dites aussi 'l'héritière du surréalisme belge'?

AN: Je suis très prétentieuse en disant cela, parce que, s'il y a bien un pays qui est allé très loin dans le surréalisme, c'est la Belgique. J'ai tellement d'admiration pour le surréalisme belge, aussi bien à travers la peinture qu'à travers la littérature, que j'aimerais m'y associer. Je ne sais pas si je mérite d'y être associée. Ceci dit, je crois que quelque part c'est un peu vrai quand même. Cette incursion du bizarre mythifié dans la vie quotidienne, est une chose qu'on voit dans mes livres. Un exemple en est les ventilateurs dans *Le Sabotage amoureux* . . . mais il y a certainement d'autres choses. Si le surréalisme belge veut bien de moi, je serais enchantée de lui être rattachée, parce que, vous savez, la question tarte à la crème des étudiants qui viennent me visiter, c'est: 'A quel courant littéraire vous rattachez-vous?' Oh, je ne sais pas, moi . . . En plus ce n'est plus vraiment vrai aujourd'hui, il n'y a plus vraiment de

deals with an earlier period. Besides, the Chinese aren't very preoccupied by what is thought of them abroad, whereas the Japanese are very preoccupied by the opinion of foreign countries so they have translated the book, which is quite remarkable. So there have been venomous articles, and I've had terrible interviews with the Japanese which were no longer even interviews, they were police inquiries. In the book, when all's said and done, I'm very nice. I don't even give the name of the firm: I hide all the names. Even if Japan remains the country in the world that I like the most, I've learned to be on my guard in Japanese interviews. On the other hand, you can understand them because all peoples are the same in that people accept criticism when it comes from the inside, but criticism from the outside, that's much harder!

SB: Speaking of the reception of your work in countries other than France, we'd like to pay particular attention to Belgium. As far as concerns the Belgian people, the term 'belgitude' is being heard more and more. What do you think of this term?

AN: What I don't like in the word 'belgitude' is the notion of suffering. Any word that ends with -tude seems to implicate something painful, whereas, frankly, I'm very happy to be Belgian. It's becoming good to say that you're Belgian. There was a time when, in France, we hid ourselves because we would come in for all the jokes. Today we still come in for all the jokes, but we're also entitled to a lot of respect. It's become good in the French intelligentsia to be Belgian. We're seen as eccentrics, which is true, for that matter. Frankly, if I compare French-language literature in France and in Belgium today, I think that we've got more originality in Belgium, quite simply because literary life in Belgium is, I believe, less organized. Literary life is so institutionalized in France that the risk of contagion between all the authors is high, and that's basically what we're seeing.

SB: Also with respect to Belgium, is it true that you call yourself the 'inheritor of Belgian surrealism'?

AN: I'm being very pretentious in saying that, because if there is a country that has taken surrealism very far, it's Belgium. I have so much admiration for Belgian surrealism, in painting as much as in literature, that I'd like to associate myself with it. I don't know if I deserve to be associated with it. All the same, that said, I think that somehow it's a bit true. The incursion of the mythicized bizarre into everyday life is something that's seen in my books. An example is the ventilators in *Le Sabotage amoureux,* but there are certainly other things. If Belgian surrealism wants me, I'd be delighted to be linked to it because, you know, the pet question from students who come to see me is: 'To what literary movement do you attach yourself?' Oh, me, I don't know . . . Besides, it's no longer really true today, there are no longer really any literary movements . . . But these high-

courants littéraires . . . Mais ces petits lycéens ont tellement besoin d'une réponse que, dans ces cas-là, je dis le surréalisme belge. Ils sont très contents d'avoir eu une réponse, mais en plus cela ne me paraît pas tout à fait faux! En tout cas, je ne vois pas à quel autre courant littéraire me rattacher. Maintenant, peut-être que d'autres gens ont de meilleures réponses à me fournir; je sais que l'on m'associe parfois au baroque, le baroque qui est quelque chose de plus ancien, pourquoi pas? Je serais enchantée. Mais qui suis-je pour me placer moi-même dans tout cela?

SB: Il serait peut-être possible de vous placer par rapport à d'autres écrivains, à d'autres œuvres. Il y a par exemple beaucoup de références intertextuelles dans votre œuvre. Considérez-vous l'intertextualité comme un aspect important?

AN: Bien sûr! Mais bien sûr! C'est un moyen pour manifester ma reconnaissance et ma gratitude. Parfois il y des intertextes plus discrets dans mon œuvre, comme lorsque je cite les auteurs sans dire leur nom, comme dans *Le Sabotage amoureux*. C'est un peu de nouveau dans le jeu de piste: autant titiller le lecteur, et qu'il aille trouver par lui-même!

SB: Vous vous référez explicitement à Stendhal, par exemple. A-t-il vraiment, comme vous l'avez mentionné ailleurs, 'fondé votre adolescence'?

AN: Il a joué un très grand rôle. Je ne vais pas dire qu'il a fondé mon adolescence à lui tout seul, parce que beaucoup d'auteurs ont fondé mon adolescence; mais il a joué un rôle particulier. Je l'ai énormément lu vers quatorze ou seize ans, en particulier *La Chartreuse de Parme,* qui est quand même le roman de la séduction par excellence. Or à 14–16 ans on s'interroge beaucoup là-dessus, et mes premières notions de séduction me sont venues à travers *La Chartreuse de Parme*. Mais aussi parce que, à 14–16 ans je ne vivais pas en Europe. Pourtant j'étais européenne, de culture européenne et j'essayais de me faire une idée de l'Europe surtout à travers mes lectures, et surtout à travers *La Chartreuse de Parme*. Donc je m'étais imaginé l'Europe sous les traits d'une gigantesque cour de Parme, où les rapports humains étaient d'une délicatesse infinie, et très subtils . . . Imaginez ma déception quand je suis arrivée!

SB: Vous explorez dans votre propre œuvre des thèmes qui jouent également un rôle dans *La Chartreuse de Parme*. Je pense par exemple aux thèmes d'enfermement et de liberté traités dans *Mercure*.

AN: Ces thèmes me renvoient à ma propre vie: j'avais aussi cette impression en même temps d'enfermement et de liberté. Je n'étais pas littéralement enfermée, mais quand on vit dans des pays qui ne sont pas du tout de sa culture, et qui en plus sont politiquement ou économiquement troublés . . . aller vers l'autre ne va pas de soi. Alors on a facilement l'impression d'être enfermé, surtout quand on est

school kids need an answer so much that, in these cases, I say Belgian surrealism. They're very happy to have had an answer, but, in addition, it doesn't strike me as entirely wrong! In any case, I don't see what other literary movement I could attach myself to. Now, maybe other people have better answers to supply me with. I know that I'm sometimes associated with the baroque, the baroque is something much older, why not? I'd be delighted. But who am I to position myself in all this?

SB: It might be possible to situate yourself vis-à-vis other writers, other works. There are, for example, a lot of intertextual references in your work. Do you consider intertextuality to be an important aspect in your writings?

AN: Of course! But of course! It's a means of demonstrating my acknowledgement and gratitude. Sometimes there are more discreet intertexts in my work, such as when I cite authors without saying their name, like in *Le Sabotage amoureux*. Once again it's the treasure hunt: might as well titillate the reader so that he goes to find it by himself!

SB: You refer explicitly to Stendhal, for example. Did he really, as you have mentioned elsewhere, 'found your adolescence'?

AN: He played a very big part. I wouldn't say that my adolescence was based on him alone because my adolescence was based on many authors, but he played a special role. I read him enormously when I was around fourteen to sixteen, particularly *La Chartreuse de Parme,* which is the novel about seduction *par excellence.* Between the ages of fourteen to sixteen we question ourselves a lot about seduction, and my first notions of seduction came to me through *La Chartreuse de Parme.* But also because at fourteen to sixteen I didn't live in Europe. Nonetheless I was European, of European culture and I tried to imagine Europe above all through my readings, and particularly through *La Chartreuse de Parme.* So I imagined Europe along the lines of a gigantic Parma court where human relations were of an infinite refinement, and very subtle . . . Imagine my disappointment when I arrived!

SB: In your work, you explore themes that also play a role in *La Chartreuse de Parme.* I'm thinking, for example, of the themes of confinement and freedom that are treated in *Mercure.*

AN: These themes refer back to my own life—I also had the impression of being at the same time imprisoned and free. I wasn't literally imprisoned, but when you live in countries whose cultures are not at all your own, and which are in addition politically or economically troubled . . . making a move towards the other is not so straightforward. So you can easily have the impression of being imprisoned,

adolescent. Adulte, je n'aurais certainement pas eu cette impression, mais adolescente, franchement, aller dans la rue parler aux gens de mon âge, c'est une chose qui n'était pas possible. Bien sûr, ce n'était pas interdit, mais quand l'autre crève de faim, ou quand l'autre ne parle pas votre langue, ou quand l'autre a des problèmes politiques ou économiques, cela ne va pas de soi. D'où une impression d'enfermement réel...

JdT: Et est-ce que la littérature, dans ce cas-là, peut jouer un rôle libérateur?

AN: Énormément! Ah, mais total. Cela a commencé à onze ans quand on est arrivés au Bengladesh. C'est au Bengladesh que j'ai découvert vraiment la misère, parce que tout le monde y meurt dans la rue, tout le monde meurt de faim, tout le monde a la lèpre... C'était l'horreur tout le temps: dès qu'on sortait dans la rue, c'était l'horreur. Et, bon, l'un des projets dont s'occupaient mes parents au Bengladesh, c'était une léproserie. Leur générosité ne me touchait absolument pas. Je me souviens, à onze ans j'étais vraiment petite; ma sœur et moi, nous étions toutes les deux dans notre petite chambre à la léproserie, et ma sœur, treize ans, lisait *Autant en emporte le vent,* et moi je lisais *Quo Vadis*. On était là, et on se disait: 'On ne va pas regarder ce qu'il y a autour de nous!' Et c'était formidable, c'était le salut, c'était continuer à vivre, et ça a commencé comme ça et ça a continué comme ça: donc moi je peux vraiment dire que la littérature m'a sauvée! Et elle n'a cessé de me sauver davantage. Je pars toujours du principe que si elle a pu me sauver moi, elle peut sauver beaucoup de gens, et j'en ai la confirmation tous les jours!

SB/JdT: Dans votre œuvre, vous n'évitez pas d'aborder des sujets difficiles, comme ceux de la violence et de la monstruosité. Lors du colloque il a été suggéré que l'humour constituerait un moyen pour aborder de tels thèmes. À votre avis quel rôle l'humour joue-t-il?

AN: J'espère ne pas vous décevoir... Je crois sincèrement que je ne fais jamais exprès de recourir à l'humour. Je n'essaie jamais d'être drôle: d'abord je ne sais pas comment on fait pour être drôle! Il paraît que je le suis souvent mais honnêtement, je ne connais pas le mode d'emploi. Je crois que l'humour, c'est un regard spécial, une distance spéciale... Je pense en effet avoir un regard spécial qui me permet de tout aborder; et je crois que la fatalité de ce regard est l'humour, mais le but, ce n'est pas l'humour. L'humour ne me dérange pas du tout, j'adore l'humour! Mais ce n'est pas fait exprès! Quand j'aborde certains sujets, je ne peux pas le faire autrement qu'avec de la distance; parce qu'en effet l'horreur est telle que sans distance il n'y a pas moyen. Et je crois que l'humour est la conséquence de cette distance, d'un regard neuf, sans aucun préjugé, mais en même temps distant, posé sur la chose.

SB: Un tel regard distancié se rapporte-t-il également à la présentation de vos personnages féminins? Serait-il possible de parler d'une certaine nostalgie de

especially when you're an adolescent. As an adult I certainly wouldn't have had this impression, but as an adolescent, frankly, going into the streets and speaking to people my own age was something that wasn't possible. Of course, it wasn't forbidden, but when the other is starving of hunger, or when the other doesn't speak your language, or when the other has political or economic problems, it's not self-evident. Hence the impression of real imprisonment.

JdT: In this case can literature play a liberating role?

AN: Hugely. Oh, totally. It started at the age of eleven when we arrived in Bangladesh. It was in Bangladesh that I truly discovered misery because people were dying in the streets there. Everyone is dying of hunger, everyone has leprosy . . . There were dreadful things all the time: as soon as we went into the streets it was horrific. And, well, one of the projects that my parents took on in Bangladesh was a leper-house. Their generosity didn't touch me at all. I remember, at eleven I was really small. My sister and I were both in our little room in the leper-house and my sister, who was thirteen, was reading *Gone With the Wind* and I was reading *Quo Vadis*. We were there, and we were saying to ourselves: 'We're not going to look at what's around us!' It was incredible, it was salvation, it was continuing to live and it started like that and it has continued like that, so I can truly say that literature saved me! And it hasn't stopped saving me since. I always start from the principle that if it could save me, it can save lots of people and I get confirmation of this every day!

SB/JdT: In your work you don't steer clear of taking up difficult subjects like those of violence and monstrosity. At the conference, it was suggested that humour constituted a means of tackling such themes. What role does humour play for you?

AN: I hope I don't disappoint you . . . I sincerely think that I never resort to humour on purpose. I never try to be funny. For a start, I don't know what to do to be funny! It seems that I often am, but, honestly, I don't know how to. I think that humour is a particular point of view, a particular distance . . . I think, in effect, that I have a particular point of view that enables me to tackle everything and I think that while the end result is humour, the aim is not humour. Humour doesn't bother me at all, I adore humour! But it's not done on purpose! When I tackle certain subjects, I can't do it otherwise than with distance because, in fact, the horror is such that without distance there's no other way to do it. And I think that humour is the consequence of that distance, of looking at something afresh without prejudice, but at the same time with a certain distance.

SB: Does the same distanced point of view also apply to the presentation of your female characters? Would it be possible to speak of a certain nostalgia for

l'enfance, de la petite fille, et d'une attitude plutôt ambivalente envers la femme plus âgée?

AN: Oui, c'est bien vu, ça me paraît bien vu. Cela vient de choses très personnelles. Enfant, j'étais vraiment dans mon élément: je sentais que j'étais faite pour être enfant, et que mon corps me convenait parfaitement. Et à l'adolescence, le corps m'échappait complètement. Et c'était une perte, et pas seulement une perte physique: c'était une perte de l'ordre de l'intensité, et la découverte aussi d'une véritable hostilité, de l'ennemi intérieur dont mon dernier livre *Cosmétique de l'ennemi* traite. L'ennemi intérieur je ne l'ai pas toujours eu: il est né en moi quand j'avais douze ans et demi. Raison de plus pour ne pas aimer l'adolescence! Enfant, je n'avais réellement pas d'ennemi intérieur . . . l'ennemi intérieur qui est en fait la culpabilité. Je suis quelqu'un d'absolument rongé par la culpabilité. Je sais que cela ne se voit pas, tant mieux, mais c'est comme ça: je suis une machine à produire de la culpabilité. Mais, enfant, pas du tout: j'ai vécu sans l'ombre d'une culpabilité pour rien. Bon, il est vrai que je n'avais pas commis de très grand crime, mais maintenant non plus. Je veux dire: il n'y pas besoin d'avoir commis des crimes pour avoir de la culpabilité, de toute façon. L'enfance, c'est l'âge parfait: plénitude absolue, pleine possession de sa propre intensité. L'adolescence vécue comme une monstruosité physique: Epiphane, c'est moi, Epiphane c'est moi adolescente et en même temps comme une découverte d'une culpabilité incompréhensible. Donc, oui, ambivalence vis-à-vis de la femme adulte, parce que en même temps d'abord objet de dégoût, mais aussi par la suite, parce que j'ai aussi découvert qu'il n'y avait pas que des désavantages à avoir un corps adulte, . . . découverte, oui, du plaisir et de tout ce qui va avec.

JdT: Cette ambivalence s'exprime-t-elle dans la manière où la femme est représentée dans vos œuvres? D'une part, elle correspond à une image stéréotypée, mais d'autre part cette image est par la suite contestée.

AN: C'est très ambigu aussi, c'est très ambigu, parce que c'est vrai qu'on y voit de pures héroïnes, en effet, tout à fait dans la lignée de la littérature classique. L'éternel féminin, et en même temps on se fiche un peu de la gueule de l'éternel féminin, par exemple à travers le personnage de Bernadette Bernardin, ou aussi, dans *Attentat,* à travers les mannequins, et le regard qu'Epiphane a sur les femmes. C'est très ambigu, mais ça correspond très bien à ce que je diagnostique comme 'une écriture paranoïaque', c'est-à-dire une écriture en partie double. J'écris en tension entre deux pôles, un pôle romantique qui est plein d'archétypes classiques (l'éternel féminin, la pure jeune fille), et l'autre pôle étant le pôle grinçant, le pôle ironique, qui coexiste simultanément au pôle romantique, et qui dit: 'mais enfin, mais tu ne vois pas que tout ceci est ridicule? Est-ce que tu crois à toutes ces énormités? Enfin, c'est grotesque!' Et ils n'arrêtent pas de se contester l'un l'autre, mais sans s'annuler pour autant, d'où en effet des phrases qui sont parfois tiraillées. Je pense par exemple à l'épisode du shampooing japonais dans *Mercure:* Hazel décrit le shampooing

childhood, for the little girl, and of a rather ambivalent attitude towards the older woman?

AN: Yes, that's well observed. That strikes me as well observed. This comes from very personal things. As a child, I was really in my element: I felt that I was made to be a child and that my body suited me perfectly. And with adolescence, the body completely escaped me. And it was a loss, and not only a physical loss: it was a loss in the degree of intensity and also the discovery of a veritable hostility, of the inner enemy that my last book, *Cosmétique de l'ennemi,* deals with. I haven't always had an inner enemy: it was born when I was twelve and a half. Yet another reason not to like adolescence! As a child, I didn't really have an inner enemy . . . The inner enemy which is, in effect, guilt. I'm someone who is absolutely racked by guilt. I know that it doesn't seem that way, so much the better, but that's the way it is: I'm a guilt-making machine. But, as a child, not at all: I lived without a shadow of guilt about anything. Now, it's true that I didn't commit any very great crimes, not now either. I mean, in any event, you don't have to commit crimes to feel guilty. Childhood is the perfect age: absolute fulfilment, full possession of your own intensity. Adolescence was lived like a physical monstrosity: Epiphane is me. Epiphane is me as an adolescent and at the same time is like the discovery of an incomprehensible guilt. So, yes, ambivalence vis-à-vis the adult woman because at the same time firstly, she's an object of disgust, but also, afterwards, because I also discovered that there were not solely disadvantages to having an adult body . . . yes, the discovery of pleasure and of everything that goes with it.

JdT: Does this ambivalence express itself in the manner in which women are represented in your works? On the one hand they correspond to a stereotyped image, but on the other this image is subsequently contested.

AN: That's very ambiguous, as well. It's very ambiguous because in effect it's true that you see pure heroines in the tradition of classic literature: the eternal feminine. And at the same time you don't give a toss about the eternal feminine, for example through the character of Bernadette Bernardin and also, in *Attentat* through the models and the view that Epiphane has of women. It's very ambiguous, but it corresponds very well to what I diagnose as 'paranoid writing', that is to say a writing that is in part double. I write torn between two poles, the one a romantic pole that's full of classic archetypes (the eternal feminine, the pure little girl, etc.), the other being a jarring pole, an ironic pole that simultaneously coexists with the romantic pole and which says: 'but, come now, don't you see that all this is ridiculous? Do you believe in all these outrageous remarks? In short, it's grotesque!' And they don't stop contesting each other, but without cancelling each other out, hence, indeed, the sentences that are sometimes drawn in all directions. I'm thinking, for example, of the Japanese hair-washing episode in *Mercure.*

des dames japonaises du passé, c'est ravissant, c'est une scène ravissante, et elle termine par une phrase qui ridiculise tout ce qu'elle vient de dire, en disant: 'vous vous rendez compte, elles avaient les cheveux dégoûtants'. Et alors l'autre lui dit: 'mais vous vous rendez compte, vous venez de poignarder toute la beauté de votre scène!' Eh bien oui, et je crois que c'est ce que je fais continuellement en écrivant: je crée de la beauté, et je la poignarde dès que c'est fini, parce que je me rends compte que c'est ridicule. Et en même temps j'y crois. Il y a en moi certainement une jeune fille romantique, mais complètement désuète et tarte à la crème—*Madame Bovary* etc.—et en même temps un diable grinçant qui dit: 'mais enfin! Regarde un peu ce que tu fais, quoi! Tu sais très bien que tout ceci c'est des histoires, et ne te moque pas de ton public, tout ceci est ridicule!'

SB: Il s'agit donc d'une sorte de dialogue intérieur?

AN: Oui, un dialogue qu'on voit de façon plus flagrante dans mes vrais dialogues; par exemple dans *Hygiène de l'assassin,* quand il y a Prétextat et Nina, vers la fin quand Prétextat raconte l'assassinat de Léopoldine, il devient complètement élégiaque, lyrique, il devient encore plus lyrique que tous ceux dont il s'est moqué. Nina est en face de lui et à chaque fois elle le rabaisse à la portion congrue, en disant: 'mais voyons c'est ridicule, tout ce que vous racontez!' Et elle a raison: c'est ridicule. Mais en même temps, je comprends Prétextat d'y croire, parce que quand on crée, on est tout à fait en rapport avec ce pôle créateur plein d'archétypes et qui est en effet tout à fait ridicule, mais peut-être également aux origines de la vie.

JdT: En ce qui concerne Prétextat, vous avez dit: 'Prétextat Tach, c'est moi'.

AN: Je suis Prétextat, oui, je vous le confirme. De tous les personnages que j'ai créés, c'est celui qui me ressemble le plus. Bon, beaucoup de mes personnages me ressemblent, mais lui c'est vraiment moi. Je suis plutôt aimable, j'ai plutôt tendance à respecter tout le monde, pourtant il y énormément de Prétextat en moi. Je crois que c'est le plus autobiographique de mes livres, parce que par exemple sa relation avec Léopoldine, c'est tellement la mienne avec ma sœur: ma sœur et moi nous avons toutes les deux cessé de manger, et ma sœur n'a jamais recommencé à manger. Donc, voilà, c'est un livre qui est particulièrement intime.

SB: Et l'intimité, est-elle d'une certaine manière toujours dangereuse? Y a-t-il forcément un conflit entre soi-même et l'autre?

AN: Oui, c'est terriblement dangereux, même les plus beaux rapports, même les plus absolus, même le rapport que j'ai avec ma sœur, qui est toujours magnifique, est un rapport très dangereux. Une des raisons pour lesquelles je suis retournée au Japon à l'âge adulte était bien évidemment pour retrouver *mon* pays, mais c'était aussi parce que je voyais qu'avec ma sœur je ne formais tellement qu'une seule personne

Hazel describes the shampooing of Japanese ladies of the past, it's beautiful, it's a beautiful scene, and she ends with a sentence that ridicules everything that she's just said by saying: 'you understand that they had disgusting hair'. And so the other says to her: 'but you understand, you've just pierced all the beauty of your scene!' Well yes, and I think that's what I do continually while writing: I create beauty and I pierce it as soon as it's finished because I'm aware that it's ridiculous. And at the same time, I believe in it. There is certainly a romantic young girl in me, completely old-fashioned and romantic—Madame Bovary, etc.—but at the same time a nasty devil who says: 'but really! Look a bit at what you're doing! You know very well that this is all just nonsense, and don't mock your audience, all of this is ridiculous!'

SB: So it's a sort of interior dialogue?

AN: Yes, a dialogue that you see more blatantly in my real dialogues, for example in *Hygiène de l'asssassin* when there's Prétextat and Nina, near the end, when Prétextat recounts the murder of Léopoldine he becomes completely elegiac, lyrical, and he becomes even more lyrical than all those who he's made fun of. Nina is opposite him and each time she brings him down to earth by saying: 'but, really, it's ridiculous everything you're describing!' And she's right, it's ridiculous. But at the same time I understand Prétextat believing it because when we create we're totally in tune with this creative pole that's full of archetypes and which is, in fact, totally ridiculous, but perhaps also at the origins of life.

JdT: As far as Prétextat is concerned, you've said: 'Prétextat Tach is me'.

AN: I am Prétextat, yes, I'll confirm it. Of all the characters that I've created he's the one who most resembles me. Well, lots of my characters resemble me, but he really is me. I'm rather kind, I have a tendency to rather respect everybody, nonetheless there's a tremendous amount of Prétextat in me. I think it's the most autobiographical of my books because his relationship with Léopoldine, for example, is so much like my relationship with my sister. My sister and I both stopped eating and my sister never started eating again. So, there, it's a book that is particularly intimate.

SB: And is intimacy always in a certain sense dangerous? Is there always necessarily a conflict between self and other?

AN: Yes, it's terribly dangerous. Even the most wonderful relationships, even the most absolute relationships, even the relationship I have with my sister, which is still magnificent, is a very dangerous relationship. One of the reasons that I returned to Japan as an adult was to find *my* country, obviously, but it was also because I saw that my sister and I were so close that if I had stayed in Belgium I would never have

que si je restais en Belgique je n'aurais jamais aucune vie. Il fallait quand même que je la quitte un petit peu, pour vivre un petit peu, parce que réellement nous ne vivions pas, ni l'une ni l'autre: jamais nous n'aurions eu d'amoureux, si nous étions restées ensemble. Je voulais quand même un petit peu voir s'il n'y avait pas autre chose!

JdT: Mais est-ce qu'il y avait aussi de la violence?

AN: Aucune, non.

JdT: Parce qu'il y a beaucoup d'autres rapports violents dans vos livres.

AN: Oui, mais c'est plutôt dans les autres rapports amoureux que je les ai trouvés! Mais pas du tout dans ce rapport parfait avec ma sœur, au contraire vécu comme une perfection, où même la parole n'est pas nécessaire.

SB: Concernant la parole et le langage dans vos œuvres, l'un des participants au colloque a parlé d'une 'poétique de l'excès'. Quelle est votre réaction à cette caractérisation?

AN: J'ai bien peur qu'il ait raison . . . Et pourtant, si vous saviez comme je fais attention!

SB: C'était un commentaire positif, je vous assure, ce n'était pas une critique!

AN: Quand j'écris, je ne cesse de me réfréner: l'impulsion est tellement forte, et tellement excessive, que je ne cesse de m'imposer des litotes. Et pourtant, vous voyez, malgré toutes mes litotes, je suis encore dans l'excès! Il y a cette pulsion très forte qui sort quand j'écris, et autant que possible je la maîtrise. Je ne la maîtrise pas complètement, bien sûr. Mais enfin, je m'efforce quand même d'enlever tout ce que je peux enlever; et malgré tout, tout en enlevant tout ce que je peux enlever, il reste en effet du baroque, de l'excès. C'est comme ça, je ne peux pas vous l'expliquer.

SB: Le pouvoir des mots est alors évident, mais votre écriture fait également preuve du pouvoir du silence.

AN: Justement, oui: c'est un double rapport continuel. J'ai tellement vécu, et je continue à tellement vivre, le pouvoir du langage: hallucinant! C'est le plus grand des pouvoirs créateurs, mais aussi le plus grand des pouvoirs destructeurs. Je ne connais rien d'aussi créateur et d'aussi destructeur que le langage. D'où le besoin de dire la chose. Voir un mot écrit peut avoir un beaucoup plus grand impact émotionnel que de voir la chose: entendre la chose prononcée peut avoir un beaucoup plus fort impact émotionnel que de vivre la chose. Le mot crée la chose

had any life of my own. I had to leave her for a little while, to live a little bit, because really we weren't living, neither the one nor the other. We would never have had any lovers if we had stayed together. I wanted to see a bit if, for all that, there wasn't anything else.

JdT: But was there also violence?

AN: No, none.

JdT: Because there are a lot of other violent relationships in your books.

AN: Yes, but it's more in other amorous relationships that I found them! But not at all in the perfect relationship with my sister which, on the contrary, is lived so perfectly that even speech isn't necessary.

SB: On the subject of speech and language in your works, one of the participants at the conference spoke of a 'poetics of excess'. What is your reaction to this characterization?

AN: I fear that they're right . . . And yet, if you knew how careful I am, how much care I take!

SB: It was a positive comment, I assure you, it wasn't a criticism!

AN: When I write I never cease to hold myself in check: the impulse is so strong, and so excessive, that I don't stop imposing understatement on myself. And yet, you see, despite all my understatement, I'm still excessive! There's a very strong impulse that comes out when I write and I control it as much as I can. I don't control it completely, of course. In a word, I even force myself to remove all that I can remove; and, despite it all, while taking out all that I can take out, there remains in effect some baroque, some excess. It's like that. I can't explain it to you.

SB: The power of words is certainly obvious, but your writing is also proof of the power of silence.

AN: Precisely, yes. It's a continually dual relationship. I have lived thoroughly and continue to live thoroughly the power of language: it's mindboggling! It's the most creative power, but also the most destructive power. I don't know anything as creative and also as destructive as language. Hence the need to say things. Seeing a word written down can have a much bigger emotional impact than seeing the thing: hearing the thing pronounced can have a much stronger emotional impact than living it. So often the word creates the thing. When certain

tellement de fois. Quand certaines personnes prononcent certains mots je reste figée, parce que je me sens plus en présence de la chose en l'entendant nommer qu'en la voyant. Je ne peux pas expliquer cela. Et encore plus en la voyant écrite. C'est un pouvoir encore supplémentaire quand la chose est écrite: elle atteint son sommet de sacré, et son sommet d'existence! Mais cela peut tout aussi bien être exactement le contraire: une chose peut totalement être détruite, justement parce qu'on l'a dite . . . et justement parce qu'on l'a écrite! Donc il faut faire très attention de rester du côté de la création, et non du côté de la destruction, puisque notre but est quand même de créer, et non de détruire. D'où l'importance du silence, une fois de temps en temps: il y a parfois des tentations de nommer la chose qui sont des tentations de détruire la chose, et à ce moment-là il faut vraiment s'en amputer.

JdT: Pour moi cela se rapporte aussi à ce qui se passe dans *Métaphysique des tubes,* où les mots du petit enfant, de la petite fille, créent son entourage.

AN: Absolument. L'un de mes rares privilèges, c'est que j'ai une très très bonne mémoire de ma toute petite enfance; c'est peut-être la seule chose spéciale que j'ai. Je me souviens très bien de ma petite enfance. Et donc je me souviens de ce moment, du moment des premiers mots, et du pouvoir . . . Je me souviens: déjà j'avais la conviction d'être un dieu, donc c'était encore plus grave. Mais vraiment quand je nommais la chose, j'étais dieu! Je donnais la chose au monde! Et en plus je voyais que c'était vrai, que bêtement on dit 'Papa, Maman' et on leur donne l'existence! Pourtant, franchement ils devaient le savoir qu'ils s'appelaient Papa et Maman . . . mais non: parce que c'est au moment où je dis le mot qu'ils existent enfin. . .

Bon, maintenant, j'ai grandi, et j'ai compris que je n'étais pas dieu, et tout et tout, mais je dois dire que, à quatre heures du matin, quand j'écris, il y a des moments où vraiment j'ai encore ce vertige. C'est peut-être parce que c'est très tôt le matin, et qu'on n'est pas dans son état normal à cette heure-là, mais il y a quand même des moments où je me dis: 'mais quel plus grand pouvoir y a-t-il sur terre que celui que j'ai en ce moment?' Je peux tout créer, en l'écrivant, ou tout détruire en l'écrivant, ou en ne l'écrivant pas.

JdT: Ce sentiment éprouvé par l'enfant dans *Métaphysique des tubes,* montre-t-il que l'autobiographie est le genre de la dissimulation par excellence?

AN: Sûrement: il n'y a pas plus dissimulateur que l'autobiographie! Je pense que je me révèle avec beaucoup plus de véracité dans mes romans non-autobiographiques que dans mes romans autobiographiques, ce qui ne signifie pas nécessairement que je mens. Mais l'autobiographie, en même temps on se dit 'Bon; là ils vont se douter que c'est moi . . . faisons attention. Disons, mais ne disons pas trop'. Tandis que dans les romans non-autobiographiques, comme par exemple dans *Hygiène de l'assassin,* ou *Attentat,* je me dis 'personne ne va savoir que c'est moi, donc je peux y

people pronounce certain words I freeze because I feel more in the presence of the thing hearing it named than seeing it. I can't explain it. And even more so seeing it written. It's yet another further power when the thing is written down: it attains the peak of its sacredness, its peak of existence! But this can just as well be exactly the opposite: a thing can be totally destroyed, precisely because it's been said . . . precisely because it's been written down! So you have to be very careful to stay on the side of creation and not on the side of destruction, because, all the same, the aim is to create and not to destroy. From there comes the importance of silence from time to time: there's sometimes a temptation to name things that is, in fact, a temptation to destroy things and at this point you really have to cut yourself off.

JdT: For me, this is also linked to what happens in *Métaphysique des tubes,* where the words of the young child, the little girl, create her family circle.

AN: Absolutely. One of my rare privileges is that I have a very, very good memory of my infancy. It's perhaps the only special thing that I have. I remember my infancy very well and so I remember that moment, the moment of those first words, and the power . . . I remember: I already had the conviction that I was a god, so it was even worse. But, really, when I named things, I was God. I gave the thing to the world! And what's more, I saw that it was true, that we stupidly say 'Mum, Dad' and we give them existence! Yet, they had to know that they were called Mum and Dad . . . . But no, because it is at the moment that I said the word that they finally existed. . .

All right, now I've grown up and I understand that I wasn't God and all that, but I have to say that at four o'clock in the morning, when I write, there are moments when, really, I still have that feeling of intoxication. Maybe it's because it's very early in the morning and you're not in your normal state of mind at that hour, but there are still moments that I say to myself: 'what greater pleasure is there on earth than the one I have right now?' I can create anything by writing it, or destroy anything by writing it or not writing it.

JdT: Does the feeling felt by the child in *Métaphysique des tubes* show that autobiography is the dissimulating genre *par excellence*?

AN: Surely. There's nothing more dissimulating than autobiography! I think that I reveal myself with much more truthfulness in my non-autobiographical novels than in my autobiographical novels, which doesn't necessarily mean that I'm lying. But in autobiography, at the same time you say to yourself: 'OK, here they're going to suspect that it's me . . . pay attention, say it, but don't say too much'. While in non-autobiographical novels, for example in *Hygiène de l'assassin* or *Attentat,* I say to myself: 'no one will know that it's me so I can go ahead, I can

aller: je peux tout déballer, déballons déballons'. Ceci dit, je vous dirais que—et ce n'est pas vraiment en contradiction avec ce que je viens de dire—que personnellement je ne fais pas tellement la différence entre les deux genres, roman autobiographique ou roman non-autobiographique. Après tout, le thème est toujours le même: le thème de l'humain: qu'est ce qu'un être humain?

SB: Et pour vous l'acte d'écrire peut-il être considéré comme cathartique?

AN: Très cathartique, très cathartique; mais pas seulement! En tout cas ce qui est certain, c'est que je n'écris pas dans le but de faire ma thérapie; je trouverais cela bien dérisoire! Le but n'est pas la thérapie, le but n'est pas la catharsis; mais c'est quand même l'un des effets. Mais je pense que le principal but est de comprendre. J'ai écrit *Stupeur et tremblements,* par exemple, en grande partie pour comprendre enfin ce qui m'était arrivé, dans cette entreprise. La raison principale, en général, pour laquelle je tombe enceinte d'un livre, c'est parce que je me suis mise face à une situation humaine courante, mais que je ne la comprends pas—que ce soit le voisinage dans *Les Catilinaires,* ou l'interview dans *Hygiène de l'assassin,* etc, etc. Voilà une situation humaine que je voudrais essayer de comprendre. Pour essayer de la comprendre, je vais l'écrire. Je crois tellement en l'écriture que pour moi elle est vraiment le souverain moyen d'investigation. Je ne crois pas tellement aux enquêtes, je ne crois pas tellement à la documentation; je me documente très peu, car l'écriture est surtout un moyen d'investigation du réel, vu de l'intérieur, pris de l'intérieur. Un exemple parmi des centaines est la scène du taureau dans *Attentat.* Dans la vie courante, je n'ai jamais été un taureau furieux, et cependant, quand j'ai écrit la scène de *Attentat,* j'étais complètement le taureau furieux, j'étais à l'intérieur de lui, je vivais ce qu'il vivait. J'étais d'ailleurs dans un état physique indescriptible! Le mot était la chose: j'écrivais le mot, et j'étais dans la chose, ça n'était même plus de l'écriture, c'était de l'acte.

SB: Une autre image très riche de signification me semble être l'escalier anachronique dans *Mercure.*

AN: Oui, c'est une métaphore de la lecture et de la construction de soi qu'on fait à travers la lecture, et aussi de la libération de soi qu'on fait à travers la lecture. La plupart du temps on lit dans le désordre. Moi, j'allais dans la bibliothèque de mes parents, personne ne me disait ce que je devais prendre, je flairais! Donc forcément je ne lisais pas dans le bon ordre ni chronologique, ni qualitatif. Et je me suis autant construite avec des mauvais livres qu'avec des bons livres. Je pense que les mauvais livres sont aussi nécessaires que les bons, puisqu'ils m'ont autant construite que les dits bons. Si la lecture libère, c'est aussi parce qu'elle permet de comprendre ce qu'on vit, et donc de s'en libérer, parce qu'on ne peut vraiment se libérer d'une situation douloureuse que quand on la comprend.

let it all out, let it out, let it out'. That said, I'll tell you that—and it's not really a contradiction with what I've just said—personally, I don't make much distinction between the two genres, autobiographical novel or non-autobiographical novel. After all, the theme is always the same: the theme of the human element; what is a human being?

SB: And for you, can the act of writing be considered to be cathartic?

AN: Very cathartic, very cathartic, but not only cathartic! In any case, what's certain is that I don't write with the aim of giving myself therapy. I'd find that very derisory! The aim isn't therapy, the aim isn't catharsis, but it's nevertheless one of the effects. But I think the principal aim is to understand. For example, I wrote *Stupeur et tremblements* in large part to finally understand what had happened to me in that firm. In general, the principal reason that I give birth to a book is because I've put myself in front of an everyday human situation, but I don't understand it—be it the neighbourhood in *Les Catilinaires* or the interview in *Hygiène de l'assassin,* etc., etc. There's a human situation that I'd like to try to understand. In order to try to understand it, I'll write about it. I believe so strongly in writing that for me it's really the supreme means of investigation. I don't really believe in investigation, I don't really believe in documentation. I document myself very little because writing is above all a means of investigating reality, seen from the inside, taken from the inside. One example from hundreds is the scene with the bull in *Attentat.* In everyday life, I've never been a raging bull and, yet, when I wrote the scene in *Attentat,* I was completely the raging bull, I was inside it, I was living what it was living. I was, I may add, in an indescribable physical state! The word was the thing: I wrote the word and I was in the thing, it was no longer even writing, it was an act.

SB: It seems to me that another very powerful image is the anachronistic staircase in *Mercure.*

AN: Yes, it's a metaphor for reading and for the construction of the self that happens through reading, and also the liberation of the self that happens through reading. Most of the time we read in a disorderly fashion. Me, I went to my parents' bookcase, no one told me what I should take, I sniffed around! So, inevitably, I didn't read in the right order, either chronological or qualitative. And I was shaped just as much by bad books as good books. I think that bad books are just as necessary as good ones because they influenced me just as much as books said to be good. If reading liberates, it's also because it allows us to understand what we're living and thus to free ourselves from it, because we can only truly free ourselves from a painful situation when we understand it.

JdT: Est-ce que, à ce moment-là, le rapport avec la réalité est très fort?

AN: Bien sûr! Moi, je m'insurge toujours quand on me dit: 'écrire, c'est une façon de se mettre dans sa tour d'ivoire'. Absolument pas! C'est au contraire une façon d'affronter complètement la réalité.

SB: Pourriez-vous nous parler de ce que vous écrivez en ce moment?

AN: Pour l'instant je ne peux pas en parler. C'est de l'ordre de l'échographie, vous savez. Écrire est pour moi un tel acte de foi que j'ai l'impression que si je pratiquais l'échographie, tout s'anéantirait. Par contre ce que je peux vous dire, c'est qu'un livre va paraître chez Albin Michel comme d'habitude le premier septembre. Je sais que, vu de l'extérieur, tout ceci est parfaitement risible, parce que c'est d'une régularité absolue! La régularité n'est qu'apparente: à l'intérieur, c'est vécu dans le chaos de la création.

JdT: La création se combine-t-elle avec des courants spécifiques tels que l'écriture féminine?

AN: Je suis très sceptique, j'avoue être très sceptique. Bon, bien sûr, je n'ai pas le fin mot de l'affaire, mais je ne pourrais accepter le terme d'écriture féminine que s'il existait une écriture masculine. Or, on ne parle jamais d'écriture masculine. Alors, pourquoi parler d'écriture féminine? C'est un peu ghettoïser l'écriture féminine. Je reviens toujours à cet exemple: il faudrait pouvoir faire une expérience de grande dimension, de dimension planétaire. On découperait des extraits de toutes les littératures, de tous les pays, de tous les temps, écrites aussi bien par des hommes que par des femmes, on les mettrait à l'aveugle dans des urnes, et on ferait passer des lecteurs hommes et femmes, et on les ferait tirer au sort les passages, et on leur dirait 'selon vous, est-ce que c'est écrit par un homme ou par une femme?' Ma conviction est que ça suffirait à prouver qu'il n'y a pas d'écriture féminine, du moins il n'y en a pas stylistiquement. Bon, c'est vrai que politiquement, historiquement, ça signifie quelque chose: les femmes n'ont pas toujours eu la possibilité d'écrire, et cela a signifié beaucoup de choses. Mais, est-ce que cela signifie encore quelque chose aujourd'hui? Je n'ai plus l'impression que, du moins pour l'écriture, les femmes aient encore besoin de se libérer. Sur d'autres plans, bien sûr qu'elles en ont besoin; mais, pour l'écriture, non, je ne pense plus qu'il y ait de censure féminine. Je ne pense pas que cela veut dire quelque chose. Je le pense d'autant moins que, quand j'écris, je me sens vraiment physiquement hermaphrodite. Je suis un homme quand je dois en être un, je suis une femme quand je dois en être une; et bien évidemment, c'est ce que je vous disais tout à l'heure, je n'ai aucune preuve que j'ai raison, puisque je n'ai jamais été un homme! C'est d'ailleurs une des merveilles de l'écriture d'avoir l'impression que je sais très bien dans quel endroit de moi je dois descendre pour trouver la masculinité. Bon, bien sûr, c'est peut-être une illusion . . . une illusion convaincante!

JdT: At those times is the link to reality very strong?

AN: Of course! I always rebel when people say to me: 'writing is a way to lock yourself in your ivory tower'. Absolutely not! On the contrary, it's a way to completely confront reality.

SB: Can you tell us what you're writing at the moment?

AN: For the moment, I can't talk about it. It's like a scan, you know. Writing for me is such an act of faith that I have the impression that if I had a scan everything would utterly vanish. On the other hand, what I can tell you is that a book is going to be published by Albin Michel on September first, as usual. I know that seen from the outside all of this is perfectly risible because of its absolute regularity! The regularity is only outward; inwardly it's lived in the chaos of creation.

JdT: Is creation combined with specific currents such as *écriture feminine*?

AN: I'm very sceptical, I avow to being very sceptical. Now, of course, I don't have the last word on the matter, but I could only accept the term *écriture feminine* if there were an *écriture masculine*. Whereas there is never talk of *écriture masculine,* so why speak of *écriture feminine*? It's ghettoizing women's writing. I always come back to this example: you'd have to carry out an experiment on a large scale, on a global scale. You'd pick out passages from all types of literature, from all countries, from all times, writing by men just as well as writing by women. You'd put them randomly in boxes, make male and female readers go and randomly pull out passages and say to them: 'in your opinion, was this written by a man or a woman?' My conviction is that this would suffice to prove that there is no women's writing, at least there isn't stylistically. Now, it's true that politically, historically, this means something: women have not always had the possibility to write and this has meant a lot of things. But does it still mean anything today? I no longer have the impression that, in writing at least, women still need to liberate themselves. On other fronts, of course, they need to; but for writing, no, I no longer think that there's any censorship of women. I don't think that this means anything. I think it even less since, when I write, I feel physically truly like a hermaphrodite. I'm a man when I need to be one, I'm a woman when I need to be one and quite obviously that's what I was telling you earlier: I have no proof that I'm right because I've never been a man! It is, for that matter, one of the marvels of writing to have the impression that I know very well where in myself I need to go to find masculinity. OK, of course, it might be an illusion . . . a very convincing illusion!

SB: Au lieu de parler de l'écriture féminine au sens stylistique, est-ce que, pour vous, l'écriture du corps pourrait représenter une prise de position politique, datant des années 70, 80?

AN: C'est qu'il y avait toujours un aspect doloriste dans tout cela, sous-entendant une écriture de la douleur, une écriture du corps en douleur; or, être femme, ce n'est quand même pas de la douleur! En tout cas moi je ne le vis pas du tout comme ça. L'écriture du corps, somme toute, tous les hommes l'ont fait aussi. Mais dans l'écriture féminine dont vous parlez, années 70–80, c'était toujours une écriture beaucoup plus doloriste, qui peut-être finalement était encore tributaire des préjugés judéo-chrétiens, à savoir la femme est un être qui souffre.

SB: Faudrait-il une revalorisation du corps féminin?

AN: Oui, oui. Et puis en plus, ce que je ne voudrais pas dans l'écriture féminine, je voudrais éviter toute forme de limitation. Je ne sais pas, moi, j'écris vraiment pour tout le monde, hommes et femmes. Et le mystère humain pour moi concerne aussi bien l'homme que la femme: alors pourquoi limiter le mystère, pourquoi le catégoriser? J'ai vu récemment dans une encyclopédie belge une catégorisation de la littérature belge. Il y avait roman policier, roman autobiographique, roman ceci, roman cela, et l'une des rubriques était: 'femmes'. Je regrette, mais quand j'ai vu cela, j'ai été affligée. Je me disais: 'mais non, ce n'est pas une catégorie à part! Il aurait fallu nous mettre dans toutes les autres catégories'. C'est déjà un ghetto; cela part peut-être d'une bonne intention, mais c'est déjà un ghetto, ce n'est pas un thème.

JdT: Vous étiez d'accord pour d'autres catégories?

AN: Ah oui, 'roman policier', tout à fait d'accord. Cela veut dire quelque chose, même si le roman policier est plus que le roman policier. Tandis que 'femme' comme catégorie, non. Mettre roman policier, roman exotique, roman autobiographique . . . puis au huitième chapitre 'Femmes', vraiment cela me choque. Cela laisserait supposer que les femmes n'ont pas écrit de roman policier? pas écrit de roman exotique, etc.? C'est une sous-catégorie, une ghettoïsation; et je pense que nous femmes autant que les hommes, nous voulons avoir accès à tout.

SB: Est-ce à cause de l'institution littéraire en France, qui privilégie toujours les écrivains masculins?

AN: Oui, enfin, enfin moi je n'ai jamais regretté un quart de seconde d'être une femme, vraiment je voulais en être une, je ne voulais pas du tout être un homme. Je suis ravie d'être un écrivain du sexe féminin, mais cela me pose plus de problèmes. Je ne veux pas du tout me présenter en victime, je suis ravie d'être qui je suis. Mais quand je vois, par exemple, mes rapports avec certains journalistes . . . bon, sans penser le

SB: Would you see *écriture féminine* dating from the 1970s and 80s as ultimately concerned with bringing the female body back into writing?

AN: It's that there was always a grief-ridden aspect in all that, implying a writing of pain, a writing of the body in pain; whereas, for all that, being a woman is not distressful! In any case, I don't live it like that at all. Writing about the body, all men have done it too. But in women's writing from the 70s and 80s that you're talking about it was always a much more painful writing which may ultimately still be a tributary of Judeo-Christian prejudices, namely that woman is a being that suffers.

SB: Do you think there needs to be a revalorization of the female body?

AN: Yes, yes. And what's more, what I don't want in women's writing, I would like to avoid any form of limitation. I don't know, I really write for everybody: men and women. And, for me, the human mystery concerns men just as much as women, so why limit the mystery, why categorize it? Recently, I saw in a Belgian encyclopedia a categorization of Belgian literature. There was the detective novel, autobiographical novel, this kind of novel, that kind of novel, and one of the headings was 'women'. I'm sorry, but when I saw that I was distressed. I said to myself: 'but, no, it's not a category of its own! We should have been put in all the other categories'. It's already a ghetto. It might stem from good intentions, but it's already a ghetto, it's not a theme.

JdT: Did you agree with the other categories?

AN: Oh, yes, 'the detective novel', absolutely in agreement. That means something, even if the detective novel is more than just a detective novel, whereas 'women' as a category does not mean anything. Putting detective novel, exotic novel, autobiographical novel . . . then in the eighth chapter 'Women', it really shocks me. Does this imply that women have never written any detective novels? Have never written any exotic novels, etc.? It's a sub-category, a ghettoization, and I think that we women just as much as men want to have access to everything.

SB: Is this because of a literary establishment in France that still favours male writers?

AN: Yes, well, well, I've never regretted for a quarter of a second being a woman. Really, I wanted to be one, I didn't want to be a man at all. I'm delighted to be a writer of the female sex, but it poses me more problems. I don't want to present myself as a victim at all; I'm delighted to be who I am, but when I see, for example, my relationship with certain journalists . . . Well, without thinking in the least

moins du monde que je suis une martyre, je vois que j'ai avec beaucoup, beaucoup de journalistes des problèmes que je n'aurais jamais si j'étais un homme. On reste plus tributaire du corps; on a besoin, par exemple, que la femme écrivain soit jolie. Excusez-moi, mais pourquoi a-t-on besoin que la femme écrivain soit jolie? Est-ce qu'on demande à l'homme écrivain d'être joli? Bien sûr ils ne vous le diront jamais! Mais c'est quand même une des premières choses qu'ils vous diront: 'Une Telle est très jolie'. Mais je regrette, dans le cas d'un écrivain, on n'a pas besoin de le savoir, on n'a même pas besoin de le dire! Cela ne serait juste que si on disait 'tel homme écrivain est très beau'. Mais comme par hasard ça on ne le dit pas. Donc la femme reste plus tributaire du corps, et cela me choque: c'est injuste! En plus c'est une question que l'on ne cesse de me poser, et qu'on ne pose jamais aux hommes écrivains, c'est: 'Avez-vous des enfants?' ou 'Aurez-vous des enfants?' La question n'est bien sûr pas insultante; elle est très gentille! Mais pourquoi est-ce qu'on ne pose pas cette question-là aux hommes écrivains? Les hommes aussi, ça peut avoir des enfants! C'est une question qu'on ne poserait qu'à la femme écrivain. Elle reste plus tributaire de son corps. Et là encore je ne vous parle que des cas les plus gentils, parce qu'il y a aussi des cas extrêmement méchants, et extrêmement réguliers. Il reste des préjugés misogynes, dans la presse française, qui sont extraordinaires! Et pourquoi parler toujours de la France? J'ai vu récemment un article flamand, où il était question de mes livres, un article très méchant où il y avait une petite caricature, un petit dessin se voulant comique. C'était sur le thème AN, et on voyait un homme écrivain qui allait chez un éditeur avec son manuscrit, et qui disait: 'Voilà, j'ai un manuscrit pour vous' et l'éditeur lui disait: 'Désolé, mais, si vous voulez vous faire publier, il faudra d'abord faire une opération de changement de sexe; comme ça vous aurez du succès comme AN'! Je me suis dit: 'ah bon! j'ai du succès parce que je suis une femme: merci'. Entre parenthèses, vous les avez vues, toutes les autres femmes qui écrivent et qui ne parviennent pas à avoir du succès? Comme s'il suffisait d'être une femme! Jamais on ne soupçonne un homme d'avoir été publié parce qu'il avait couché avec quelqu'un; je ne compte plus le nombre de gens qui m'ont demandé si j'avais réussi parce que j'avais couché avec quelqu'un. Des choses qui ne m'effleurent pas. Je vous rassure, ça ne m'effleure pas; mais c'est pour vous dire que cela existe toujours.

SB: J'ai l'impression que l'on rencontre de telles situations dans tous les métiers—dans le milieu politique, par exemple.

AN: Dans le milieu politique aussi; c'est pour ça que je suis 'chienne de garde'. Vous avez peut-être entendu parler des chiennes de garde? Bon, je ne le suis plus trop aujourd'hui, parce que je trouve que souvent elles se trompent d'objectif. Mais à la base les chiennes de garde sont nées pour un objectif très spécifique, qui était en réaction contre l'insulte sexiste en politique. On peut très bien injurier les femmes politiques, comme on peut injurier les hommes politiques, mais pas parce qu'elles sont des femmes! Parce qu'on n'aime pas leurs idées, ça, on peut le faire. Mais il faut voir en France l'injure sexiste politique: c'est extraordinaire!

that I'm a martyr, I see that with many, many journalists I have problems that I would never have if I were a man. We're more tied to our bodies. For example, the woman writer needs to be pretty. Excuse me, but why do women writers need to be pretty? Do we ask of male writers that they be handsome? Of course they'll never tell you that! But even so, it's one of the first things they'll say to you: 'so and so is very pretty'. I'm sorry, but in the case of a writer you don't need to know, you don't even need to say it! It would only be fair if they said: 'such and such a male writer is very handsome'. But as if by chance this is never said. So the woman remains tied to her body and this shocks me: it's unfair! What's more, there's a question that they never cease to ask me and that is never asked to male writers, it's: 'Do you have any children?' or: 'Will you have any children?' Of course the question's not insulting, it's very nice! But why isn't that question asked to male writers? Men, too, can have children! It's a question that would only be asked to women writers. They're more tied to their bodies. There, again, I'm only telling you about the nicest cases because there are also extremely nasty cases that happen very regularly. There are misogynistic prejudices in the French press that are extraordinary! And why always stick to France! I recently saw a Flemish article about my books, a very nasty article where there was a small caricature, a small drawing that was supposed to be funny. It was on the theme of AN and there was a male author who was going to an editor with his manuscript and who was saying: 'here, I have a manuscript for you' and the editor said to him: 'sorry, but if you want to get yourself published, you'll have to have a sex-change operation first, that way you'll be successful like AN'! I thought to myself: 'OK, then! I'm successful because I'm a woman. Thanks'. Incidentally, have you seen them, all the women who write and who don't manage to be successful? As if it were enough to be a woman! Never would a man be suspected of being published because he had slept with someone. I can no longer count the number of people who've asked me whether I've been successful because I'd slept with somebody. These things don't bother me. I assure you, it doesn't bother me, but it's just to tell you that it still exists.

SB: I have the impression that such situations are encountered in all professions, in political circles, for example.

AN: In political circles, as well, which is why I'm a 'chienne de garde'. Have you heard of the 'chiennes de garde'? Well, I'm not very much of one any more because I find that they often set their sights wrong, but at heart the 'chiennes de garde' were born for a very specific purpose, which was in reaction to sexist insults in politics. You can very well insult female politicians, as you can insult male politicians, but not because they're female! Because you don't like their ideas, that you can do. But you have to see the sexist political insults in France, it's extraordinary!

JdT: Et cela a changé maintenant?

AN: Disons que un petit peu quand même. Je suis devenue membre signataire, pas membre militant, mais membre signataire, parce que cela me semblait une cause extrêmement juste. Et pour moi, c'est du civisme: j'aurais été un homme, j'en aurais fait autant! Je préfère le mot 'civisme' au mot 'féministe', parce que cette notion me paraît beaucoup plus vaste. Mon attitude féministe s'inscrit dans une attitude civique, qui regroupe bien d'autres attitudes, qui sont comme le racisme ou toute forme d'inégalité. Mais le féminisme en fait partie.

JdT: Votre féminisme est-il beaucoup plus clair dans votre vie sociale que dans vos livres?

AN: Non, parce que je ne suis pas quelqu'un de très engagé. Mais je crois qu'à ma manière, dans mes livres, j'en parle quand même un petit peu! Bon, j'essaie de le faire discrètement, parce que, un rien, et tout le monde est excité. J'ai découvert aussi que les gens me traitent de provocatrice; mais je ne suis pas provocatrice. Les gens sont tout le temps provoqués! Dans *Mercure,* par exemple je présente des petites choses ironiques sur l'homme et la femme; j'y vais vraiment sur la pointe des pieds, ce n'est même pas un roman féministe. C'est simplement un petit questionnement, comme par exemple, à un moment où le capitaine dit: 'oui, mais la femme n'a pas besoin que l'homme soit beau pour tomber amoureuse'. Vieux lieu commun, mais je l'entends tous les jours. Et là, l'autre lui dit: 'Ah bon, vous croyez vraiment cela? vous croyez vraiment que la femme n'a pas besoin que l'homme soit beau?' Bon, c'est dit très doucement, mais peut-être que certaines personnes comprendront que bien sûr . . . pourquoi est-ce que l'exigence de beauté ne serait que d'un côté?

JdT: La beauté constitue un thème très important dans votre œuvre, n'est-ce pas?

AN: Oui, et j'ai bien peur de ne pas pouvoir vous en parler de façon très éclairante, parce que je ne comprends pas tout moi-même. Bon, j'imagine que l'une des raisons pour lesquelles la beauté compte tant pour moi et dans mes livres, l'une des raisons doit être le Japon. Le Japon est quand même le pays qui a le plus élevé l'exigence esthétique, et je suis née en plein dedans; je ne suis pas née à Tokyo, je suis née dans le beau Japon. Je suis née dans la montagne, dans une maison japonaise: autour de moi tout était beau . . . et cela me paraissait naturel, que tout soit beau. A cinq ans, j'ai brutalement quitté le Japon pour la Chine populaire qui à cette époque, et je crois que cela a dû empirer—je ne parle pas ici des monuments chinois, qui sont sublimes, bien évidemment—mais à l'époque Pékin était d'une laideur, c'était horrible! J'étais poursuivie par l'extrême beauté et l'extrême laideur. Et mon œil s'y est habitué, si bien que mon œil est devenu extrêmement simpliste, en ayant tendance à ne voir que ce qui est très beau et que ce qui est très laid, et à ne pas très bien voir ce qu'il y a entre les deux. Et en même temps, ces chocs esthétiques ont

JdT: Has this changed now?

AN: Let's say a little bit, for all that. I became a signatory member, not a militant member, because it seemed to me to be an extremely just cause. And for me, it's public-spiritedness: had I been a man I would also have done as much! I prefer the word 'public-spiritedness' to 'feminist' because this notion seems much more vast. My feminist attitude is part of a civic attitude that groups together many other attitudes, such as racism or any form of inequality. But feminism is part of that.

JdT: Is your feminism any clearer in your social life than in your books?

AN: No, because I'm not someone who's very politically committed. But I think that in my own way, in my books, I talk about it a little bit, all the same! OK, I try to do it discreetly because the slightest thing and everyone gets excited. I've also discovered that people think of me as provocative, but I'm not. People are always being provoked! For example, in *Mercure* I make a few ironic comments on men and women. I'm really tiptoeing, it's not even a feminist novel. It's simply a little questioning, like for example, at one point when the captain says: 'yes, but women don't need men to be handsome to fall in love with them'. An old commonplace, but I hear it everyday. And then the other says to him: 'Oh really, do you really believe that? Do you really believe that women don't need men to be handsome?' Right, I say it very gently, but maybe certain people will understand that, of course . . . why would beauty only be required on one side?

JdT: Beauty constitutes a very important theme in your work, doesn't it?

AN: Yes, and I'm afraid I won't be able to speak to you in an enlightening way about it because I don't understand it all myself. All right, I imagine that one of the reasons why beauty counts for so much for me and in my books, one of the reasons has to be Japan. Japan is the country that has the most elevated aesthetic requirements and I was born right in the middle of it. I wasn't born in Tokyo, I was born in the beautiful Japan. I was born in the mountains, in a Japanese house: around me everything was beautiful . . . and it seemed natural to me that everything should be beautiful. At the age of five, I suddenly left Japan for communist China which, at that time, and I think that this must have worsened—I'm not talking here about Chinese monuments, which are magnificent, obviously—but at the time Peking was so ugly, it was horrible! I was dogged by extreme beauty and extreme ugliness. And my eye got used to it, so much so that my eye became extremely simplistic by having the tendency to only see what is very beautiful and what is very ugly and not to see very well what lies in between the two. And at the

certainement eu un impact sur ma pensée et ma vision du monde. Même une conception de la vie vue comme une traversée de l'horreur, ponctuée d'émerveillements; et d'une nostalgie d'une beauté première à retrouver.

SB/JdT: Voilà une pensée riche de signification sur laquelle nous proposons de terminer. Nous vous remercions vivement de cet entretien et nous espérons vous revoir à Édimbourg dans le proche avenir.

AN: Vous m'en avez certainement donné très envie, ça c'est certain. En plus l'Écosse me fait tellement rêver!

same time, these aesthetic clashes have certainly had an impact on my thoughts and my world view. Even a conception of life seen as a horror to be lived through, punctuated with marvels, and a nostalgia about recapturing a youthful beauty.

SB/JdT: There's a thought that's rich in meaning on which we'd like to end. Thank you very much for this interview and we hope to see you in Edinburgh in the near future.

AN: You've certainly made me want to, that's for sure. What's more, Scotland makes me dream so much!

Translated by Dr Katherine Ashley

SELECT BIBLIOGRAPHY

The Works of Amélie Nothomb

All works are published in Paris by Albin Michel.

Hygiène de l'assassin (1992)
Le Sabotage amoureux (1993), trans. *Loving Sabotage* by Andrew Wilson, New Directions, NY, 2000
Les Combustibles (1994)
Les Catilinaires (1995), trans. *The Stranger Next Door* by Carol Volk, Henry Holt & Co., 1998
Péplum (1996)
Attentat (1997)
Mercure (1998)
Stupeur et tremblements (1999), trans. *Fear and Trembling,* by Adriana Hunter, St. Martin's Press, 2001
Métaphysique des tubes (2000), trans. *The Character of Rain,* by Timothy Bent, St. Martin's Press, 2002
Cosmétique de l'ennemi (2001)

Interviews with Amélie Nothomb

Ahmad, Nusrat, 'Amélie Nothomb et le surrealisme bruxellois', in *Railissimo,* magazine de la SNCB, 1999.
Amanieux, Laureline, 'Un entretien avec Amélie Nothomb' (27 avril 2001), available online at http://membres.lycos.fr/fenrir/nothomb.htm.
Berto, Michel, Interview in *Bruxelles, ma région,* 2, available online at http://www.bruxelles-maregion.com.
Bourton, William, 'Amélie chez les doux-dingues', *Le Soir,* 14 mars 1998.
Corinne Le Brun, 'Amélie, Madame pipi des Nippons', *Le Soir illustré,* available online at http://membres.lycos.fr/fenrir/nothomb.htm.

Lortholary, Isabelle, 'Amélie Nothomb: Chapeau noir pour manteau blanc', *ELLE*, 30 juillet 2001.

Tombeur, Madeleine, Gilles et Laurent, 'Amélie Nothomb et Christine Delmotte', *Le Logographe,* le 3 avril 1998, available online at http://membres.lycos.fr/fenrir/nothomb.htm.

Turpin, Etienne, 'Une histoire belge à la sauce nippone', *Top Ouest,* 1999, available online at http://membres.lycos.fr/fenrir/nothomb.htm.

'Mémoire d'un jeune bébé dérangé', available online at http://www.opinion-ind.presse.fr/archives/texte/nothombbebe.html.

'J'ai un ennemi en moi', *Psychologies* magazine, 2000, available online at http://membres.lycos.fr/fenrir/nothomb.htm.

Articles and Book Chapters

Amanieux, Laureline, 'Des romans à double-fonds', *La Revue française,* 12 (décembre 2001), 149–56.

La présence de Dionysos dans l'œuvre d'Amélie Nothomb', *Religiologiques,* 25 (printemps 2002) (no page reference available).

Lecture analytique de l'incipit du *Sabotage amoureux*', *L'École des lettres,* 11 (15 mars 2002), 39–54.

Campagnoli, Ruggero, '*Mercure* d'Amélie Nothomb au sommet de la tour livresque', *Les Lettres belges au présent,* Actes du Congrès des Romanistes allemands (Université d'Osnabruck, du 27 au 30 septembre, 1999) (Frankfurt: Peter Lang, 2001), pp. 309–18.

Chung, Ook, 'Une Enfance épique', *Liberté,* 36, 3, 213 (June 1994), 221–26.

Clisson, Isabelle, 'Le Japon d'Isabelle, le Japon d'Amélie', *Lesbia* Magazine, 192 (April 2000), 29–31.

de Decker, Jacques, 'Amélie Nothomb', *La Brosse à relire: Littérature belge d'aujourd'hui* (Avin/Hannut: Éd. Luce Wilquin, 1999), pp. 146–153.

Gorrara, Claire, 'Speaking Volumes: Amélie Nothomb's *Hygiène de l'Assassin*', *Women's Studies International Forum,* 23, 6 (2000) 761–66.

Helm, Yolande, 'Amélie Nothomb: "l'enfant terrible" des lettres belges de langue française', *Études Francophones,* 11 (1996), 113–120.

'Amélie Nothomb: Une écriture alimentée à la source de l'orphisme', *Religiologiques,* 15 (Spring 1997), 151–63.

Hutton, Margaret-Anne, ' "Personne n'est indispensable, sauf l'ennemi": l'œuvre conflictuelle d'Amélie Nothomb', in *Nouvelles Écrivaines: nouvelles voix?,* ed. by Nathalie et Catherine Rodgers (Amsterdam: Rodopi, 2002), pp. 111–27.

Libens, Christian, 'Chère Amélie', *Revue Générale,* 131, 3 (March 1996), 91–95.

Wilwerth, Evelyne, Amélie Nothomb: Sous le signe du cinglant', *Revue Générale,* 132, 6–7 June–July 1997), 45–51.

Websites

http://membres.lycos.fr/fenrir/nothomb.htm
http://www.mademoisellenothomb.com/
http://www.amelienothomb.com/home.html
http://www.livresse.com/Auteurs/nothomb-amelie.shtml
http://www.chez.com/guidelecture/peplum.html

NOTES ON CONTRIBUTORS

Laureline Amanieux is a qualified French teacher in Paris, currently preparing a DEA in French (at the University of Nanterre, Paris X), on the theme of the double and duality in the works of Amélie Nothomb. She has published a number of articles on this subject in *La Revue française* and *Religiologiques*.

Susan Bainbrigge is Lecturer in French at the University of Edinburgh. Her research interests include 20th century French literature, in particular women's writing, feminist theory, autobiography studies, francophone writing, women in politics. She has published articles on Simone de Beauvoir's autobiographies, feminist theory and the 'parité' debate.

Philippa Caine graduated from the University of Stirling in 1997 and has just completed a Doctoral Thesis on the inscription of female corporeality in recent women's writing in French. She is currently working on questions of body image and eating disorders in contemporary French women's writing. She will be teaching English at the University of Nancy from October 2002.

Jacques de Decker, Permanent Secretary of the *Académie royale de langue et de littérature françaises de Belgique,* is the author of numerous novels, plays and translations including *La Grande roue, Parades amoureuses, Le Ventre de la baleine, Petit matin, grand soir, Tranches de dimanche, Le Magnolia*. He is the well-known literary critic at *Le Soir* newspaper and a regular contributor to Belgian radio and television programmes as well as writing for Belgian and foreign publications.

David Gascoigne is Senior Lecturer at the University of St Andrews. He is the author of a study of the novels of Michel Tournier (Berg, 1996). He has also published on writers such as Malraux, Grainville, Le Clézio and Michel Rio and on feminist fiction. He is currently working on a book on the writings of Georges Perec.

Claire Gorrara is Senior Lecturer in French in the School of European Studies, Cardiff University. She has published on French women's writing and the Second World War, most notably *Women's Representations of the Occupation in Post-1968 France* (Macmillan, 1998) and *European Memories of the Second World War,* co-edited with H. Peitsch and C. Burdett (Berghahn, 1999). She is currently completing a monograph on post-war French crime fiction to be published by Oxford University Press.

Adriana Hunter took a 1st in French & Drama at University of London, Goldsmiths College and worked in film publicity before becoming a freelance writer and translator in 1989. Her first book in translation was Geneviève Jurgensen's harrowing, autobiographical *La Disparition* (*The Disappearance,* Flamingo, 1999). Since then she has concentrated on literary translation and on scouting for promising new French fiction. As well as Nothomb's *Stupeur et tremblements,* her work has included two novels by Agnès Desarthe, Frédéric Beigbeder's acerbic *99F,* Sophie Marceau's experimental first novel *Menteuse* and Catherine Millet's explicit autobiography, *La vie sexuelle de Catherine M.*

Hélène Jaccomard is Senior Lecturer at the University of Western Australia. Her research centres around contemporary literary autobiographies and testimonies, in particular AIDS and 'Beur' literature. She has published two books (*Lecteur et lecture dans l'autobiographie contemporaine,* Geneva, Droz, 1993; and *A Guide of Influential Literary Texts on AIDS,* Nedlands, UWA Press, 1998, online) with another one in process (*Les femmes qui écrivent le sida*) and articles, opening the way to a feminist reading of AIDS literary texts. Her research interests also cover teaching and learning innovations, in particular the use of multimedia.

Shirley Ann Jordan is Senior Lecturer in French at Oxford Brookes University. She publishes on Francis Ponge, on French women's writing and ethnography. Her recent projects have focused on Marie Darrieussecq, Virginie Despentes and Amélie Nothomb and she is currently writing a monograph on six contemporary French women writers.

Victoria B. Korzeniowska is Senior Lecturer in French at the University of Surrey. Her research interests include the works of Jean Giraudoux and writing by contemporary French women writers. Her book *The Heroine as Social Redeemer in the Plays of Jean Giraudoux* was published in autumn 2001. She is currently working on Marie Rouanet, Amélie Nothomb and Virginie Despentes.

Mark D. Lee is Associate Professor of French at Mount Allison University in Canada where he teaches modern French literature and film. He reviews new French writing and cinema for *The French Review* and has published a number of articles on Nathalie Sarraute. He is currently finishing a book manuscript, tentatively entitled

Les vies et les morts de Nathalie Sarraute, and planning a book-length study of the works of Amélie Nothomb.

Lénaïk Le Garrec works at present for the publishing house *Éditions Actes Sud* in Arles. Her thesis in modern French literature focused on the works of Serge Doubrovsky. She has participated in numerous conferences and specializes in contemporary fiction.

Désirée Pries is Visiting Lecturer in French at Indiana University, Bloomington. Her interests include French women's writing, Gender studies, the novel, and film studies. Secondary interests include applied linguistic and materials development in the foreign language classroom. Her recent projects have focused on Nothomb, Reader-Response theory in the foreign language classroom, and materials development including computer-assisted language learning.

Catherine Rodgers, Senior Lecturer in French at the University of Wales, Swansea, has research interests in French feminist theory and the contemporary novel in which fields she has several publications. In particular, she is the co-editor of *Marguerite Duras: Lectures plurielles* (Rodopi, 1998). *Le Deuxième Sexe: un héritage admiré et contesté* (L'Harmattan, 1998), her second book, is a collection of interviews with leading French feminist writers. Her next co-edited book *Nouvelles écrivaines, nouvelles voix?* is a collection of essays on contemporary French women writers (Rodopi, 2002).

Marinella Termite is a graduate in Literature and Foreign Languages with a PhD in French Literature from the Università di Bari, Italy (1999). Her research deals with authors and works of French literature associated with the *extrême contemporain.* An essay from her PhD has been published by Peter Lang (Bern, 2002), entitled, 'L'écriture à la deuxième personne. La voix ataraxique de Jean-Marie Laclavetine'.

Jean-Marc Terrasse is a writer and journalist, contributing regularly to publications such as *Les Nouvelles Littéraires, Le Monde de la Musique* and *Libération.* He has also produced many radio and television programmes, and has written both essays and plays (for example, *Génération Beur,* 1989). His involvement in Arts administration has taken him to Vienna, Austria, where he was Cultural attaché, and to Edinburgh, Scotland, where he was Director of the *Institut français d'Ecosse.* He is currently responsible for Cultural events (lectures, conferences, concerts. . .) at the *Bibliothèque nationale de France.*

Jeanette den Toonder was Lecturer in French at the University of Edinburgh from October 1998 until March 2002 and is currently Lecturer in the Department of Romance Languages and Cultures at the University of Groningen. Her research interests include contemporary French and francophone literature focusing on the contemporary novel in Quebec, the autobiographical genre and questions of identity. She has published a book on autobiography entitled, *'Qui est-je?' L'écriture autobiographique des nouveaux romanciers,* and numerous articles.

Andrew Wilson is a freelance writer, editor, policy analyst and speechwriter. Born in Vancouver, Canada, he worked in educational publishing in Central America for three years in the 1980s, and has since worked extensively for UN organizations (WHO, UNESCO, UNAIDS, UNICEF) in Paris and Geneva. He currently lives in London.

BELGIAN FRANCOPHONE LIBRARY

Edited by Donald Flanell Friedman

As Belgium has become a center and focal point of the resurgent new Europe, the Belgian Francophone Library was founded at Peter Lang Publishing, New York, as a special series devoted to the rich and varied literature and cultural life of the French-speaking community in Belgium. The series will publish English translations of important works of Belgian Literature, as well as critical studies, principally in French and English, of Belgian literature, culture, and social history. It is the hope of series editor, Donald Flanell Friedman of Winthrop University, and the initial contributors to the series to broaden knowledge of the specificity, fascination, and enduring artistic contribution of this crossroads country.

For additional information about this series or for the submission of manuscripts, please contact:

Peter Lang Publishing
Acquisitions Department
275 Seventh Avenue, 28th floor
New York, New York 10001

To order other books in this series, please contact our Customer Service Department at:

(800) 770-LANG (within the U.S.)
(212) 647-7706 (outside the U.S.)
(212) 647-7707 FAX
CustomerService@plang.com

or browse online by series at:
WWW.PETERLANGUSA.COM